ALCOHOL, POLITICS AND SOCIAL PO

To Debbie, Mark, and Panky

Alcohol, Politics and Social Policy

ROB BAGGOTT
Leicester Polytechnic

Avebury

Aldershot · Brookfield USA · Hong Kong · Singapore · Sydney

Published by

Avebury

Gower Publishing Company Limited,
Gower House, Croft Road, Aldershot,
Hants. GU11 3HR, England

Gower Publishing Company,
Old Post Road, Brookfield, Vermont 05036
USA

Printed and Bound in Great Britain by
Athenaeum Press Ltd., Newcastle upon Tyne.

ISBN   0-566-07075-8

Contents

List of tables

Preface

This book is based upon my PhD thesis, *The Politics of Public Health: Alcohol, Politics and Social Policy*. Since the submission of the thesis in February 1987 there have been many important developments in alcohol policy. Alcohol issues - such as licensing law reform, drinking and driving, alcohol-related hooliganism, and alcohol abuse among young people - have all received considerable media attention of late. At the same time there also appears to be a growing public awareness about the problems of alcohol abuse. Government and Parliament are also taking a much greater interest in alcohol matters, as indicated by the establishment of a high level Ministerial committee on alcohol abuse in the autumn of 1987.

These recent developments may create a wider interest in this book. But apart from the general reader, three groups in particular will find it useful. First of all, for students of politics it provides an excellent case study of the political system. It clearly illustrates how issues move on and off the political agenda and examines the roles played in this process by various political actors such as pressure groups, parties, politicians, and government officials. Secondly, students of social policy and administration will appreciate its value as a case study of how social policy is made. Of particular interest to them will be the way in which social policy considerations conflict in practice with other policy objectives pursued by government - in short, the clash between 'health' and 'wealth'. Third, this book will interest those involved in the delivery of health and social services related to the prevention and treatment of alcohol problems. For these people, not only does the book outline the policy framework within which they operate, but also illustrates how this framework originated and indictates what pressure may be needed to change policy in the future.

There are a number of people I would like to thank for their help and assistance in this project. I have received a great deal of cooperation from individuals and organisations in the alcohol industry, the professions, and the voluntary sector. In addition a number of government officials and politicians past and present have been most helpful in assisting my research. So many people have been involved that it would be impossible to mention all by name, but I am nevertheless extremely grateful to all who have cooperated.

I must also thank former colleagues in the ESRC Addiction Research Centre based at the Universities of Hull and York: Professors Alan Maynard and David Robinson; Researchers Roy Boakes, Mark Booth, Christine Godfrey, Geoff Hardman, Larry Harrison, Melanie Powell, and Phil Tether. My PhD supervisor, Steve Ingle (University of Hull) and my examiners, Andrew Cox (Hull) and Mike Calnan (Kent) have also provided valuable advice and deserve mention. I am also grateful to Professor Albert Weale, now of the University of East Anglia, for pointing me in the right direction at the outset. I would also like to thank Mel Collier and Roy Freer of Leicester Polytechnic for their assistance in the submission and preparation of this work for publication. Finally, on the home front a big thanks to Debbie, Mark and Panky for their support and tolerance during the completion of the book, and to apologise for the loss of many a Sunday afternoon.

Rob Baggott, Leicester Polytechnic, April 1989.

1 Alcohol politics in perspective

The Politics of Public Health

In Victorian times, public health was a highly contentious political issue. The public health movement believed that health and other related problems were largely caused by the social and physical environment in which people lived. (Brockington, 1965; Flinn, 1968; Frazer, 1950; Hodgkinson, 1973) The movement was eventually successful in pressing for legislation designed to prevent ill-health by altering this environment. This led to the provision of good housing, clean water supplies, and food and hygiene regulations, amongst other things. Though advances in medicine were not unimportant, most observers agree that it was the provision and protection of a healthy environment which was crucial to the overall reduction in the incidence of disease in the nineteenth century.

From the turn of the century, up until the nineteen-seventies, public health was a relatively uncontroversial matter. In the developed world at least rising material standards of living have generally been accompanied by better standards of health. The provision of comprehensive health care and welfare systems in many countries assisted this trend. For the industrialised nations the appalling levels of morbidity and mortality experienced in the nineteenth century became a distant memory. Accordingly, the political significance of public health diminished.

1

Today, however, public health is back on the political agenda. This can be attributed in part to a growing recognition that developments in medical technology alone cannot solve the major health problems of today. Many now believe that the so-called 'diseases of Western civilisation' - such as heart disease, cancer, alcoholism, sexually transmitted diseases, to name a few - can only be significantly reduced by altering the social environment and individual habits and lifestyles. (O'Neill, 1983; World Health Organisation, 1981, 1985)

As in the last century, renewed awareness of the connection between environment, lifestyles and public health has produced a heated political debate. A wide range of health and environmental groups have in recent years called for government intervention on public health grounds. Such demands have not, as might be expected, fallen entirely on stony ground. Modern governments, faced with funding increasingly expensive health care services, have been strongly attracted to the idea of a more cost-effective public health strategy, at least in principle.

Official support for such a strategy was particularly evident in the UK during the seventies. The government was caught between the need for public expenditure restraint on the one hand and increasing demands for health services on the other. These circumstances encouraged a series of policy statements which emphasised the importance of public health measures aimed at preventing ill-health. (DHSS, 1976; Cmnd 7047, 1977) The policy has since been continued by the Conservative Government which found such an approach highly compatible both with its policy of public expenditure restraint and its desire to shift the burden of responsibility for health towards the individual and away from the state. (DHSS, 1981a)

Studies of modern public health have, however, illustrated the wide gulf between policy statements and practice. This gap is particularly evident where health appears to be in conflict with wealth. The ability of commercial interests to obstruct preventive health strategies has been well documented. Studies of UK government policy on smoking for example have arrived at the general conclusion that the tobacco industry has on the whole successfully opposed policies which might have been more effective in preventing smoking related diseases. (Baggott, 1987,1988a; Calnan, 1984; Popham, 1981; Taylor, 1984) Whilst studies of government policy on food additives and diet (Cannon and Walker, 1984; Millstone, 1986), airborne lead (Wilson 1983), pesticides (Cook and Kaufman, 1982) have confirmed that commercial priorities have often predominated at the expense of public health and welfare.

Public health issues, particularly where commercial interests are involved, have a clear political dimension. In such cases government, if it is to tackle the problem effectively, has to take on powerful vested interests. Moreover even where public health measures have not been strongly opposed by commercial interests, they may still raise controversy. Issues such as the flouridation of water supplies (Brand, 1971) and the compulsory wearing of seat belts in motor vehicles, for example have not involved commercial interests to a great extent. But they have still raised important political questions concerning the liberty of the individual.

This study seeks to contribute to the growing literature on the politics of modern public health by examining an important policy issue which has until now been relatively neglected. It focuses on the British government's response to the post war growth in alcohol abuse, which is regarded by many today as one of the greatest public health problems facing the nation. Following the pattern of other studies of public health policy mentioned above, it seeks to explain why the government has adopted certain approaches to the problem whilst at the same time rejecting other policy options which some believe might be more effective in preventing ill-health and other social problems.

Alcohol - A Social and a Political Problem

In the UK, alcoholic drink is produced and distributed commercially, and is consumed by around 90% of the population. (OPCS, 1986a) It is therefore not only profitable but popular. Although the majority of people drink without causing harm either to themselves or to their fellow citizens, it is nevertheless generally recognised that alcohol is a major factor behind a number of major health and social problems.

* Mortality: According to the official figures, there were 3,054 deaths directly caused by alcohol consumption in England and Wales during 1985. (OPCS, 1986b) This represents a mortality rate of approximately 6.11 per 100,000 population. In Scotland the rate stands even higher at 11.04. (Registrar General Scotland, 1986) These figures, it should be noted, exclude deaths indirectly caused by alcohol, such as road accident fatalities due to drunken motorists. There are great difficulties in estimating the overall number of deaths where alcohol has been a significant cause. But some believe that as many as 25,000 (Royal College of Physicians, 1987) or even 40,000 (Royal College of General Practitioners, 1986) deaths in the UK every year could be alcohol-related.

* Morbidity: In 1983 there were 15,222 admissions to NHS mental hospitals and alcoholism treatment units in England alone. (DHSS, 1987) Yet this represents only the tip of an iceberg. In 1981 the Office of Health Economics estimated that around 150,000 people in Britain were in some way dependent on alcohol, whilst 700,000 (2% of the adult population) suffered from some form of alcohol problem.

* Accidents: Convictions for drinking and driving in Britain totalled 113,000 in 1984. (Harrison, 1987) Yet despite this deterrent, a quarter of the drivers killed in road accidents in England (and 40% in Scotland) are over the legal alcohol limit. It has recently been estimated that around 25% of road accidents are attributable to excess alcohol consumption. (Foster et. al. 1988) Alcohol is also a significant contributory factor in other accidents such as do-

3

mestic fires and drownings. (Harrison and Tether, 1986)

* Crime: In Britain there were 80,000 offences of drunkenness (excluding drinking and driving offences) in 1986. (Home Office, 1987a; Scottish Office, 1988) In addition alcohol has been associated more generally with criminal activity. (Murphy, 1983) Other anti-social and criminal behaviour such as domestic violence (House of Commons, 1975) and football hooliganism is also believed to be alcohol-related. Furthermore there is some evidence which suggests that the possibility of being the victim of a violent assault also increases with the degree of alcohol intoxication. (Shepherd et. al. 1988).

* Children and Young people: There is particular concern that young people are especially vulnerable to the problems associated with alcohol. (Home Office, 1987b) In England and Wales every year around a thousand chidren below the age of fifteen are admitted to hospital with acute alcohol intoxication. (O' Beattie, 1986) By the age of fifteen, 52% of boys and 37% of girls are drinking weekly in England and Wales. (OPCS, 1986c) The low level of convictions for under age drinking fail to reflect the true incidence of this activity. A Health Education Council survey in 1986 showed that the number of under age drinkers was high and rising. 80% of men and 70% of women admit that they started drinking below the age of eighteen. By the age of fifteen most young people purchase alcohol from licensed outlets. (OPCS, 1986c; Hawker, 1978)

* Economic Costs: Finally the social cost of alcohol has been estimated at over £1,846 million at 1985 prices. (McDonnell and Maynard, 1985; Maynard, Hardman, and Whelan, 1987) Approximately £110 million of this represents the cost to the National Health Service of providing services for alcoholics. But the vast majority of the cost (approximately £1,600 million) falls upon industry in the form of losses such as the costs of absenteeism. In 1981 for example according to a DHSS estimate somewhere between 8 and 15 million working days were lost as a result of employees experiencing alcohol problems.[1]

It should be pointed out though that estimates of the social costs of alcohol misuse can vary, and the figures are often disputed. An alternative estimate of social cost by Professor Jackson of Leicester University puts the figure much lower at £900 million (1988 prices). (*Brewing Review* Summer 1988 p20-1)

The Development of Alcohol Policy in Britain

Alcohol-related problems in Britain have reached an alarming level following a rapid growth during the post-war period, particularly in the sixties and seventies. The government's initial response was to tackle some of the more obvious manifestations of the problem. It responded with measures such as the drink-driving laws and by encouraging an expansion of specialist health services for alcoholics. But as the level of alcohol problems continued to rise, the search began for a

4

deeper explanation. Many began to identify the overall consumption of alcohol - which had also risen dramatically in the post-war period - as the common denominator behind the range of alcohol problems. Accordingly, the focus began to shift from the specific problems associated with alcohol to the general use of the substance itself.

The recognition of an apparent correlation between the level of alcohol misuse and overall alcohol consumption, both in Britain and abroad, raised the possibility of preventing alcohol misuse to some extent by controlling the level of consumption. As a result the government has since come under increasing pressure to adopt policies capable of achieving this. But whereas policies designed to tackle the symptoms of alcohol misuse were largely uncontroversial, alcohol control policies, as they have become known, are much more contentious. Consumption can be discouraged in many ways: by penal taxation on alcohol to raise prices, through stricter licensing controls, and by imposing restrictions on the promotion of alcoholic drink, to name a few possibilities. But such measures have been vigorously opposed by the alcoholic drinks industry, amongst others. Consequently the problem of alcohol misuse has been increasingly seen as a political problem requiring a political solution.

The issue of whether or not special controls should be imposed on alcoholic drink is not by any means new to British politics. (Baggott, 1986, Wilson, 1940, Weir, 1984) In the nineteenth century there was a massive campaign against alcohol in the form of the temperance movement. Following the formation of the pressure group UK Alliance in 1853, the movement adopted the objective of 'legislative suppression' - the restriction of drinking through more stringent licensing laws. This was the signal for the start of a running battle between the drinks industry and the temperance movement, which was eventually resolved around sixty years later when restrictive licensing was introduced as part of the government's wartime emergency restrictions.

Strict controls on alcohol have also been imposed in other countries at various times in history. In the United States between 1919 and 1933 the sale, manufacture, and transport of alcohol was prohibited by the constitution. (Coffey, 1975) The Eighteenth Amendment illustrated how far a liberal democratic government may choose to go in its attempts to discourage alcohol consumption. Indeed the General Secretary's current drive to combat alcohol misuse in the USSR appears liberal in comparison with the Prohibition period in the USA.[2]

It is important to bear in mind the wider international perspective when considering alcohol policy in Britain. (Davies and Walsh, 1983) Although the use of alcohol in Britain is still formally subject to a relatively high degree of regulation, largely for historical reasons, some other countries have gone much further. The Scandanavian countries for example have adopted stringent alcohol control policies, as illustrated by the case of Sweden.

In Sweden the production, importation and distribution of alcoholic drink is largely controlled by a state monopoly. Strict licensing laws govern the retail trade, whilst the advertising of wines, spirits and strong beers is prohibited. In addition alcoholic drink is heavily taxed, in a conscious attempt to prevent drink prices from falling in real terms. There is also a central coordinating council on alcohol questions located within the agency responsible for health policy, the National Board of Health and Welfare. Finally there is an organisation funded by government, the Swedish Council for Information on Alcohol and other Drugs, which promotes education about alcohol and alcohol problems. In 1980 this body spent approximately 13% of the governments revenue from alcoholic drink. In Britain by contrast around £3 million was spent by the government in 1987 on health education about alcohol, a negligible percentage of the £6 billion raised in tax revenue from alcoholic drink in that year.[3]

In Britain, alcohol policy is not as well developed as in many other countries like Sweden. Recently however, for reasons to be discussed later, British policy makers have decided to take a fresh look at the nation's drink problem. The issue of alcohol abuse has consequently become something of a priority. New initiatives have been launched and the government has set up a special committee of ministers to consider and monitor policy. This has been welcomed almost universally. Even so the government continues to steer clear of some of the more controversial policies associated with the regulation of overall alcohol consumption. A comprehensive alcohol policy, incorporating control policies, still appears to be some way off.

The Politics of Alcohol: An Overview

Essentially this book attempts to answer two main questions. First, why have successive British Governments refused to adopt control policies ? Secondly, why has government bothered to do anything at all about alcohol abuse?

The structure of the book is as follows. Chapter two opens with an examination of how the issue of alcohol misuse arrived on to the political agenda in the postwar period. The main aim here is to explain why the state initially began to respond to the growth in alcohol problems, and to outline the factors which shaped this policy.

Chapter three deals with the growing controversy surrounding the alcohol issue during the seventies. The main aim here is to account for the shift in government policy which took place during this period, from treatment to prevention. There is also a re-assessment of the situation here in the light of the government's recent initiative on alcohol abuse.

This is followed by a chapter devoted to the political organisation of the drinks industry and its role in the formation of policy. Of particular interest here are the characteristics of this industrial lobby, its reaction to the growing politicisation of the issue, and the ways in which it has attempted to influence government policy on alcohol.

Whilst these three chapters are concerned with broad questions, such as the emergence of the issue and the formation of the government's general policy on alcohol misuse, chapters five to eight deal with more specific policy issues. The aim is to construct a picture of the pattern of influence in this policy area, through a detailed analysis of salient issues in the alcohol policy debate. Chapter five examines the so-called 'consensus' issues of education and training, the early identification of problem drinkers, and the presentation of alcohol in the media. Chapter six looks at the question of regulating the price of alcohol. Chapter seven examines licensing law reform. Chapter eight considers the issue of drinking and driving.

In the final chapter these various strands are brought together in an attempt to arrive at a coherent explanation of alcohol policy in Britain. There is also an attempt at this stage to place this study in a wider context by discussing important similarities and differences with other public health issues.

Notes

1. *House of Commons Official Report* Volume 997 Column 306w 26 January 1981
2. *The Economist* 20 December 1985 p51-2
3. The figure of £3 million includes central government money spent on drinking and driving campaigns but excludes the money spent on alcohol education by government-funded voluntary organisations and by local health authorities.

2. Alcohol abuse on the political agenda

The present unease about the level of alcohol-related problems in Britain originated out of a specific concern over the quality of services for alcoholics in the fifties and sixties. In this chapter we examine the sources of this concern, the political pressures generated, and the sequence of policy responses which emerged. The main purposes of this exercise are to discover how the issue of alcohol abuse arrived on the political agenda, and how far the government's initial response to the problem has shaped subsequent policy on alcohol services.

We begin by looking at how the concern over services was originally articulated. This is followed by an analysis of the government's response to what became a rapidly deteriorating situation during the early seventies. The third part deals with the subsequent development of services for alcoholics, and the relationship between government and the voluntary organisations which supplied these services. The next section charts the shift in policy which took place during the seventies, whereby the government backed down from its commitment to expand services. Finally, there is a brief account of the reorganisation of the voluntary organisations in the alcohol field, which took place in the early eighties.

Attracting the Government's Attention

The government's initial reaction to the post-war growth in alcohol problems came in response to the demands of a number of professional and voluntary organisations during the sixties. These demands arose from three main sources. The temperance movement and religious organisations; the medical profession; and the law enforcement and penal professions.

Temperance

The temperance movement originated and developed during the nineteenth century, when, as mentioned in the last chapter, the abuse of alcohol was an important political issue. Despite the declension of the alcohol issue after the first world war, the movement was far from moribund. As alcoholism and drunkenness began to grow in the fifties, its campaign took on a renewed relevance. By 1960 the temperance movement could still count on the support of 98 MPs - the total membership of the Parliamentary Temperance Committee.[1] But in contrast its popular support - which had been its strength in the last century - had all but withered away. This was partly because of the declining popular appeal of the church in the post-war period: the temperance movement drew much of its support from churchgoers.

The temperance movement realised that its limited popular appeal was a liability, and created a number of new organisations which, it hoped, would have a more satifactory public image. In September 1961 for example, the Church of England Temperance Society initiated a process which led to the creation of a new voluntary organisation, the National Council on Alcoholism (NCA) in 1962. The NCA's main objectives were to campaign against alcohol abuse, to act as a forum for discussion within the alcohol field, and to coordinate and improve local councils on alcoholism. At the time the NCA was created only two local councils were in operation. It was evisaged that a network of councils would eventually result. These would provide a wide coverage of counselling services for alcoholics; referring them where necessary to other services (such as those provided by hospitals and Alcoholics Anonymous - see below).

Two other important organisations created by the temperance movement in the sixties also deserve mention: the Christian Social and Economic Research Foundation (CSERF) and The Teachers Advisory Committee on Alcohol and Drug Education (TACADE). The CSERF was formed in 1966 on the initiative of the UK Alliance, a temperance organisation. The CSERF was to conduct and publicise empirical studies of the level of alcohol problems in Britain. The aim behind this move was to try and create a greater awareness by society, and by policy makers in particular, of the extent of these problems. Three years later the UK Alliance helped to promote the formation of TACADE. This body, which also seeks to create a wider awareness of alcohol (and other drug) problems, focuses specifically on promoting such an awareness amongst the teaching profession.

The influence of the temperance movement, in view of its rather insiduous strategy, has proved difficult to detect. Even so it is clear that the main organisations within the movement, the UK Alliance and the Church of England Temperance Society, exerted little direct influence on policy in the sixties. This was illustrated for instance by their lack of success in attracting government funding for the NCA during this period.

The medical profession

Whilst the direct influence of the temperance movement appears to have been neglible, the medical profession in contrast seems to have made some impact upon policy makers during this period. The medical profession's awareness of alcohol problems was stimulated by two reports from the influential World Health Organisation (WHO) in 1951 and 1966. In between these two reports there were further signs that the profession was beginning to take a greater interest in these problems. At the British Medical Association's (BMA) Annual Conference in 1965 for example, doctors called on the government to provide more funds for research into alcoholism. But by far the most significant development was the recommendation in 1962 by the Standing Mental Health Advisory Committee (SMHAC), that the government should encourage the expansion of specialist treatment facilities for alcoholics.

SMHAC was an influential advisory body whose members were largely drawn from the psychiatric branch of the medical profession. Its function was to advise the Health Ministry on a wide range of matters concerning mental health services. Alcoholism was at this time regarded by the medical profession as primarily a mental illness, and clearly fell within SMHAC's brief.

Following the recommendation of SMHAC, the Ministry issued a memorandum (Ministry of Health, 1962) to the Regional Hospital Boards (RHBs), which called on them to expand the provision of specialist alcohol treatment units (ATUs) But although the SMHAC recommendation was crucial in the adoption of the new policy, other factors were also favourable. (Robinson and Ettore, 1962) The original impetus for a policy on ATUs came from the BMA and the Magistrates Association (1961). The two associations had set up a joint committee to examine the growing problem of alcoholism. Its main recommendations were incorporated in both the SMHAC advice, and the Ministry of Health memorandum. A further factor may have been the WHO's interest in alcoholism, mentioned above. As Peters (1984) has noted, worldwide organisations such as the WHO 'are responsible for spreading ideas about what government's should do and in turn serve as sources of policy ideas for bureaucracies.'

How significant was the new policy? According to Dr. Max Glatt (1982, p437), one of the original exponents of the ATU, it 'constituted a clear reversal of the former official policy on scattering alcoholics haphazardly in numerous local hospitals.' Yet the actual impact of the new policy was far from spectacular. By 1968, only thirteen ATUs were operational, and three of these were already in existence when the Ministry's memorandum was issued in 1962. The slow development of these services can be partly explained in terms of the general difficulties faced by central government in attempting to implement health policy at the local level. (Haywood and Alaszewski, 1980) But another reason was the unwillingness of the Health Ministry itself to earmark resources specifically for the expansion of specialist units. If it had been prepared to do this, there would have been a greater incentive to expand these services. The failure to provide such funding then suggests that whilst the Ministry was prepared to support a policy of expanding ATUs, it did not in this period consider them a priority.

One reason why the expansion of treatment facilities for alcoholics was not a high priority lies in the internal politics of the medical profession. Within medicine some specialties are considered more prestigious than others. (Ham, 1985, p25) The psychiatrists - at this time the specialists most concerned about the growth of alcoholism - often lacked the status needed to bring about a shift in resources to expand their services. So although the psychiatrists were able to influence alcohol policy within their own area of expertise, they were unable to obtain a significant shift in resources from other areas of medicine on a scale necessary to promote a significant expansion in the provision of ATUs.

It became increasingly obvious that greater resources would only be attracted when other parts of the profession became more aware of alcohol problems and began to join in the call for improved services. This realisation prompted a number of doctors in 1967 to create a new voluntary organisation, the Medical Council on Alcoholism (MCA). The MCA was to act as a pressure group within the profession. It has since tried to create a wider awareness of alcohol problems in two main ways. By disseminating research on alcoholism; and by attempting to persuade those responsible for training doctors to include instruction on the diagnosis and treatment of alcohol problems.

The need to form a body like the MCA suggests that although the medical profession did exert some influence over policy in the sixties, and was an important force behind the movement of alcohol problems on to the agenda, its actual influence was less than it might have been. More pressure could have been brought to bear had the more prestigious parts of the profession taken a greater interest in alcohol problems.

The law enforcement and penal professions

The third major source of concern about alcohol problems in this period, alongside doctors and the temperance movement was the law enforcement and the penal professions. The Magistrates Association, as we have already mentioned, established a joint committee with the BMA to examine the problems associated with alcoholism. As the sixties progressed the Association became particularly concerned about the habitual drunken offender - the alcoholic who was constantly being arrested for public drunkenness. It believed that such offenders should be treated for their illness rather than punished as criminals - a view shared by the police associations,

11

whose members generally resented the time and effort spent in arresting drunks and taking them into custody.

Others groups were also in favour of decriminalising the habitual drunk, including the Probation Officers Association (NAPO), the Prison Officers Association (POA), and NACRO (the National Association for the Care and Resettlement of Offenders). Together these bodies called upon the Home Office, the department responsible for law enforcement and the penal system, to review the situation. Partly because of this pressure, and partly because of a belief within the department that 'decriminalisation' might reduce the burden on both the police and prison service, the Home Office established a working party in 1967 to examine the issue of the habitual drunken offender.

The working party, though established under the auspices of the Home Office, was in effect an interdepartmental committee; containing, in addition to four Home Office officials, three civil servants from the Health Ministry (Department of Health and Social Security from 1968). A recognition of the medical aspects of the problem under consideration was also reflected by the appointment to the working party of two psychiatrists specialising in the treatment of alcoholics. The working party sought evidence from police, magistrates, prison officers, probation officers, and from voluntary organisations. The evidence given reflected a consensus that a much more comprehensive range of treatment and rehabilitation services was needed to tackle the problem.

Four years passed before the working party's report was eventually published. (Home Office, 1971) Yet the enquiry had finished taking evidence as early as May 1968. It appears that the delay was due, at least in part, to disagreement within the committee over the content of the report itself. There was also some dispute over which department should be responsible for the implementation of the report. The Home Office believed that the Department of Health and Social Security (DHSS) should ultimately take responsibility for what it saw as a socio-medical problem, whilst the DHSS was wary of taking on this extra burden.

The main recommendations of the working party's report were as follows. First of all it recommended a pilot scheme of detoxification centres - places where drunken offenders could be 'dried out' as an alternative to the police cells. Secondly, the report called for an expansion in the hostel sector: the Home Office at this time funded a number of hostels which provided a residential service for alcoholic offenders, where they could undergo a process of rehabilitation. Third, the working party urged a greater level of coordination between the agencies involved, so as to promote a better service. It did not however specify how this improvement in coordination was to be achieved and said nothing about tranferring the responsibility for habitual drunken offenders to the DHSS - which had been discussed as a possible option. Later in this chapter we shall return to consider the impact of these these recommendations upon government policy.

Alcoholics

It is evident that the initial calls for action on alcoholism did not come from those directly suffering from alcohol problems, but from other organisations having an indirect interest in the issue. The temperance movement was mainly motivated by moral considerations - the desire to protect the public from the moral (or immoral) consequences of excessive drinking. The medical profession on the other hand saw alcoholism as a disease which needed adequate service provision. Whereas the law enforcement professions saw it mainly as a public order problem which could be prevented to an extent by the provision of rehabilition and treatment services. But what about the alcoholics themselves? Why have they had to rely on others to represent their 'interests'?

There are several reasons why alcoholics did not collectively assert their demands. First of all, alcoholism is a debilitating condition which even today carries a lot of social stigma. Even those alcoholics who were able to coherently articulate their demands may have chosen not to do so in fear of being labelled publicly as an alcoholic. The adverse public image of the 'skid row' alcoholic in particular has inhibited high profile collective action by alcoholics themselves to draw attention to their problems. The widely acknowledged success of Alcoholics Anonymous (AA) does not contradict this reasoning. (Robinson, 1979) AA is a self-help organisation which brings alcoholics together and helps them develop the will to overcome their drink problems. Although it is in regular contact with the DHSS (it has quarterly meetings with the department) and other services for alcoholics, it is prevented by it own internal rules from undertaking any form of political campaign. AA's low profile is moreover essential to its philosophy of anonymity.

The case of AA illustrates that the growth of a social problem in society does not automatically lead to the formation of organisations campaigning politically for the correction of the problem. As a result the interests of alcoholics have been largely represented by those organisations indirectly affected by the growth in alcohol problems: the temperance movement, the medical profession and the law enforcement and penal professions. It is these groups which articulated the demand for action on alcohol abuse in the political arena. It was these groups, particularly the professions, which were influential in getting the issue on to the political agenda during the sixties.

Overlapping memberships

Although the activities of the temperance movement, the medical profession, and the law enforcement and penal professions in this period can be clearly distinguished, there was a considerable overlap between them. They did not operate in splendid isolation from each other. The joint committee of the BMA and the Magistrates Association exemplifies a formal link between groups on this issue. But there were also important informal links which should be mentioned. Some individuals for instance were members of more than one organisation.

Dr Douglas Acres for example has been an influential figure in the Magistrates Association over the last twenty years, and has done much to stimulate the interest of the Association in alcohol misuse. He has also been the chairman of the Churches Council on Alcohol and Drugs (CCAD) an organisation within the temperance movement. He also at one time served on the Executive Committee of the National Council on Alcoholism (NCA). Furthermore he is a qualified General Practitioner and therefore has a medical interest in alcohol abuse. Another individual involved in a number of organisations concerned about alcohol abuse is Dr. Max Glatt, the pioneer of the ATU and vice-chairman of the Medical Council on Alcoholism (MCA) since its inception. He was also a member of the steering committee which paved the way for the formation of the NCA, and has since served on its executive committee. A further example is Derek Rutherford, currently director of the Institute of Alcohol Studies (a temperance-funded body created in 1983). He has been an active member of the temperance movement for many years, and was formerly the director of the National Council on Alcoholism. It is personalities such as these which form the basis of an informal network of communication between the various organisations concerned about alcohol abuse. As is often the case such contacts and links are often more significant than any formal committee.

A Degree of Commitment

Moving into the seventies, the Government's policy on alcoholism began to change in two important respects. First of all, the policy took on a greater significance than it had before, with the government giving it a much higher priority. Secondly, the emphasis of the policy moved away from a hospital-centred treatment approach and towards a more comprehensive community care strategy.

Alcohol: a higher priority

The increasing importance of alcohol policy was reflected in the organisational changes which followed the publication of the Home Office working party's report on habitual drunken offenders in 1971. In the interdepartmental discussions which took place after the report was completed, it was decided that the DHSS would assume the main burden of responsibility for drunken offenders on the grounds that 'facilities for persons who are habitually drunk in public places ought normally to be provided as part of a comprehensive counselling, treatment and rehabilitation service.'[2] As a result the DHSS took responsibility for the residential hostels catering for alcoholic offenders, previously funded by the Home Office. But perhaps more importantly, it took on the responsibility of formulating a response to the recommendations of the working party, outlined in the previous section.

The reshuffling of departmental responsibilities in relation to alcohol problems marked an official recognition that alcoholism and drunkenness were symptoms of the same problem, and that this required a more comprehensive and coordinated strategy than ever before. Hitherto alcoholism and drunkenness had been treated by government as two distinct problems. The new line of thinking was that a more effective policy would result by bringing them under one department. Moreover by placing the responsibility upon the DHSS, the government demonstrated that it now believed alcohol problems to be principally a socio-medical issue, rather than a criminal or public order matter.

These organisational changes, ostensibly at least to improve coordination and thereby producing a more effective policy, indicated that the government was taking alcohol problems more seriously than it had before. This was confirmed by the decision of the DHSS to earmark resources specifically for the development of services in this area. Departmental funds first became available in 1970 when the Secretary of State for Social Services, (Sir) Keith Joseph, granted £2m (£10m at 1986 prices) to the statutory and voluntary organisations involved in the provision of services for alcoholics.[3] Then, in 1972 the DHSS began to give annual grants to the major voluntary organisations in the alcohol field, like the NCA and the MCA. These grants, which were given in order to help these organisations expand their activities, were made under section 64 of the Health Services and Public Health Act of 1968. In addition the government earmarked NHS resources between 1972 and 1975 to encourage a further expansion in ATUs.

But by far the biggest commitment of resources came in 1973, when the DHSS announced its new policy document on alcohol abuse, *Community Services for Alcoholics*. The document, which became more familiarly known by its reference number, 'Circular 21/73' proposed action along similar lines as recommended by the Home Office working party. It made three main commitments. First of all, the DHSS would seek to expand the residential hostel sector it had inherited by granting 'pump-priming' financial assistance to any suitable voluntary organisation willing to provide residential care. Second, it would encourage the growth of local counselling services (such as those supported by NCA, described earlier) to which those suffering from drink problems could turn for advice and information. The third main commitment was to fund an experimental detoxification scheme for drunken offenders, as recommended by the Home Office Working Party.

From treatment to care

Circular 21/73 not only announced the commitment of new resources to the field: it also marked an important shift in policy. The governments previous response to the increase in alcohol problems had been to encourage the development of specialist hospital-based treatment services. Now it emphasised the importance of community care and sought to expand services outside the hospitals. It was envisaged that from now on the community services would play a much greater role than before. But this did not mean that ATUs were now to be discouraged. On the contrary, the DHSS believed that the whole range of services needed to be improved and for this reason continued to earmark funds in an attempt to encourage the growth of ATUs.

The origin of the shift in the emphasis of alcohol policy towards community services can be traced back to 1968, when the Ministry of Health issued further advice to health authorities. (Ministry of Health, 1968) This document repeated the call made in 1962, for an expansion of ATUs in the health service. But whereas the 1962 document was essentially concerned with hospital treatment, the advice given in 1968 mentioned the importance of community services, as a back up for hospital treatment. Indeed the difference in emphasis is suggested in the title of the two documents: the 1962 memorandum was entitled *The Hospital Treatment of Alcoholism*; whereas the 1968 document was simply called *The Treatment of Alcoholism*, the word 'hospital' being significantly omitted.

The expansion of community services foreshadowed by the 1968 memorandum and Circular 21/73 was in line with medical thinking. The 1968 memorandum, was also based on the advice of the Standing Mental Health Advisory Committee (SMHAC). But the shifting emphasis in alcohol policy also reflected wider developments, and in particular the attempt to promote community care in many other areas of the health service in the sixties and early seventies. This policy initiative was particularly evident in mental health services. A series of policy announcements were made in this sector, encouraging services geared to community care rather than to hospital treatment. (see for example DHSS, 1971, 1975) As alcohol problems were still seen as a mental health issue during this period, by the medical profession and by policy makers alike, it is perhaps not surprising that alcohol policy was sensitive to policy developments in the wider field of mental health.

Explaining the government's response

Having now explained the changing content of alcohol policy in the late sixties and early seventies, one must now explain why alcohol abuse became more important in the government's scale of priorities at this time. The increased importance of alcohol abuse was reflected in two main developments, discussed earlier: the reorganisation of government responsibilities in relation to alcohol problems, and the allocation of specific resources to alcohol services.

Perhaps the most obvious explanation for the government's reaction was that the problem was becoming visibly worse. At the beginning of the seventies there was a marked rise in the indicators of alcohol misuse. For example, in England and Wales drunkenness offences in 1970 were almost 14% up on the 1965 figure; the increase over the previous five years had been much lower - approximately 6%. Even when one takes into account the growth in population over this period, the increase is still significant.[4]

Yet it was not so much the growth of the alcohol problem as the growing attention that it began to receive from the media, pressure groups and Parliament, which helped to promote action. The media's interest in alcohol problems increased sharply from around 1970. During this year the media's attention was attracted by the three reports on the extent of alcohol problems in Britain which appeared with-

16

in months of each other. These were the NCA's publication *The Alcohol Explosion*, which came out in January; *Alcohol Abuse*, a report by the Office of Health Economics, which emerged in April; and the annual report of the MCA, which was published in July. The reports all carried basically the same message: that alcoholism was a social problem requiring urgent attention. The media's interest was stimulated and the reports were given plenty of coverage. Newspapers and periodicals began to run feature articles on alcoholism during the early seventies. (see for example *The Times* 22 November 1971, p3: *The Economist* 24 January 1970: *New Society* 20 May, 1971) The broadcast media also took a greater interest, and the subject was covered both by documentaries and in drama. A fine example of the latter was the play *Edna the Inebriate Woman* screened in 1971 by the BBC, which did much to raise public awareness about the plight of homeless alcoholics.

The alcohol problem also became a much more important issue for many pressure groups during the early seventies. The groups already mentioned - the temperance movement, the medical profession, and the law enforcement and penal professions - intensified their efforts to persuade government to take the problem more seriously. In particular the activities of the Medical Council on Alcoholism began to create a wider awareness of alcohol problems within the medical profession. But other groups also began to take an interest in the alcohol issue. Established cause groups such as the Howard League for Penal Reform (HLPR, 1974), the Campaign for Homeless and Rootless (CHAR, 1971), and the National Society for the Prevention of Cruelty to Children (Stewart, 1974) became concerned about the implications of alcohol problems for their particular cause. Although these groups did not become closely involved in campaigning for action on alcoholism, their concern demonstrated that the constituency of support for further government intervention was now wider.

Parliament also became more interested in alcohol problems during this period. One indicator of this is the number of Parliamentary Questions tabled on the subject. In the Commons during the period 1960-70, 5.3 PQs per session on average were asked on matters concerning alcoholism and drunkenness (calculated from table one) This compares with an average of 19.8 per session for the period 1970-5. During the seventies 27.5 PQs per session were tabled on the subject of alcoholism and drunkenness. This trend is also reflected by the increase in the number of debates on alcoholism after 1970. There was only one debate in Parliament (Lords and Commons) during the sixties. Whilst in the seventies, alcoholism was debated on seven occasions, three times in the Lords and four times in the Commons.

Table 1

Parliamentary Questions on Alcohol Problems

Session	Alcoholism and drunkenness	Drink-driving	Total
1960-1 to 1964-5	28 (5.6)	19 (3.8)	47 (9.4)
1965-6 to 1969-70	25 (5.0)	102 (20.4)	127 (25.4)
1970-1 to 1974-5	99 (19.8)	31 (6.2)	130 (26.0)
1975-6 to 1979-80	176 (35.2)	67 (13.4)	243 (48.6)
1980-1 to 1984-5	177 (35.4)	56 (11.2)	223 (44.6)

Note: Figures in brackets represent average number of PQs per Parliamentary Session.

Source: *House of Commons Official Report*

The growing Parliamentary activity on the subject of alcohol abuse reflected the interests of a number of MPs who were allied to pressure groups in the alcohol field. Sir Bernard Braine, who later became the chairman of the NCA, and Ron Lewis, who was linked with temperance organisations, were particularly active in tabling PQs and motions. But others were involved, and as the seventies progressed their activities expanded leading to the creation of an all-party group of MPs on alcohol misuse.[5]

The increased political salience of the alcohol issue may partly explain why the government decided to give it a higher priority than before. Even so it is important to maintain a sense of proportion. The pressure on government to expand alcohol services was by no means irresistable. Alcohol problems still had a much lower profile than other social problems, such as illicit drug addiction for example. This is clearly reflected in evidence from public opinion polls. In 1967 one survey asked members of the public if they believed drug taking in Britain to be a serious problem or not. 87% of the respondents said it was, and only 8% believed the opposite to be the case. But by contrast another survey, taken in 1973, found that only 19% of public believed that excessive drinking was a very serious social problem, a further 38% believing it to be moderately serious. (Gallup, 1976) Moreover, the DHSS, in its circular on the development of alcohol services in 1973, observed 'the reluctance of public opinion to recognise the scale and nature of the (alcohol) problem.' Finally, the public's view of the value of services for alcoholics was reflected in a more recent survey of Scottish attitudes in 1976. According to this survey only 14% of the public believed that such services were 'something well worth spending money on.' (Scottish Home and Health Department, 1976, p173) Since alcoholism and drunkenness are more widespread north of the border, one might guess that the support for such services in England and Wales is even lower.

The absence of widespread public support could have seriously undermined the case for an expansion of service provision in this sector. But any effect this might have had was offset by the favourable disposition of the DHSS towards action on alcohol problems in the seventies. Indeed the DHSS began to take a far more active role in relation to alcohol policy than it had previously. During the sixties, as we have seen, the department responded in a rather passive fashion to its medical advisors. In the seventies this approach was replaced by a more active, interventionist style. As one observer has remarked 'the surge of enthusiasm for all matters alcoholic which overtook the DHSS during the period has known no equal before or since.' (Steele, 1984)

One possible explanation for this transformation is that the reorganisation of departmental responsibilities in 1972, mentioned earlier, gave the DHSS a clear brief to formulate and implement a comprehensive policy on alcohol problems. There are however two problems with this line of reasoning. First of all, as we have already noted, there was some evidence of conflict between the DHSS and the Home Office in the late sixties over the transfer of the responsibility for drunken offenders. The DHSS change of heart in the early seventies is therefore left unexplained by this account. Second, the reorganisation itself was, as we have argued above, an indication of a growing awareness by government that alcohol problems were of increasing significance. To say that the new brief promoted the new policy in effect puts the cart before the horse.

Both the reorganisation of responsibilities in relation to alcohol problems, and the allocation of new resources to this area are best explained in terms of ministerial initiative. Significantly the rise of alcohol policy in the government's scale of priorities appears to coincide with the appointment of Sir Keith (now Lord) Joseph as Secretary of State for Social Services in 1970. In fact this was something more than a coincidence. According to many in the field at this time Keith Joseph was certainly taking a personal interest in alcoholism. He himself claims to have had a personal concern, though he adds that this was not exclusive of other more general concerns about the scale of alcohol problems.[6] It seems clear that the new policy was not being sold to the Minister by his senior civil servants. The Senior Medical Officer (SMO) responsible for alcohol abuse has since spoken of the reappraisal of policy which followed the Secretary of State's initiative. (Sippert, 1975)

Why did Keith Joseph take such an interest? It may be significant that his cousin, Harry Vincent, was chairman of the National Council on Alcoholism at the time. No doubt he had access to the Secretary of State and was able to inform him of the scale of the problem and the difficulties facing the organisation. But whatever the reason, it is clear that the Secretary of State's personal interest, rather than powerful pressure from media, Parliament and organised groups, was the key factor behind the higher priority given to alcohol policy during the early seventies. Though this is not to deny the importance of these other factors in maintaining a political and social climate highly conducive to action on alcohol abuse.

The Impact of the New Policy

Consultation and relationships

The government's greater commitment to services for alcoholics brought it into closer contact with the voluntary organisations and it began to consult them on a regular basis on matters concerning alcohol policy. For example, when the Secretary of State announced the special allocation of resources for the development of alcohol services in 1970, the MCA and the NCA were both consulted on the question of how the money should be spent. Previously, advice on alcohol policy had been taken mainly from the medical profession. But the successful implementation of the new policy, with its emphasis on community services, now depended on the cooperation of the voluntary organisations. They were in effect acting as agents of the DHSS, supplying a service on its behalf. But the department was still responsible for overall policy and for this reason had to establish lines of communication, accountability and control in this area. This meant that it had to cast its consultative net much further than before, and as a result the voluntary organisations gained greater access to the policy making process.

The incorporation of the voluntary organisations within the policy making process was further illustrated in 1974 when, on the initiative of the DHSS, a new voluntary organisation was formed to represent the interests of the growing hostel sector. The Federation of Alcohol Residential (later Rehabilitation) Establishments (FARE) was created largely because the department preferred to consult a single body rather than the thirty or so separate organisations which provided this service. The department also believed that a body such as FARE would provide a more effective channel of communication between the government and the hostels, and would therefore promote better coordination of services in this sector.

The voluntary organisations became even more closely involved with the health department as the seventies progressed. In 1974 the Secretary of State announced the establishment of an Advisory Committee on Alcoholism, which would provide specialist advice on how best to tackle the problem. The committee was set up initially for an experimental period of three years and its membership was drawn from a wide range of organisations having an interest in alcohol problems. The medical bias of the commitee's membership indicated that this profession, of all those involved, still carried the most weight. Out of the thirty one members of the committee, nine - including the chairman, Professor Kessel - were drawn from the medical profession. A further three members had a background in nursing, four in

the probation and social work services, and four were drawn from the voluntary organisations. The police and magistrates were also represented. The remainder were
lay members and academics. The Advisory Committee contributed to the development of policy in this area chiefly through its three reports on alcoholism, which
will be discussed later in this chapter and in the next.

The development of services

What was the actual impact of the government's new policy and the new relationships which it encouraged? Table two illustrates the development of services for
alcoholics in the seventies compared with the previous period. From this one can
see how the provision of services began to expand, particularly after 1970. Alcoholic Treatment Units (ATUs) had been encouraged for almost a decade before the
new initiative. Yet despite the emphasis on community services, the ATU sector
grew faster in the seventies than it had in the previous decade. This was mainly because NHS resources were earmarked for the expansion of ATUs between 1972
and 1975. The rapid development of local councils on alcoholism is also clearly indicated in the table. During the sixties, as we saw earlier, the NCA had been unsuccessful in its attempts to obtain the necessary government funds to support an expansion of local counselling and information services. In contrast the injection of
resources into this sector in the seventies stimulated a fourfold increase in the number of local councils between 1973 and the end of the decade.

Table 2

The Development of Alcohol Services (England and Wales)

	ATUs/NHS units	Local Councils	Hostels
1962	3	2	-
1964	-	5	-
1968	13	5	10
1970	14	9	-
1973	18	9	21
1974	-	-	30
1975	22	-	-
1976	-	-	44
1978	25	-	65
1979	-	26	-
1980	34	35	70
1986	35	80	86

Sources: *Department of Health and Social Security, National Council on Alcoholism, Federation of Alcohol Rehabilitation Establishments, Alcohol
Concern.*

The expansion in the number of residential hostels was also significant. The DHSS inherited 21 hostels from the Home Office After Care Scheme in 1972. By 1980 there were seventy hostels with a combined capacity of 800 places, a seven-fold increase in less than ten years. In addition the DHSS funded three experimental detoxification centres during the seventies, as recommended by the Home Office Working Party. The first was opened in Leeds in 1976.

These achievements though appear less significant in the context of the continued growth in alcohol problems during the decade. In 1981 the Office of Health Economics estimated that 150,000 people in Britain were dependent on alcohol, and that in all 700,000 suffered from some form of drink problem. Yet in the same year the ATUs and the hostels together could only provide 1,550 places for problem drinkers.[7] Moreover according to one source the turnover of all the alcohol services in any one year amounted to no more than 20,000 individuals, a mere fraction of those believed to be suffering from alcohol problems. (National Council on Alcoholism, 1982, p8)

The Commitment Falters

More might have been achieved in this sector if the original commitments had been followed through. But as the seventies progressed the DHSS began to reassess its policy of expanding alcohol services. This led to four main developments in the late seventies and early eighties.

New developments

First of all the Advisory Committee on Alcoholism was wound up in 1978. When it was established in 1975 ministers evisaged that it would operate on a temporary basis.[8] But few outside government believed that it would be wound up within the three year period originally set. Moreover, according to several members of the Advisory Committee, it did not automatically lapse but was disbanded on the explicit initiative of Health Ministers in 1978.

A second development occurred partly as a result of one of the Advisory Committee's reports. In its report on alcohol services in 1977, the committee emphasised the importance of detecting and treating drinking problems at an early stage. (DHSS, 1977a) It also favoured a more localised service to provide primary care for problem drinkers. This had implications for the ATUs which were based at regional level: the report recommended that ATUs should be seen as part of a broad range of services available at a local level. This represented a further shift away from the philosophy of specialised treatment for alcoholics. It was against this background that the DHSS decided that no new ATUs would be funded after 1980.

A third development occurred around 1980. This was the DHSS decision to get local councils on alcoholism to stand on their own feet, and not to rely on central government funds channelled through the NCA. The NCA was told by the DHSS to cease its funding of local councils within twelve months. Eventually a compromise was worked out between the department and the NCA and central funding was cut rather than cut off. Even so the restriction of central funds, especially at a time when local government spending was being squeezed, tended to discourage further growth in local councils. This notably went against the Advisory Committee's report on services, which had recommended an expansion of local councils.

Fourthly, the expansion of the hostels sector was also checked by the lack of available resources. Again the Advisory Committee's recommendations were ignored when in 1979 the DHSS announced that hostels would have to obtain finance from elsewhere. Between 1973 and 1980 the DHSS had provided £2.4m in capital and revenue grants to the hostels sector under the terms set out in Circular 21/73.[9] It was however intended at the outset that central government funding of this sector would be temporary. The original idea was that DHSS funding would be used to pump-prime the development of hostels for a period of five years. It was assumed that after this time the hostels would be supported by local authority grants. But the reality was quite different. By 1979 many hostels were still dependent on central government finance by and faced closure if the DHSS went ahead with its plans to end central funding. The original pump-priming scheme had in fact been scheduled to end in 1978. But the difficulties which hostels had faced in obtaining local funds persuaded the government to extend central funding until March 1980. (DHSS, 1978a) In a repeat of their earlier attempt to avert the closure of hostels, the voluntary organisations, with local authorities in support, made representations to the DHSS in December 1979. The minimum demand was for another short term extension of central funding, though in one meeting at the DHSS, FARE, CHAR and NACRO, called for permanent central funding. There was also some pressure from MPs on this issue: in the 1979-80 session of Parliament, 39 Questions were tabled on the subject. All supported the voluntary organisations' case.

These demands met with a measure of success. Reluctantly the DHSS agreed to give limited aid to those hostels which had been unable to secure local funding by March 1980. But the DHSS reiterated its intention to end central funding by stating that under no circumstances would it fund hostels after April 1981. At the FARE Annual Conference in 1980 the DHSS was accused of intransigence. It was claimed that the department had backed out of commitments, set out in Circular 21/73. The Conference also criticised the DHSS for refusing to fund a third experimental detoxification centre in London, as earlier promised.

Why did the commitment to services falter?

A number of the above developments had been foreshadowed, notably the winding up of the Advisory Committee on Alcoholism and the curtailment of hostel grants. But new pressures had also emerged in the seventies which forced a reappraisal of the DHSS policy on services.

23

First of all the services were hit by government policies on public expenditure in the late seventies and early eighties. The Labour government initially was forced to clamp down on public spending in view of the general economic situation. As a result many programmes, particularly those recently established, came under threat. The election of the Thatcher Government in 1979 added momentum to moves to cut central government funding of alcohol services.

Secondly, the new initiative on preventive medicine, began by the Labour Government in the mid-seventies and continued by its Conservative successor, represented a further threat to alcohol services (see chapter three below). Alcohol abuse fell into that category of health problems which the government believed would be tackled more effectively by a strategy of prevention. This had serious consequences for the developing network of services for alcoholics, since most of these services focused upon the treatment, care, and rehabilitation of those already suffering considerably from alcohol problems. This was particularly true of the treatment units and the hostel sector. The counselling services, such as those operated by the National Council on Alcoholism, were however more prevention-oriented. As were the education and training functions undertaken by one of the newer voluntary organisations in the field, the Alcohol Education Centre (AEC). The commitment of the NCA and the AEC to prevention meant that they were more favourably placed than the treatment and care-oriented services in the light of this new development in health policy.

Thirdly, there were also more specific doubts about the effectiveness of care and treatment services. The government was becoming increasingly dissatisfied with the hostels sector in particular. The DHSS, in its evidence to the House of Commons Expenditure Committee in 1976, referred to the development of services in this sector as 'disappointingly slow.' (House of Commons, 1977b p340) There were also growing doubts in government, shared by some in the field, about the effectiveness of ATUs. As government became more conscious of the need to be cost-effective, the future of care and treatment services looked increasingly bleak.

Recriminations and Reorganisation

Recriminations

By the early 1980s the relationship between the DHSS and the voluntary organisations had turned rather sour. This was due in no small part to the cuts in central government funding discussed above. In addition to this many organisations felt more excluded from the policy making process than had been the case in the seventies. There was growing tension in particular between the department and the hostel sector. FARE, the organisation which represented this sector, had at first enjoyed a fairly close relationship with the DHSS; but this gradually changed. For example, in 1983 FARE had to persuade an MP to ask the Secretary of State for Social Services why his department had not replied to a letter from FARE received six months earlier.[10]

The department nevertheless was still responsible for the voluntary organisations. Despite the deteriorating financial situation it continued to give resources to the main national voluntary bodies. It also maintained its informal links with these organisations, and in the case of the NCA for instance continued the practice of sending official observers to the meetings of its executive committee. But above all the department was highly sensitive to criticism that the voluntary sector was uncoordinated and that the organisations involved duplicated each other's work. The House of Commons Expenditure Committee in 1977 had recommended that the 'inevitable overlap of preventive work being done by various bodies existing to counter alcoholism should be reduced by coordinating these bodies under one umbrella organisation.' Following this the department raised the possibility of a merger with the voluntary organisations. Although some agreement was reached, the merger never materialised; the most that could be achieved was a decision to house three of the organisations- NCA, MCA and FARE- in the same building.

Reorganisation

The question of a merger returned to the agenda in 1981 amidst widespread rumours that the organisations were fighting amongst themselves. This time the DHSS, along with the National Council for Voluntary Organisations (NCVO), set up an enquiry in March 1981 to examine the role of the voluntary organisations and their relationships with each other. The DHSS/NCVO report (DHSS, 1982) concluded that the present situation was far from satisfactory, and noted in particular that '....competition rather than cooperation seems to predominate. FARE tends to fight the corner for residential services, NCA, counselling services, MCA, the medical viewpoint.' The report went on to recommend a rationalisation of activities along the following lines.

First of all it recommended that the government should replace NCA, MCA, FARE, and AEC with a single organisation. This new body would be responsible for the provision of information and advice about alcoholism, the planning and development of alcohol services, training of local counsellors, and the development of alcohol and work policies (see chapter five). It was envisaged that the new organisation would receive a government grant to help it carry out its duties.

The second recommendation was for a small campaigning body to inform the public on the issue of alcohol misuse. The report called on the Royal Colleges of Medicine to take a lead role in establishing such an organisation, and made a case for it to be supported by public funds. It would therefore be rather similar to the pressure group, Action on Smoking and Health (ASH), a small organisation formed in 1971 by the Royal College of Physicians to campaign on the smoking and health issue. Since 1973 ASH has received a grant from the DHSS to help it perform this role more effectively.

The third main recommendation was that the Health Education Council (HEC) should assume the responsibility for education about alcohol. The HEC, an existing quasi-governmental agency funded by the DHSS, would therefore assume the educational functions of the NCA and the AEC.

The DHSS responded to these and other recommendations and by setting in motion a process that would lead to the creation of a new voluntary organisation. It tried to force the existing organisations to accept the need for reorganisation by making it clear that those wishing to remain outside the reorganisation process would lose their central government grant. The DHSS prompted the four organisations involved - NCA, MCA, FARE and AEC - to set up a steering group as a means of paving the way for the new organisation. Originally the department believed that the new organisation could be established by April 1983, but the steering group discussions took longer than expected. One reason for the delay was the refusal of the MCA to join in the reorganisation. This ultimately resulted in the withdrawal of the MCA's grant; although it should also be noted that, of the four organisations involved, the MCA was the least dependent on government funds, 60% of its income coming from other sources.

In time, out of the steering group's deliberations came a new voluntary organisation, Alcohol Concern, which was launched in November 1983. NCA, FARE and AEC were wound up, and their aggregrate grant (albeit slightly reduced) passed to the new organisation. The DHSS was not prepared however to allocate public funds in similar fashion to a campaigning organisation, as recommended by the DHSS/NCVO report. In part this reflected the department's fear of a backlash from the drinks industry, which was firmly opposed to creation of such an organisation. The department clarified its position in a response to a Parliamentary Question tabled on the 16th of November 1983 by Barry Porter MP. At the time, incidentally, Porter was chairman of an all-party group of MPs which had been formed to defend the interests of registered drinking clubs.

But this did not prevent the emergence of the new campaigning body. In 1982, following the DHSS/NCVO report, the conference of Royal Medical Colleges decided to establish such an organisation. This led directly to the creation of Action on Alcohol Abuse (AAA), which was launched shortly before Alcohol Concern in September 1983. Don Steele, the former director of FARE, became its first director.

So by the end of 1983, there were three main national voluntary bodies in the alcohol field. Alcohol Concern, which was government funded; Action on Alcohol Abuse and the Medical Council on Alcoholism, which were not. They were joined by the Institute of Alcohol Studies, which had been established in 1983 by the temperance movement as a forum for generating research and debate about alcohol issues.

Conclusion

From the early sixties onwards the DHSS (and its predecessor, the Ministry of Health) became ever more closely involved with the problems of alcohol abuse.

The main policy response until the mid-seventies, as we have seen, was to expand and develop services for those individuals suffering from drinking problems. This official willingness to intervene reflected not just the growth in magnitude of alcohol problems, but an increased awareness of these problems both within government and in society at large. Alcohol abuse had during this time become an issue, attracting the attention of the public, the media, and Parliament. It therefore required a much more active response from government than before. This process was helped considerably by the personal interest in the issue taken by Lord Joseph, the senior health minister in the early seventies.

But although alcohol abuse as an issue had grown in stature, it was still comparatively speaking a dwarf among giants, certainly until the late seventies. One indicator of the issue's relative lack of importance was its slow return to the political agenda. It crept quietly on to the political agenda during the late sixties, and even a decade later appeared far less significant politically than many similar health and social policy issues, in particular 'hard drugs.'

As we have seen, alcohol abuse arrived on the political agenda largely as a result of concern about services. This concern was voiced by a range of professional groups having an indirect interest in the problem of alcohol abuse, and a number of voluntary organisations. The medical profession, and the law enforcement and penal professions, did much to attract the attentions of policy makers, and exerted considerable influence over policy. Even so it is clear that the issue of alcohol abuse was not central to the interests of any single professional group. Moreover, the voluntary organisations, to whom alcohol abuse was a central issue, were weak and fragmented. It would be wrong therefore to say that alcohol services were supported by a strong, well organised, and coherent lobby. This did not matter so much when the political climate to service development was favourable. But when this climate began to change in the latter part of the seventies, services became extremely vulnerable, and the political constituency which supported them was shown to be relatively weak.

Notes

1. *The Times* 17th November 1960 p8
2. *House of Commons Official Report* Volume 831 Column 178-9, 18 February 1972
3. *House of Commons Official Report* Volume 806 Column 392, 11 November 1970
4. Home Office Offences of Drunkenness London HMSO
5. Personal Correspondence with Sir Bernard Braine
6. Personal Correspondence with Sir Keith Joseph
7. Figures supplied by DHSS and FARE.
8. *House of Commons Official Report* Volume 889 Column 199-200w 26 March 1975

9. *House of Commons Official Report* Volume 971 Column 697-8w

10. *House of Commons Official Report* Volume 35 Column 287w 24January 1983

3 From treatment to prevention

As we saw in the last chapter, the provision of services for alcoholics and problem drinkers was a relatively uncontroversial matter. Even where the development of services was inhibited, this was not the result of direct opposition from organised interests, but a reflection of the relative political weakness of those demanding expansion. During the seventies, however, the emphasis of alcohol policy shifted away from the provision of treatment-oriented services towards an approach based on prevention. This new approach was in contrast highly controversial and provoked strong opposition from a number of quarters, including government departments, politicians, and organised interests.

In this chapter we shall examine closely the more recent and controversial phase of alcohol policy in Britain. First of all, we focus upon the trend in overall alcohol consumption, which was identified by many in the seventies as the common factor behind the continued growth of alcohol problems. We then move on to relate this to the increasing pressure on government during the late seventies and subsequently, to adopt a comprehensive and coherent policy to prevent alcohol misuse. The second section goes on to deal with the response of the Department of Health and Social Security - the department having overall responsibility for alcohol abuse - to this pressure. This is followed by a look at how the government as a whole responded to the implications of a policy designed to prevent alcohol misuse by controlling consumption. Next, we discuss the problems of coordinating government policy on issues such as alcohol abuse, which cut across formal departmental responsibilities. In the final section we examine the government's recent initiative to coordinate alcohol policy.

The Changing Demands of the Alcohol Misuse Lobby

We have already seen that during the sixties and early seventies the demands for action on alcohol problems were fragmented. These demands involved a number of diverse groups, each drawing attention to one particular aspect of the problem. Doctors pointed out the medical problems associated with alcohol abuse; the law enforcement professions highlighted the implications for crime and public order, and so on. In short, the government was called upon to adopt specific policies to tackle the particular problems identified by these groups. During the seventies however, these diverse concerns became more integrated. This was partly due to the identification of a common factor which appeared to be responsible for the continued growth of these problems.

Alcohol consumption

This common denominator was the level of alcohol consumption. The relationship between overall consumption and the level of alcohol problems was first discovered by the French statistician Ledermann (1956) in the fifties. The Ledermann Hypothesis, as it became known, suggested a fixed relationship between the average (per capita) level of alcohol consumption and the level of alcohol misuse in society. Although Ledermann's work was later criticised on the grounds that his statistical assumptions were far too unrealistic, (Duffy and Cohen, 1978; Miller and Agnew, 1974) cross-national evidence collected during the seventies, after a prolonged period of increasing alcohol consumption, suggested that there was indeed a link. (Bruun, 1975; Davies and Walsh, 1983; de Lindt and Schmidt, 1971; Schmidt, 1977) The general argument of these studies was that changes in the overall consumption of alcoholic drink by society as a whole had a bearing on the level of alcohol problems in that society. Table three reproduces cross national data for overall consumption and liver cirrhosis deaths (an indicator of the general level of alcohol problems). This indicates an apparent link between consumption and alcohol abuse.

Table 3

Alcohol Consumption and Liver Cirrhosis Deaths

	(a) Alcohol Consumed Per head (litres)	(b) Deaths from Cirrhosis of Liver per 100,000 pop.	Ranking by(a)	Ranking by(b)
France	17	33	1	1
Spain	14	21	2	4
West Germany	13	28	3	3
Austria	12	32	4	2
Hungary	11	20	5	5
Switzerland	10	13	6	9
Belgium	10	15	7	7
Czechoslovakia	9	18	8	6
Denmark	9	10	9	13
Yugoslavia	8	13	10	8
East Germany	8	12	11	10
Holland	8	5	12	15
Poland	8	11	13	12
England and Wales	8	4	14	17
Finland	6	7	15	14
Sweden	6	12	16	11
Norway	5	3	17	15
Iceland	4	2	18	18

Source: *Office of Health Economics (1981).*

An examination of the indicators of alcohol misuse in Britain during the post-war period reveals a similar connection. As table four shows, there appears to be a positive correlation between alcohol consumption and problems. The doubling of alcohol consumption per head since the fifties has been paralleled by significant increases in drunkenness offences and deaths from alcohol.

Table 4

The Relationship between Alcohol Consumption and Misuse

Year	Consumption(a)	Drunkenness(b)	Deaths from Alcohol(c)
1950	9.1	1.10 (-)	2.3 (-)
1955	9.5	1.22 (2.55)	2.6 (-)
1960	10.7	1.48 (2.78)	2.8 (-)
1965	11.3	1.53 (2.86)	3.1 (4.8)
1970	13.2	1.68 (2.75)	3.1 (5.7)
1975	16.3	2.11 (2.26)	4.6 (8.4)
1980	18.6	2.48 (2.68)	5.3 (11.0)
1985	17.1	1.51 (3.1)	6.1 (11.0)

Notes

(a) Consumption of pure alcohol per head in pints for population aged fifteen and over in the UK
(b) Findings of guilt per hundred thousand population, England and Wales (Scottish figures in brackets)
(c) Deaths per hundred thousand from alcohol psychoses, alcohol dependence, chronic liver disease and cirrhosis, and alcohol poisoning, England and Wales (Scottish figures in brackets)

Sources: *Brewers Society; Home Office; Scottish Office; Office of Population Censuses and Surveys, General Register Office, Scotland.*

The identification of alcohol consumption as the common denominator and the potential causal factor behind the growth in alcohol problems led naturally on to the question of how consumption could be controlled. A range of measures were suggested including tighter liquor licensing laws to regulate the use and availability of alcohol, high taxation to raise the price of drinks, and education and restrictions on the promotion of alcoholic drinks to moderate consumption. Research was soon being generated on the effectiveness of such measures in regulating the consumption of alcohol. (see, for example, Popham, Schmidt, de Lindt, 1975) This in turn produced a growing realisation that the systematic application of consumption control measures could help prevent alcohol problems emerging in the first place.

The support for alcohol control policies, as these measures became collectively known, began to emerge during the late seventies. There were four sources of potential support for such policies: the medical and caring professions, the temperance movement, the law enforcement professions, and the voluntary organisations - all of which, as we saw in the last chapter, had reasons to be concerned about the continued growth of alcohol misuse.

The medical profession

As it happened, medical opinion began to move in favour of control policies towards the end of the seventies. This was reflected in a number of papers published in the major medical journals. One of the most significant of these was a paper by Robert Kendell, Professor of Psychiatry at the Royal Edinburgh Hospital, which appeared in the *British Medical Journal* in 1979. He attacked the traditional view, that alcoholism was a disease, and suggested that the problem of alcohol misuse was political than a medical. According to Kendall a political solution was therefore needed: government should intervene to reduce the overall level of alcohol consumption. He went on:

"There are sound reasons... for believing that all the consequences of alcohol abuse would be reduced if total population consumption could be reduced; and that within fairly broad limits, total population consumption could be reduced by legislative changes to increase the price or restrict the availability of alcoholic beverages... Until we stop regarding alcoholism as a disease and therefore as a problem to be dealt with by the medical profession, and accept it as an essentially political problem, for everyone and for our legislators in particular, we shall never tackle the problem effectively." (Kendall, 1979)

The Lancet also began to carry articles with a similar message. An editorial early in 1981 supported a greater level of intervention in the alcoholic drinks market and observed that '... the liquor supply is too important to the public's wellbeing for it to be left entirely to market forces.' (Anon. 1981)

The Royal Colleges of Medicine and the British Medical Association appeared to be of a similar opinion. The BMA, in its evidence to the House of Commons Expenditure Committee in 1976, supported legislative intervention in conjunction with a programme of public education about alcohol. (House of Commons, 1977b p357-60) In 1979 and 1980 the BMA leadership was forced to take an even harder line on alcohol misuse. Resolutions passed by the Representative Body of the BMA committed the leadership to press for effective alcohol control measures including a ban on alcohol advertising.

The Royal Colleges were also by this time taking a greater interest in control policies. The Royal College of Psychiatrists' committee on alcohol problems in 1979 considered a number of measures and came down firmly in support of control policies. The main recommendation of the committee's report was for a new emphasis on prevention, based on a commitment by government to restrain the growth in alcohol consumption. In particular the report urged that government should be prepared to use taxation to influence drink prices. Similar conclusions were reached by the Royal College of Physicians' Faculty of Community Medicine (1980). Its report on alcohol abuse went on to recommend a reduction in the level of consumption - to be brought about mainly by a ban on alcohol advertising, a reduction in the number of licensed outlets selling drink, and higher taxation to increase the price of alcoholic drinks.

In the last chapter we saw that during the sixties and the early seventies the issue of alcohol misuse failed to attract the attention of the higher status elements of the medical profession. But by the end of the decade most of the Royal Medical Colleges had begun to show much more concern. In the aftermath of the Royal College of Psychiatrists' report, there followed a dialogue involving all the Colleges. Out of this came the initiative to foster the campaigning organisation, Action on Alcohol Abuse (Triple A) whose emergence was discussed further in the previous chapter.

The law enforcement and penal professions

In contrast the law enforcement and penal professions did not show the same degree of enthusiasm for control policies during this period. Although concern about the continued growth in alcohol problems was voiced by several organisations in this area, including the Association of Chief Police Officers (ACPO), the Magistrates' Association, and the Justices' Clerks' Society (JCS), only one, the National Association of Probation Officers (NAPO) openly favoured a policy of reducing alcohol consumption. Moreover,it was not until 1982 that the NAPO executive approved a programme of alcohol control which included raising drink prices, banning the advertisement of alcohol on TV, and reducing the number of licensed outlets.

It appears that the fairly neutral position taken by the other organisations on this question was mainly due to internal divisions of opinion, rather than an ignorance of the policy options. But whatever the reason, their failure to support control policies was significant. ACPO, the Magistrates Association, and the JCS are all highly regarded by government. They are frequently consulted by government departments, and the Home Office in particular, on a wide range of law and order issues, and therefore have the opportunity to put forward views on policy. One can conclude from this that the case for control policies was substantially weakened by the failure of these groups to support such an approach in the late seventies.

The voluntary alcohol bodies

Surprisingly perhaps, the voluntary organisations were also divided on the subject of control policies. Indeed only the National Council on Alcoholism (NCA) arrived at a clear position on this. In 1979 the NCA Annual Conference endorsed a programme of action which included an increase in the price of drink and a freeze on plans to relax the licensing laws. Although the NCA was still concerned about the inadequacy of services for alcoholics, and continued to campaign for more funds for counselling services in particular, it nevertheless became more prevention-oriented during the late seventies. Its support for control policies represented a clear movement in this direction.

Meanwhile the other voluntary organisations, whose main interests lay in research (The Medical Council on Alcoholism - MCA), treatment and rehabilitation (FARE), and education (MCA and the Alcohol Education Centre - AEC), were much less enthusiastic about control policies. The MCA still saw alcoholism as disease, caused mainly by factors related to the individual's personal background, and rejected consumption theory. Whilst FARE, as we saw in the last chapter, was preoccuppied with protecting hostel services, in the light of the shift in policy away from the provision of services. Finally, the AEC, although taking a greater interest in the consumption theory debate, and being more prevention-oriented than either FARE or MCA, did not openly endorse control policies.

The temperance movement

Perhaps the least equivocal of all the groups concerned about alcohol misuse during the seventies was the temperance movement. The movement has had a traditional commitment to control policies of one form or another. During the nineteenth century the temperance bodies supported and campaigned for a policy of 'legislative suppression of the liquor traffic' (Baggott, 1986) In the nineteen-seventies the two main organisations in this area, the Churches Council on Alcohol and Drugs (CCAD), and the UK Alliance (UKA), maintained this tradition by reaffirming their opposition to a relaxation of the licensing laws, and by supporting measures to increase the price of alcohol and to restrict alcohol advertising.

In the public eye the temperance movement is hampered by what some may refer to as a 'killjoy persona'. Moreover, policy makers in recent years have tended to attach less weight to the opinions of the movement in view of its rather 'antiquated' image. But as we noted in the last chapter, the movement has sponsored a number of new organisations in an attempt to overcome these problems. The NCA for example was created by the temperance movement, and more recently the Institute for Alcohol Studies. So although the movement has carried little influence in its own right, it has been able to press its views through contact with and influence over other organisations in the field.

The alcohol misuse lobby

Together these four groups: the medical profession, the law enforcement and penal professions, the voluntary organisations, and the temperance movement, constituted a potential lobby - the alcohol misuse lobby. Although, as we have seen, the support for control policies varied considerably amongst these groups, they nevertheless comprised a more integrated and coherent lobby during the late seventies. In the previous decade the different aspects of alcohol misuse were perceived as distinct problems: social, legal, medical, or moral. The concern about these problems, and the demands that something be done about them, was therefore compartmentalised and fragmented. The catalyst which helped integrate these concerns and demands was the growing recognition of the relationship between alcohol consumption and harm. This effectively provided the logical connection between the diverse consequences of alcohol misuse. As a result the groups involved no longer saw these consequences as separate problems, but as symptoms of the same problem. And this in turn made for a more integrated lobby.

But although most groups within the alcohol misuse lobby accepted that the higher levels of alcohol consumption during the post-war period were, in part at least, responsible for the increased incidence of alcohol problems, fewer groups actually came out in support for policies designed to reduce consumption. In particular, as we have seen, the law enforcment professions and some of the voluntary bodies did not openly endorse control policies in seventies. As a result the pressure for control policies was not as strong as it might have been.

Lobbying and pressure

As well as achieving a higher level of integration and coherence, the alcohol misuse lobby also became more active towards the end of the seventies. This was reflected in Parliament where matters concerning alcohol misuse in general, and control policies in particular, were discussed more frequently than before. For example, the number of Parliamentary Questions (PQs) tabled on the subject of alcohol misuse in the period 1975-80 was twice that tabled in the previous five years. (see table one, above) The new emphasis on preventing (rather than treating) alcohol problems through control policies was indicated by the changing nature of the questions asked. The issues of price regulation, advertising control and licensing law reform were increasingly raised, particularly by MPs who had a connection with one or more of the groups which supported control policies. These MPs included Sir Bernard Braine, chairman of the NCA; Ron Lewis, the treasurer of the UKA; Frank Hooley, a vice president of the UKA; and Tristan Garel-Jones, a member of both the NCA Prevention Committee and the UKA Parliamentary Liaison Committee. In addition two MPs with medical backgrounds: Dr Roger Thomas, a GP, and Dr. Brian Mawhinney, a lecturer in medicine, tabled PQs on alcohol-related topics on a number of occasions.

Parliamentary interest in the prevention of alcohol misuse was further stimulated by an enquiry into preventive medicine by a sub-committee of the House of Commons Select Committee on Expenditure in 1976. The committee selected alcohol misuse as one of several public health issues to be examined in detail. After receiving evidence from a wide range of individuals and organisations in the alcohol field, ranging from the NCA to the Brewers Society, the committee arrived at the conclusion that alcohol consumption was indeed related to the level of alcohol misuse. It also implicitly recognised the need for control policies by recommending amongst other things that the price of alcohol should not become cheaper in real terms; and that the licensing law provisions relating to drink and young people should not be relaxed. (House of Commons, 1977a) The Expenditure Committee's report not only created a wider awareness in Parliament of the problem of alcohol misuse, but also added considerable weight to the arguments of those within the alcohol misuse lobby who favoured the adoption of control policies.

Parliament was an important channel through which the lobby could raise the issue of alcohol misuse and attract support for control policies. This was particularly true in the case of the temperance and voluntary organisations. The medical profession on the other hand was much better placed politically and did not have to rely on Parliamentary pressure to convey its views. The medical organisations preferred instead to represent their views directly to the Department of Health and Social Security. It is understood that the Royal Colleges and the BMA have been consulted by the DHSS on the subject of alcohol misuse on a number of occasions since the mid-seventies.

This does not mean, however, that non-medical groups were not consulted. The NCA for example had regular contact with the department. But it and the other voluntary organisations lacked the professional status of the medical bodies and were also dependent on the DHSS for its annual grant. Their political leverage was as a result much lower.

The voluntary organisations, along with other groups having an interest in alcohol misuse, were represented on the DHSS Advisory Committee on Alcoholism, mentioned in the previous chapter. The Advisory Committee played a significant role in the development of alcohol policy during the seventies. Its report on the subject of preventing alcohol misuse, was an important catalyst in this respect. (DHSS, 1978b) The Committee gave a clear endorsement to the consumption theory of alcohol misuse and made a number of recommendations, which included the following:

1. A programme of health education about the dangers of alcohol.
2. The modification of the presentation of alcohol in advertisements and the media to produce a less one-sided picture of its effects.
3. The use of fiscal powers to ensure that alcohol would not become cheaper in real terms.
4. The rigorous enforcement of existing legal controls over the availability of alcohol, and a freeze on plans to relax the law until such a time as it could be proved that such changes would not increase alcohol misuse.
5. The encouragement of drinkers with alcohol problems to seek help at an early stage.

This five point plan represented a comprehensive policy for the prevention of alcohol problems. In the next section we shall examine how the DHSS viewed this approach and how it responded to the growing pressure for a policy along these lines.

The Prevention of Alcohol Misuse: The DHSS View

During the seventies the Government, and the DHSS in particular, made an attempt to give preventive medicine a much higher priority. This was reflected in the publication of a DHSS consultative document on the subject during 1976. In the following year the government published a White Paper which confirmed its commitment to a policy of preventing ill-health. (Cmnd 7047, 1977) Both Labour and Conservative Governments have since sought to put these policy initiatives into practice by issuing policy advice to local health authorities, stressing the need to develop effective prevention progammes at this level. (DHSS, 1977b; 1981a)

One justification for a policy aimed at preventing illness is that much of the morbidity and mortality in Britain and in other developed countries today can be attributed to individual lifestyles and the environment in which people live. Such factors are now widely believed to be mainly responsible for the high incidence of cancer and circulatory disease found in the developed world. In Britain for example cancer and circulatory disease are currently responsible for around 74% of all deaths. (Central Statistical Office, 1985)

It is now recognised that the best way of tackling these and other chronic diseases is to seek to prevent them, rather than relying on treatment services to provide a cure. But in the post-war period health services have been mainly geared to the treatment, rather than the prevention, of disease. In England and Wales for example, during the mid-seventies, less than 2% of NHS expenditure was devoted to preventive medicine. In view of this it became increasingly obvious that the balance between curative and preventive medicine was inappropriate. The government's decision in the seventies to place a greater emphasis on prevention can be seen as a rational attempt to redress this imbalance.

But narrower financial considerations also had some bearing on this decision. During the seventies resource constraints were imposed on the health and social services in view of the general economic climate. (Ward, 1983) The situation was exacerbated by the increasing demands being placed on the health service by an ageing population and the rising cost of medical technology. A policy of prevention appeared to offer a way out of the impasse. Prevention was not only better than cure, but it was also cheaper. The DHSS believed that such a policy would not only be more effective (since many cases of cancer and heart disease are incurable), but would also be more cost-effective, by hopefully reducing the demand for treatment services in the future.

Against this background one might have expected that the DHSS, as the government department responsible for health and social policy, would favour alcohol control policies. After all, these policies were aimed at preventing a wide range of health and social problems, and would in this sense be in line with the governments new policy initiative. How did the DHSS respond therefore to the pressure, outlined in the last section, for a more comprehensive policy of preventing alcohol misuse?

The first thing to note was that many DHSS civil servants were indeed becoming increasingly concerned about alcohol misuse during the seventies. Those who gave evidence to the House of Commons Expenditure Committee (see above) admitted that they believed that the problem was becoming very serious. (House of Commons, 1977b, p420-5) Alcohol misuse also began to attract attention from other officials in the department, who were not directly responsible for alcohol policy. For example in 1977 the Senior Nursing Officer at the DHSS reported that alcoholism was causing increasing concern amongst the nursing profession. (Friend, 1977)

Civil servants at the DHSS were in fact considering the use of alcohol control policies. In her evidence to the Expenditure Committee the Assistant Secretary responsible for alcohol policy, whilst stressing the need for public debate on the use of such measures, nevertheless clearly believed that such an approach should be used prevent the situation from getting worse. (House of Commons, 1977b, p431) This departmental view appears to have become stronger towards the end of the decade and was reinforced by a further report on alcohol misuse by the influential World Health Organisation (WHO) in 1980. The WHO report endorsed control policies by recommending that member governments take steps to reduce the overall consumption of alcholic beverages.

Table 5

Health Ministers

Date	Party in Office	Secretary of State for Social Services	Minister of Health	Under Secretary of State for Health
1970-4	Con	Keith Joseph	Lord Aberdare	Michael Alison
1974-6	Lab	Barbara Castle	David Owen	
1976-9	Lab	David Ennals	Roland Moyle	Eric Deakins
1979-81	Con	Patrick Jenkin	Gerard Vaughan	George Young
1981-2	Con	Norman Fowler	Gerard Vaughan	Geoffrey Finsberg
1982-3	Con	Norman Fowler	Kenneth Clarke	Geoffrey Finsberg
1983-4	Con	Norman Fowler	Kenneth Clarke	John Patten
1984-5	Con	Norman Fowler	Kenneth Clarke	Ray Whitney
1985-6	Con	Norman Fowler	Barney Heyhoe	Ray Whitney
1986-7	Con	Norman Fowler	Tony Newton	Edwina Currie
1987-8	Con	John Moore	Tony Newton	Edwina Currie
1988-	Con	Kenneth Clarke	David Mellor	Edwina Currie

Notes:

In Autumn 1988 the Department of Health and Social Security was split into the Department of Health and the Department of Social Security.

Baroness Trumpington served as Under Secretary for Health between 1984 and 1987.

Lord Skelmersdale has served as Under Secretary for Health since 1987.

There is however no concrete evidence that DHSS officials actually advised ministers to adopt a more comprehensive policy on alcohol misuse, including the use of control policies. Though some sources have suggested to me that civil servants were in fact active in this respect. It is worth noting that such advice is officially secret. In this case, as in many others, the Official Secrets Act along with the conventions of civil service anonymity and neutrality have obscured the role of the civil servants in the making of policy.

Similarly another constitutional convention, the doctrine of collective responsibility, makes it difficult to discover the precise views of successive DHSS ministers on this issue. As we shall see later, the opposition of the government as a whole to control policies has prevented DHSS ministers from supporting these policies in public. Three different ministerial teams served in the period 1974-81. These are shown in table five above.

We have already discussed the role played by Keith Joseph in the previous chapter. His successors, David Owen and Barbara Castle were far from ignorant of the problems caused by alcohol misuse and were strongly in favour of a preventive approach. Barbara Castle, as Transport Minister in the 1966-70 Labour Government, had introduced the breathalyser in an attempt to reduce drink-related road accidents. (see chapter eight) Whilst David Owen, a qualified medical practitioner, was a firm supporter of preventive medicine. When giving evidence to the Expenditure Committee in 1976 Owen clarified his position on the question of alcohol misuse as follows:

"... an emphasis on the prevention of excess drinking need in my view to be very much greater than before." (House of Commons, 1977b, p314-339)

David Ennals and Roland Moyle were also in favour of prevention. They broadly agreed with the recommendations of the Expenditure Committee and the Advisory Committee, that prevention was the way forward. But on the specific issue of control policies they believed, along with their civil servants, that greater public support was needed before such measures could be introduced. In 1977, shortly after the Advisory Committee's report had been passed to him, Ennals made a public speech in an attempt to stimulate debate (and public support for action) on the issue.[1] He referred to the possibility of a higher level of tax on drink, greater enforcement of the licensing laws, and a more restrictive code of practice for drink advertisements. He went on to call for a public response to these questions. This action indicated that DHSS ministers were prepared to press for control policies, providing the opposition both within and outside government to such an approach was not too hostile. It also suggested that the DHSS feared it would lose the inter-departmental battles which would have to be fought on this issue, if public support was not forthcoming.

The Conservative health ministers, who entered office in 1979, went further than their predecessors. In opposition the conservatives had established a special committee to examine the whole area of preventive medicine. This committee was chaired by Sir George Young, who also had taken a personal interest in the prevention of alcohol and tobacco related problems. Young believed that strong measures were needed in this area. In 1979 he was given the chance to put his ideas into practice when appointed Under Secretary at the DHSS with special responsibility for preventive medicine. He lost little time. In a speech during 1979 to the NCA Annual Conference he pledged his support for a comprehensive prevention policy.

"Preventing alcoholism is not a medical but a political problem... the answer may not be cure by incision at the operating table but prevention by decision at the cabinet table."[2]

It must be remembered that Young was only a junior minister, yet his views gave encouragement to those who felt that the government should commit itself to a more comprehensive policy on alcohol misuse involving the use of control policies. Moreover Young's senior minister, Patrick Jenkin, appeared to be thinking along similar lines. In June the following year in a speech to the International Conference on Alcoholism at Cardiff he emphasised the need for action:

"There is no doubt we are facing a major and indeed an increasing epidemic in our midst. There is a great need to tackle it with urgency, with insight and with a real sense of commitment."[3]

These and other statements by DHSS ministers could of course be dismissed as being nothing more than rhetoric. Indeed one looks in vain for a ministerial statement explicitly backing specific control policies. But one has to remember that ministers were unable to pledge their commitment to specific policies because of the doctrine of collective responsibility. Their statements to Parliament and in public had to be vague because their hands were tied by this convention.

Despite the lack of official statements, circumstantial evidence suggests that by the late seventies the DHSS was in favour of a tougher approach to alcohol problems. There is little doubt that it supported a comprehensive policy to prevent alcohol misuse, involving the use of control policies. Moreover the indications were that the department was arguing for such a policy within central government. It is to this interdepartmental conflict that we now turn.

The Government's Response

Departmental conflict

In the sixties and early seventies, when alcohol policy was concerned almost wholly with the provision of services for alcoholics, policy making on this issue was located within the DHSS. This situation changed with the movement on to the agenda of policies designed to prevent alcohol misuse. These new policies encroached more on the responsibilities of other departments. As a result the decisions concerning alcohol misuse were now being made in interdepartmental committees, where other departments could exert a greater influence over policy.

One problem facing the DHSS was that most of the instruments which were essential to a comprehensive prevention policy lay outside its control. Licensing law and alcohol advertising in the broadcast media were the responsibility of the Home

41

Office. Non-broadcast media advertising was the responsibility of the Department of Trade (merged with the Department of Industry in 1981). Whilst the Treasury and Customs and Excise were responsible for the taxation of alcoholic drinks. Only health education could be directly influenced by the DHSS, and even here responsibility was shared with the Department of Education and Science.

If control policies were to be adopted the DHSS would have to persuade these other departments of the merits of such an approach. But it seems that these departments were not open to persuasion: on the contrary, they showed considerable hostility towards the idea of controlling alcohol consumption. The Home Office, for instance, did not take a favourable view. The department's opposition to control policies was indicated in a paper published in 1980 by its research unit, which attacked the basis of the consumption theory of alcohol misuse, outlined above. (Home Office, 1980) More specifically, during the seventies, the Home Office favoured relaxing the licensing laws, contrary to the wishes of the DHSS. This issue is discussed in more detail in chapter seven.

The Treasury and Customs and Excise were also hostile to control policies. These departments did not want to sacrifice their control over the taxation of alcoholic drinks, which they viewed as a useful instrument for raising revenue rather than a means of regulating alcohol consumption. (see chapter six, below) Moreover, the Treasury, in view of its responsibility for the economy, was also concerned about the wider economic side effects of control policies. The output of the drinks industry has on average contributed directly to around 5% of Gross Domestic Product. If control policies were effective, alcohol consumption would fall and the economic side effects of this according to the Treasury would be significant.

Control policies were also opposed by the Departments of Trade and Industry, Employment, and the Ministry of Agriculture (MAFF). The Department of Employment had reservations about the effect of control policies on jobs. As the drinks industry was a major employer, falling consumption would be likely exacerbate the growing problem of unemployment. The Departments of Trade and Industry were concerned about the side-effects of these policies upon manufacturing and retail sectors and also upon the tourism and leisure industries, whose economic fortunes were linked to the welfare of the drinks industry. The Department of Trade also sponsored the advertising industry, and shared its view that severe restrictions on alcohol advertising, as part of an attempt to reduce consumption, would be damaging. In addition both Trade and Industry were concerned about the effect of control policies on the export performance of the drinks industry. Finally MAFF, in its role as the sponsoring department of the alcoholic drinks industry, was also opposed to any measures that might damage this sector's industrial performance.

Despite this opposition, the DHSS was committed to producing a consultative document on alcohol policy. Its intention to do so was mentioned in the White Paper on Prevention and Health in 1977. But because alcohol policy was now cutting across departmental interests and responsibilities more than ever before, the substance of the document had to be agreed with these other departments. This set the scene for a lengthy interdepartmental battle within Whitehall.

Much of the conflict between the departments was sparked off by a report on alcohol policy from the Central Policy Review Staff (CPRS), known colloquially as 'the Think Tank'. This body, abolished in 1983, conducted in-depth reviews of policy often on issues which cut across departmental lines.

The CPRS report and the consultative document

The CPRS began its study of alcohol abuse in 1977. It was envisaged that its report would provide a basis for the forthcoming consultative document by transcending the sectional interests of the government departments mentioned above. The report emerged in March 1979 and came down firmly in favour of control policies. (Central Policy Review Staff, 1982) Its main recommendations were, first that government should adopt the objective of preventing an increase in alcohol consumption. Second, its policies should reflect this objective. Third, that the government should publish a consultative document reflecting this position. More specifically the CPRS recommended that the real price of alcohol should be maintained; that the licensing laws should be better enforced, and should not be relaxed as long as increased consumption and harm appeared likely to result; and that advertising and the presentation of alcohol in the media should reinforce, not undermine, moderate drinking habits. In addition the report urged the implementation of further restrictions on drinking and driving.

In spite of the CPRS endorsement of control policies, the opposition within Whitehall remained strong. The hostile departments continued to fight over the contents of the consultative document. It was this conflict which caused the considerable delay in the publication of this document. According to the 1977 White Paper the document was originally due in 1978. In that year the Senior Medical Officer at the DHSS responsible for alcohol policy told MPs that the document would appear next year. (House of Commons, 1979 p19) But, in a debate during 1979, a DHSS minister informed the Commons that the document was still being drafted.[4] The process appeared to be no further forward in 1980 when, in reply to a Parliamentary Question from Tristan Garel-Jones the DHSS minister confirmed that 'the question of publishing a consultative document is still under consideration with my right honourable and honourable friends.'[5] The document was still under consideration in February 1981, according to a further Ministerial statement, four years after its appearance was first presaged.[6]

The DHSS and the health ministers began to show increasing signs of frustration with the interdepartmental bargaining process. A change of government in 1979 brought no immediate change in policy. But matters came to a head in the latter part of 1979 when the CPRS report was leaked to the media. Questions in Parliament followed and a request to the Prime Minister to publish the report from Clive Soley, the chairman of AEC, was rejected.[7] The CPRS report was never actually published in Britain, although in 1982, much to the embarrassment of the British

Government, it was published in Stockholm and copies became readily available worldwide.

The leaking of the CPRS report, and the accusations of a government conspiracy of silence which inevitably followed, led to renewed pressure for government action. This strengthened the hand of the DHSS and led to speculation that the consultative paper, when it eventually emerged, would after all endorse control policies. For example, a *Sunday Times* report in December 1980 claimed that Cabinet opposition to a tougher anti-drinks line was crumbling in the light of the relationship between excessive drinking and crime, poor work performance and health costs.[8] The same article understood that the forthcoming consultative document would amongst other things argue that alcoholic drink should be more expensive, that tougher controls over advertising would be necessary, and that further restrictions on drinking and driving were required.

Eventually, in December 1981, the government's long-promised consultative document on alcohol policy, *Drinking Sensibly* was published. (DHSS, 1981b) According to one source the seventy-page document had been redrafted three times before a form of words agreeable to all Whitehall departments had been found. As one might expect in view of the interdepartmental conflict involved the document was equivocal on many important issues. On the central question of regulating consumption for example it urged:

"continued recognition by Parliament and Government that health and social implications should be among the factors taken into account when any action affecting consumption of alcoholic drinks is under consideration."

Yet elsewhere the document stressed the point that:

"While the misuse of alcohol may cause serious health and social problems, the production of and trade in alcoholic drinks form an important part of our economy in terms of jobs, exports, investment, and as a source of revenue for the Government - all of which could be adversely affected by any measures designed to restrict consumption."

It was clear that the government had come down against control policies, refusing for example to use taxation explicitly as a means of influencing drink prices and thereby consumption. But the document did make some concessions to the alcohol misuse lobby. It confirmed that the government had no plans to relax the licensing laws. In addition it urged the drinks and advertising industries to modify their practices so as to encourage sensible and moderate drinking. The document also endorsed a programme of health education about alcohol misuse. So *Drinking Sensibly* did not represent a total defeat for the alcohol misuse lobby. But in the light of the recommendations made by the Advisory Committee on Alcoholism and the CPRS, more was expected. The policies proposed in the document did not represent the kind of comprehensive policy on alcohol misuse that had been envisaged by many.

44

A Problem of Coordination ?

Better coordination

The apparent difficulty which the government faced in attempting to resolve the interdepartmental disputes over the consultative document raises questions about its ability to coordinate policy on issues, such as alcohol policy, which cut across departmental interests and responsibilities. According to the CPRS report for example almost every government department has some interest in alcohol policy. (CPRS, 1982) At least seven of these (Customs and Excise, DHSS, Treasury, Trade and Industry, Home Office, MAFF, and Employment) have a considerable interest. Moreover, as we have indicated, the nature of these interests have been such that agreement between the departments concerned has been difficult to achieve. But this difficulty may be less a problem of conflicting interests than one of coordination. Indeed the lack of an explicit framework of coordination appears to have been partly responsible for the governments refusal to adopt a comprehensive policy on the prevention of alcohol misuse.

Britain is fairly unusual in not having an official body specifically charged with the task of coordinating policy on alcohol misuse. A number of countries have established such bodies in recent years. In Sweden for example the government set up a Council on Alcohol in 1980 to perform this function. Similar organisations can be found in most European countries including France, Swizerland, Norway, and Denmark. (Davies and Walsh, 1983) The CPRS believed that such a body was needed in Britain and recommended the adoption of an Advisory Council on Alcohol Policies (ACAP) which would be 'a standing advisory council of outside experts working with officials and serviced in a way which enable it to assemble information and to monitor policies as well as to help formulate them.' (CPRS, 1982 p86) This proposal was welcomed by many within the alcohol misuse lobby who believed that the creation of such a body was a necessary precondition for the introduction of control policies.

A similar idea was put forward by the Magistrates Association in 1981. In a paper sent to the Home Office, the Association called for the establishment of a National Alcohol Affairs Commission, to coordinate alcohol policy. This would consist of experts in the field of law, health, economics, and representatives from the voluntary organisations. In addition every government department having an interest in alcohol policy would be represented. Finally, it was suggested that such a commission should be the responsibility of a cabinet minister with special responsibility for alcohol policy.

The kind of body suggested by the CPRS and the Magistrates Association would have had a much wider scope than the erstwhile Advisory Commitee on Alcoholism. This committee, it will be remembered, was established to advise DHSS Ministers. At first it appeared that the winding-up of the Advisory Committee in 1978 was a prelude to the creation of an interdepartmental advisory body. This was not however to be the case. The government made its position clear subsequently in

45

Drinking Sensibly:

"Well established arrangements already exist for all the interested departments to inform each other about matters of mutual concern, to coordinate their advice to ministers and to implement the government's policies. In each case the responsibility for the necessary coordination rests firmly on the department with the leading interest in the aspect of policy under consideration. The government agrees coordination on all aspects of alcohol is essential; it believes, however, that this can be more effectively secured through the well-established processes described above than by the creation of a new non-departmental public body." (DHSS, 1981b, p67)

Why no interdepartmental body?

There were two main reasons why the government did not establish a new interdepartmental body. First of all, the same departments which had prevented the emergence of control policies were also opposed to the creation of such a body. They believed that it would increase the threat of control policies in the future. Since, as the CPRS report had illustrated, any body which was able to transcend departmental interests, would be likely to recommend the adoption of such policies, their fears were well founded. The second reason is more general, being related to the government's overall view of non-departmental public bodies around this time. The Conservative Government, elected to office in 1979, was committed to reducing the number of such bodies. Nearly seven hundred were abolished between 1979 and 1986. (Cabinet Office and Treasury, 1986) The political climate has therefore been clearly unfavourable to those urging the creation of a new non-departmental body in the field of alcohol misuse.

In his speech to the Annual General Meeting of the NCA in 1981, the Secretary of State for Social Services, Patrick Jenkin re-iterated the government's view that an official policy coordinating body would be inappropriate. He also hinted at the pressures within government, mentioned above, which militated against such an approach:

"While my department is consulting the other Government departments concerned, I must make it clear that there would have to be a very powerful case indeed for creating a new public body at a time when all the pressure is in the other way."[9]

He went on however to endorse moves to establish a free standing alcohol forum where non-governmental groups could discuss a common approach to the problem of alcohol misuse:

"I believe the time has come for the representatives of the drinks trade... and representatives of the bodies concerned with the misuse of alcohol, to sit around the table in a common forum."

Since government departments would not be directly involved in such an arrangement it would not carry any real implications for the coordination of policy within government, and would not therefore constitute a threat to existing departmental interests. In 1984, in order to promote a body along these lines, the DHSS encouraged a series of meetings between the drinks industry and a number of voluntary organisations in the alcohol field. This led to the creation of the Alcohol Forum, a committee which was to examine a range of non-controversial issues where the drinks industry and the alcohol misuse lobby could work together to their mutual interest. On this committee were representatives from the medical profession, Alcohol Concern (the newly created voluntary organisation in the alcohol field), the Health Education Council, the Scotch Whisky Association and the Brewers' Society.

This initiative later suffered a serious setback, much to the embarrassment of the DHSS who were providing the secretariat to the committee. In 1986 the department felt obliged to remove the chairman of the Alcohol Forum, Sir John Crofton, following his suggestion that the drinks industry should provide £50 million over the next five years to help prevent alcohol problems. The industry objected strongly to this and other plans put forward by the alcohol misuse lobby and is understood that their indignation influenced the decision to remove Crofton.

The governments refusal to establish a non-departmental body for alcohol misuse effectively meant that control policies would not be adopted in the foreseeable future. The structure of departmental power on this issue would not be challenged by a non-government body, particularly one where the drink industry apparently exercised considerable influence. But there were other reasons why control policies began to slip from the political agenda after 1981. The most important being the arrival at the DHSS of ministers who, unlike their predecessors, were highly unsympathetic to the case for control policies. (See table five above) In a ministerial reshuffle of September 1981, Sir George Young was replaced by Geoffrey Finsberg, The alcohol misuse lobby were dismayed by this appointment, as Finsberg had formerly been employed as Parliamentary advisor to the National Union of Licensed Victuallers - the public house licensees trade association. The lobby also viewed the appointment of Kenneth Clarke as Minister of State for Health in 1982 with some concern. Clarke had some years earlier introduced a private members bill to relax the licensing laws. (see chapter seven) Finally, it should be noted that the head of this new ministerial team, Norman Fowler, had a particular interest in illicit drug misuse. Given that alcohol is a drug, one might have expected Fowler to press for a tougher policy on alcohol abuse. But the new emphasis on tackling illicit drug misuse appeared to have a negative effect on alcohol policy. It served merely to push alcohol misuse further down the department's scale of priorities.

The shift in policy which accompanied these ministerial changes became obvious when the new junior minister at the DHSS, Geoffrey Finsberg, addressed a BMA symposium on alcohol misuse in 1982. He stressed that whilst prevention was the only way forward 'the key to preventing misuse is for individuals to recognise and accept the responsibility for their own health.'[10]

This was a far cry from his predecessor's assertion that the prevention of alcohol misuse was mainly a political problem requiring political decisions. The new policy of distancing the government from the problem was further confirmed in a speech during two years later by John Patten, who had by this time replaced Finsberg in yet another ministerial reshuffle. Patten emphasised that 'doctors could play a more central role in tackling alcohol misuse' because there was 'no way central government alone could tackle the problem'[11] Central government, it appeared, was now trying to shift the main burden of responsibility for dealing with the problem back on to the shoulders of the medical profession. It was seeking to redefine the alcohol misuse once again as medical not a political problem.

A New Initiative

Alcohol policy in the period 1981 to 1987 was very much in the doldrums. This was partly because of the priority given to illicit drugs, mentioned above, and the appointment of health ministers generally unsympathetic to an assault on the alcohol problem. There was also a slight decline in the incidence of alcohol related problems between 1980 and 1983. This was to some extent due to a fall in alcohol consumption in Britain in this period, partly the result of the economic recession. Ironically, this experience confirmed the consumption control theory - though the government did not appear to heed this.

As the recession bottomed out, alcohol consumption began to rise once more. The indicators of alcohol misuse also began to show an increase. In the meantime efforts to put alcohol back on the political agenda were being stepped up. The newly-formed voluntary alcohol organisations, Alcohol Concern, Action on Alcohol Abuse, and the Institute for Alcohol Studies had by now overcome their initial teething problems (see chapter two) and were putting more pressure on government and Parliament to take action. At around the same time no less than four medical organisations, the Royal College of General Practitioners, the Royal College of Psychiatrists, the Royal College of Physicians, and the British Medical Association, began to prepare reports on the subject of alcohol abuse.

The emergence of these four reports attracted considerable media attention. Three of the reports were published in 1986: *Young People and Alcohol*, from the BMA, *Alcohol: Our Favourite Drug*, from the Royal College of Psychiatrists, and the Royal College of General Practitioners' report *Alcohol: A Balanced View*. The fourth report, *The Medical Consequences of Alcohol Abuse: A Great and Growing Evil*, by the Royal College of Physicians emerged the following year. These reports were all very much in the same vein, calling on government to recognise the extent of the problem, particularly amongst young people. All the reports recommended the adoption of alcohol control policies alongside less controversial proposals, such as an expansion of health education about alcohol.

This overt demonstration of concern by various branches of the medical profession indicated that the support for some form of official action on alcohol was becoming even broader. Alcohol problems were definitely no longer the preserve of the psychiatrist, as had been the case in the sixties and early seventies. The medical establishment was now uniting against alcohol in a similar way as it had against smoking. This strengthened the alcohol misuse lobby immensely.

The alcohol misuse lobby was further strengthened by the growing support for control policies in non-medical organisations that had not previously been in favour of such an approach. These included the police, magistrates', and justices' clerks' associations. Such organisations were increasingly worried about the growth of alcohol related crime and began to make representations to government on this matter.

By the middle of 1987 the alcohol and crime issue was becoming ever more prominent. Law and order is traditionally a sensitive issue for conservative governments, and the Thatcher government has been no exception. It was therefore becoming difficult for the government simply to sit back and ignore the evidence on alcohol related crime, and the representations made by the law enforcement professions.

In response to these pressures the Home Office in 1987 set up an independent working party on young people and alcohol. This committee, chaired by Baroness Masham, had a wide membership drawn from law, medicine, social services, the police, probation service, education, alcohol services, the drinks industry, and the Home Office itself. The committee reported in November 1987, and made a number of recommendations which endorsed control policies. It called for a ban on all TV advertising of alcoholic drinks, increased taxes on strong beers, and a tightening of the law on under age drinking. Less controversially, the Masham report called for a new initiative on health education about alcohol, and made a number of recommendations about improving the role of agencies and professions in preventing alcohol abuse among young people.

Somewhat paradoxically, whilst considering this report, the government was preparing to relax the law on liquor licensing (see chapter seven). This caused concern amongst a number of conservative backbench MPs who felt that the government was being rather inconsistent in its handling of the alcohol issue. Some, such as Sir Bernard Braine - the former chairman of the NCA, were against a relaxation in the licensing law. Others were simply concerned about the law and order implications of alcohol abuse. These MPs made representations through the conservative whips (the MPs responsible for ensuring that the government gets its measures through Parliament) and to the Home Secretary, Douglas Hurd. These representations were evidently persuasive, leading the government to create an interministerial group on alcohol abuse in September 1987.

This committee, under the chairmanship of the Leader of the House of Commons, John Wakeham, contains ministers from a number of goverment departments including DHSS, MAFF, DTI, Transport, the Treasury, Education and Science, Employment, and Scottish and Welsh Offices. The ministers involved mainly hold junior posts in the government. For example, the Health Department is represented on the committee is by the Parliamentary Under Secretary for Health. There are one or two other members, who do not not represent a particular department, including Hartley Booth, one of the Prime Minister's advisers. The committee is served by civil servants from the DHSS and the Home Office.

The stated aims of the Wakeham Committee are to review the government's strategy for alcohol problems; to develop proposals to implement such a strategy; and to identify priorities in the allocation of resources to alcohol services and programmes. Since it was established the group has met regularly and has initiated a number of proposals on a wide range of alcohol policy issues, including under-age drinking, drink advertising and drinking and driving. Some of these proposals are examined in more detail in later chapters.

Conclusion

It is perhaps too early to evaluate the contribution of the Wakeham Committee to the development of alcohol policy. Some of its recommendations have been adopted, though as we shall see later these have been fairly uncontroversial. The committee has not backed some of the more radical proposals put forward by the recent reports of the Masham Committee and the Royal Medical Colleges and the various reports on alcohol abuse in the seventies. Whether or not the committee will be able to maintain the momentum it now has, and whether it will venture into more controversial policy issues, remains to be seen.

The creation of the Wakeham Committee illustrates the government's new willingness to consider alcohol problem in a rational manner. It can also be seen as a response to the pressures for better coordination of alcohol policy which had until recently been rejected. This pressure in turn reflects the growing concern about alcohol problems amongst the public and, more importantly perhaps, the increasing strength and coherence of the alcohol misuse lobby.

The alcohol misuse lobby has come a long way since the sixties. It is is now a much more integrated and effective lobby than before. The key development was the gradual acceptance by those groups involved of the need to control alcohol consumption. Yet the debate over alcohol control policies has perhaps on reflection proved to be a mixed blessing. On the positive side, it has brought a large number of diverse groups together by offering a set of common solutions to a range of health and social problems with which they were all concerned. But it could be argued that the alcohol control debate was disadvantageous to the alcohol misuse lobby in that it transformed a health department issue into one which had implications for all major government departments. In consequence alcohol policy became a matter not just for the DHSS but for the government as a whole to decide. As we have seen, the opposition of other departments to a full-blooded prevention policy on alcohol misuse was a key factor in the rejection of control policies.

Notes

1. *The Times* 8 November 1977 p4
2. Annual Conference of the National Council on Alcoholism, 10 July 1979
3. *The Times* 10 June 1980 p6
4. *House of Commons Official Report* Volume 964 Column 1978 23 March 1979
5. *House of Commons Official Report* Volume 981 Column 140w 18 March 1980
6. *House of Commons Official Report* Volume 999 Column 306w 23 February 1981
7. *House of Commons Official Report* Volome 973 Column 506w 13 November 1979
8. *The Sunday Times* 14 December 1980 p1
9. National Council on Alcoholism, Annual General Meeting July 1981
10. An Absence of an Alcohol Policy *British Medical Journal* Volume 285 11 December 1982 p1680-1
11. Institute for Alcohol Studies, Conference on Alcoholism, London 28 November 1984

4 The alcoholic drinks industry

The main concern so far has been with the development of alcohol policy in the context of the changing demands of the alcohol misuse lobby. In this chapter however the focus is upon the alcoholic drinks industry's response to the problem. Three aspects of this response are particularly important, and each will be examined during the course of this chapter. These are: the industry's view of the causes of alcohol misuse; its role in the policy making process; and its ability to influence alcohol policy. We begin, however, with an analysis of the alcoholic drinks market in the UK. This discussion provides a useful background to the political organisation of the industry, the subject of the following section. Next, we take a look at the response of the drinks industry to the growth of alcohol misuse during the seventies. This is followed by an analysis of the political links between the industry and policy-makers in government, Parliament and the Conservative Party. Finally we consider two other groups which have an interest in the alcohol industry, namely consumers and the trade unions, and examine their position on the alcohol misuse issue.

The Alcoholic Drinks Market

The main features of the alcohol market are: private production for profit; diversification; concentration; size and economic importance.

Private ownership and the profit motive

In the UK both alcoholic drink is produced for profit by privately owned companies. This has been the case since 1971 when state management of the drinks industry in a small number of areas (Carlisle, Gretna and Cromarty Firth) ended. Full scale nationalisation of the drinks industry was on the agenda during the first world war, but was not followed up. Even so it is worth noting that in a number of other countries today, including some capitalist countries, the alcoholic drinks industry is in state ownership. In Norway for example, the state has a monopoly of wines and spirits production.

It would be impossible here to enter into the highly ideological debate about the comparative performance of state and private enterprise. Suffice it to say that there is little evidence to suggest that ownership makes a big difference in practice to the level of alcohol misuse in the country in question. This is largely because, particularly in capitalist states, most public enterprises are generally market-oriented. As a result the objectives of most state-owned alcohol firms are broadly in line with their private sector counterparts.

Even so public ownership does appear to give more scope for the introduction of social objectives alongside commercial targets. For example one notes that 20% of the profits made by Norway's nationally owned wines and spirits monopoly are channelled into prevention and treatment programmes. (Davies and Walsh 1983) But the actual extent to which this kind of potential is exploited is in most cases limited.

Moreover, it would not be true to say that private ownership precludes the achievement of social objectives. It is possible within the framework of the private market to give incentives and disincentives, through subsidies and taxation for example, in an attempt to encourage and discourage certain forms of business activity which are socially harmful. Also, one should not forget that private companies have public images, which if tarnished could have implications for long term profitability. We shall return to this point later in the chapter.

Diversification

Alcohol companies worldwide have diversified in recent years, and the UK companies are no exception. This should come as no surprise since three out of the top four drinks companies in the world (Allied-Lyons, Grand Metropolitan, and Guinness) are based in the UK. There are two types of diversification to consider: internal diversification, where companies move into the production of other alcoholic drinks; and external diversification, where companies become involved in activities other than selling alcohol.

Taking internal diversification first, we must first note that the alcohol market is divided into a number of sectors: beer, wines, spirits, and cider. Beer is still the largest single sector in the UK, accounting for 54% of spending. The market share of spirits is currently around 24% The share of beer and spirits has fallen over the last twenty or so years as a result of the growth in the consumption of wine and cider, which together now account for around a quarter of expenditure. (Godfrey, Hardman, and Maynard, 1986) Within each sector, drinks are further differentiated by product (for example, red and white wine; beer and lager) and by brand name.

In view of the relative decline of the beer market, the brewers have increasingly moved into wines and spirits, Grand Metropolitan for example which has a large stake in the brewing industry is also involved in the wines and spirits markets through its subsidiary, International Distillers and Vintners (IDV). Other major wine importers, such as Grants of St. James, Stowells, and Hedges and Butler are also owned by major brewers (Allied-Lyons, Whitbread, and Bass respectively). This kind of diversification, as we shall see later, has increased the degree of concentration of ownership within the industry.

Drinks companies have also expanded their alcohol-related service operations, and this has led more recently to a movement into leisure services, such as hotels and restaurants. Bass, for example, owns the Crest Hotel chain; and Watney Mann, through its parent company Grand Metropolitan, is linked with the Berni Inn restaurant business. Diversification into non-alcohol products is greatest among the larger drinks companies. In 1986 the top five British drinks companies derived 71% of their profits from alcohol. For the smaller companies howver alcohol contributes anywhere between 80% and 100% of total profits.[1] As with internal diversification, the movement into non-alcohol product markets has increased in recent years.

Concentration

As well as being increasingly diversified, the largest companies have come to dominate the domestic alcohol market. (Booth, Hardman, and Hartley, 1986) The wines and spirits market is generally regarded as more competitive than the beer market in that more companies are involved and each tends to have a smaller market share. It is worth pointing out however that Distillers (before it was taken over by Guinness in 1986) controlled around 20% of the domestic market in Scotch Whisky and 60% of the market in Gin. Moreover, the diversification of the larger brewers into wines and spirits, noted earlier, has increased the level of concentration in these sectors. Subsidiaries of the major brewers control over half of the domestic market in Scotch Whisky; three-quarters of UK Gin and Vodka sales; and around a third of the wine market. As a result individual companies hold significant market shares in all domestic alcoholic drinks markets: Grand Metropolitan, through its various subsidiaries holds 12% of the beer market, 10% of the gin market; 50% of the vodka market and 5% of the wine market in the UK. whilst Allied-Lyons' 14% share of the beer market is actually smaller than its 15% slice of the Scotch Whisky market; Allied controls 8% of the wine market as well.[2]

In the beer sector, the top six companies (Bass, Allied-Lyons, Whitbread, Grand Metropolitan, Scottish and Newcastle, and Courage) control 80% of the market. (*The Guardian* 18th October, 1988) One reason for the high concentration of production in beer in particular has been the low level of imports. This suggests little competition from abroad. Beer imports have generally stayed below 6% of domestic sales. But increasingly all alcohol sectors, including beer, are becoming international in scope (See for example *The Economist* 1988 p75-6). This has been reflected in recent merger activity, which has seen Courage taken over by an Australian brewer (Elders IXL, in 1986) in addition to a number of unsuccessful takeover bids for other British brewers. The opening of European markets in future is likely to give further impetus to the internationalisation of the drinks market.

Whilst beer has traditionally been a closed market, Britain has imported most of her wine from abroad. Although one should note that the share of domestically produced wine had increased to 10% of the British wine market by 1983.[3] Britain is less reliant on imported spirits, domestic production supplying 75% of the market.[4] But in contrast the spirits producers are highly dependent on overseas markets. For example the Scotch Whisky industry exports 80% of its output (by value) abroad.[5] Whilst exports account for around two thirds of the British gin industry's sales revenue. (National Economic Development Office, 1982)

Turning now to the retail alcohol trade, there appears at first sight to be much less concentration in the market than is the case on the production side. Alcohol is sold through a wide range of outlets (see chapter seven): on-licensed premises, like public houses, restaurants and hotels (99,600 in Britain in 1980); off-licensed premises, like supermarkets, grocery stores, and specialist off-licences (42,200), as well as registered clubs (29,600).[6] But the retail trade in alcohol is not as fragmented as it might first appear, for three reasons.

First, the licensing system regulates the retailing of alcohol and limits to some extent the overall number of outlets (see chapter seven). Secondly, the brewers' ownership of licensed premises leads to a considerable degree of concentration in the retail sector. Brewers own over 60% of on-licensed premises and just under 10% of off-licensed establishments. (Brewers' Society, 1984). Such 'vertical integration', where producers control aspects of the retail trade, has tended to undermine the economic independence of the retail sector, and this partly explains why the producers are the most powerful element within the industry. This is offset however to some extent by the growing proportion of the retail alcohol trade captured by the independent food retailers and grocers. These now control around 40% of off-licence alcoholic drink turnover.[7] This. moreover, represents a larger slice of a bigger cake: the market share of the off-licence sector is around 30% of total sales: it was only around 20% in the early seventies.[8]

The most important part of the off-licence retail trade today are the supermarket chains. These outlets have considerable economic leverage and represent an important countervailing force against producer power. But at the same time they also serve to increase the degree of concentration within the retail sector, and their growing involvement is a further factor behind the increasing concentration in this sector.

Size and economic significance

The market for alcoholic drinks, as we have already suggested is large. Around 90% of the population drink alcohol. Alcohol consumption has also grown rapidly over the past three decades, as we saw in the previous chapter, with expenditure on alcohol doubling between 1960 and 1984. (Godfrey, Hardman and Maynard, 1986)

The alcohol industry is also important in terms of the wider economy. Alcoholic drink accounts for 7% of consumer spending. Alcohol taxes make a huge contribution to national revenue. The spirits industry is a major exporter (the Scotch Whisky industry is the largest exporter in the food and drink sector by value. (NEDO, 1988) Table six summarises these statistics. In addition, one has to be aware of the importance of the alcohol industry to other sectors like engineering, agriculture, packaging, and advertising. A few examples illustrate this point. Around a fifth of UK barley production and around two thirds of domestic hop production is used by British brewers and distillers. On average this represents around 6% of the value of British crop production, and 2% of agricultural output.[9] Another industry whose fortunes are closely related to alcohol is advertising. Approximately 5.4% of press and television advertising expenditure is attributable to alcohol and tobacco. (see chapter five)

Table 6

The Economic Significance of the Alcohol Industry (1986)

Number of Companies in the UK Top 50	4
Annual Profits from Production(£m)	1300
Employment (000)	512
Sales as % of UK Consumer Spending	7.0
Indirect Taxation as % of Exchequer Revenue	4.5
Exports as % of Visible Exports	1.8

Sources: *Company Reports; The Times Top 1000 Companies; Central Statistical Office UK National Accounts Department of Employment Employment Gazette; Department of Trade and Industry Overseas Trade Statistics.*

The Political Organisation of the Industry

Producer organisations

The firms having an interest in alcohol are organised into producer and retail trade associations. The drink producers are, as one might expect, organised on product lines. The 83 British brewers are represented by the Brewers' Society. This organisation is governed by a Council, most of whom are either nominated or elected by the member firms. The Council, which meets ten times a year, elects an executive committee to deal with major issues. The Executive Committee in turn appoints sub-committees which formulate policy on issues of current importance. The establishment of a special executive sub-committee on social problems of alcohol therefore reflects the importance which brewers attach to this issue.

The Council elects a chairman (and a vice-chairman) every year and he is invariably drawn from one of the major brewers. This illustrates the weight which the larger brewers carry within the Society. Indeed the largest seven brewers (the 'big six' mentioned earlier, plus Guinness) nominate half the Executive; around a third of the Council members are also drawn from these companies. The major brewers pay larger subscriptions than the smaller companies, a factor which no doubt adds to their influence within the Society.

The decisions of the Executive and Council are implemented by permanent officers, headed by the director of the Society. The officers are in turn accountable to the Council and to various standing committees. The standing committees, not to be confused with the executive sub-committees mentioned a moment ago, are partly elected by the members and partly co-opted. They examine issues within their particular brief and recommend appropriate action to the executive. Currently there are ten standing committees, covering matters such as technology, the retail trade, public relations, law, and finance, to name a few.

The other trade associations are similar in structure and organisation. But there are some differences. The Wines and Spirits Association (WSA) for example - which organises wine and spirits importers, merchants and the domestic wine producers - has a much larger membership, organising around five hundred wine and spirit traders. Like the Brewers' Society, most of its work is done in specialist sub-committees, whose briefs reflect the specialised interests of the membership. The supermarkets group of the WSA for example deals with issues arising out of members' trade in this retail sector. Whilst the domestic wine industry has its own standing committee to consider the main issues affecting this sector.

The other main producer organisations are the Scotch Whisky Association (SWA), the Gin Rectifiers and Distillers Association (GRD) and the Vodka Trade Association (VTA), which together represent the interests of the domestic spirits producers. The GRD and the VTA are very small organisations: the GRD for example has only thirteen members. The SWA is by contrast much larger, having 120 members who are engaged in the distilling, blending, bottling, and marketing of Scotch Whisky. Some of the larger and more important members of the SWA, such as the Grand Metropolitan subsidiary, International Distillers and Vintners (IDV), and Guinness (through its ownership of Distillers) are also involved in the production of gin and vodka, and are also members of the GRD or the VTA. Partly because of this overlap, and partly because of the limited resources of the smaller trade assocations, the SWA often makes representations on behalf of the GRD and VTA on issues of common interest.

In summary, the most powerful producer organisations are the Brewers' Society, the WSA, and the SWA. These organisations have overlapping memberships, given the fact that the larger drinks companies are now involved in more than one product. They are, moreover, in regular contact with each other on common issues and serve to coordinate the collective response of the industry as a whole, where necessary. As we shall see later these organisations have been at the heart of the industry's response on the issue of alcohol misuse.

Retailers' organisations

The Brewers' Society, through its ownership of the retail alcohol trade, can also claim to speak for this sector, as well as for beer producers. The Wines and Spirit Association also has a substantial interest in retail matters, as a number of its members operate off-licences. But a number of other assocations exist to represent the independent retailers, and it is to these we now turn. The retail alcohol sector, as we mentioned earlier, is more fragmented than alcohol production, and the organisation of this sector reflects this. In the on-licensed trade there are several organisations, each catering for a particular type of premises.

Public house tenants and freeholders are fairly well organised. Their association, the National Union of Licensed Victuallers (NULV), has approximately 20,000 members, over half the potential membership. The organisation's governing body, the National Council, is elected by six regional councils, which are in turn elected by local Licensed Victuallers Associations (LVA). The National Council, which is a large and somewhat inflexible body, delegates reponsibility to the national president and the NULV officers who are elected by the Council for a two year period. Much of the day to day work is however performed in sub-committees, such as the Parliamentary Committee, which are serviced by the permanent staff of the association.

Since the creation of the NULV in 1976, the public house landlords have been able to speak with a single voice. Prior to this there were a number of organisations claiming to represent their views. Indeed this kind of situation still persists in the registered club sector where several separate representative organisations can be found, including the Association of Conservative Clubs, the Working Men's Club and Institute Union, the Royal British Legion, and the National Union of Labour Clubs.

Hotels and restaurants on the other hand have been mainly represented by a single organisation since the turn of the century. The British Hotels, Restaurants and Caterers Association (BHRCA) has approximately 15,000 members, many of whom now sell alcoholic drink. In view of this, the association has taken a closer interest in alcohol matters, particularly in recent years.

Turning now to the off-licensed sector, the larger general retailers are organised by the British Retailers Association (BRA). This organisation was formed in 1983 following a merger between the British Multiple Retailers Association (BMRA) and the Association of Retail Distributors (ARD). Its 300 members include the larger multiple stores and together account for just over half the total retail trade in Britain. Although alcohol is only one of many products sold by the Association's members, it has been significant enough to warrant the creation of a special Wines and Spirits Group within the organisation. This group caters specifically for those companies heavily involved in retailing these beverages. There is also a Wines and Spirits Committee within the Association's decision making structure, which meets about five times a year, and which monitors issues affecting the retail trade in alcohol. The chairman of this committee is automatically a member of the food and drink steering committee, which formulates the Association's overall policy on these matters.

The smaller general retailers are organised by the British Independent Grocers Association (BIGA), a much less powerful organisation than BRA and its precursors. BIGA also includes members who operate specialist off-licences, although the National Off-Licence Federation is the main organisation for this kind of outlet.

There are, then, at least nine major organisations which claim to represent the interests of alcohol retailers. But as with the producer organisations, some are more active, and some carry greater weight, than others. The most powerful organisation in this area is the BRA. Its influence is largely due to the fact that it represents the largest firms in the general retail trade. The NULV follows, some distance behind. Its main strength is its representativeness: its actual membership is a relatively high proportion of the total potential membership. But in general, and with the possible exception of the BRA, NULV, and pehaps also the BHRCA, the independent retailers are not as effectively organised as the producers. They also have less economic and political power as we shall see later.

The Industry's Response to the Alcohol Problem

It is the producer organisations which have taken the lead role in formulating and coordinating the industry's policy on alcohol problems. Each producer association has in recent years publicly accepted that alcohol abuse is a serious social problem (see House of Commons, 1977b; House of Lords, 1985). The Brewers' Society, for example, has stated that 'the brewing industry is aware that a small but significant minority cause harm to themselves and others through the misuse of alcohol and shares the concern about this problem.' (Brewers' Society, 1983) Similarly, the Scotch Whisky Association has recognised 'the existence of social and medical problems arising from excessive drinking... (and) has always wished to play a responsible and active part in their resolution.' (House of Commons, 1977b) Whilst the Wines and Spirit Association is 'always concerned by the misuse of the products of its members and is active in promoting their proper use.' (Wines and Spirit Association, 1984)

The drink industry's concern about alcohol abuse was further demonstrated by the creation of special standing committees within each of the main producer associations during the seventies. The Brewers' Society has a special executive sub-committee, the Social Problems of Alcohol Committee, to formulate its policy on alcohol abuse. A similar function is performed within the Scotch Whisky Association by the Alcohol Education and Research Committee, and in the Wines and Spirits Association by the Social Aspects of Alcohol Committee. These three committees are in regular contact with each other, mainly through the chairmen, and are thus able to coordinate the industry's overall policy on alcohol misuse. Coordination is also facilitated by the larger drinks companies having members on all three committees.

It has been suggested by some within the industry that the Brewers' Society has a central coordinating role within the ranks of the producers. There are a number of reasons why brewers may have taken on such a responsibility. First, they appear to have a stronger incentive to defend the industry: beer is the largest single sector in the market. The brewers are also more heavily dependent on domestic markets than on exports, compared with the other producers. Secondly, they have the ability to perform a lead role. The brewers exert considerable influence over the retail trade through the tied house system. Moreover, the diversification of brewery firms into wines and spirits, and their membership of the relevant trade associations, has enabled them to exert influence over the policies of the SWA and the WSA on the issue of alcohol abuse.

Whilst the producers recognise alcohol problems, and have sought to coordinate a response to these problems, they disagree strongly with some of the measures that have been proposed by the alcohol misuse lobby. The producer asociations have been particularly critical of control policies, such as advertising controls, taxation, and licensing restrictions. The industry's opposition is based on two premises. First, that such measures infringe personal (and of course, commercial) liberty; and secondly, that their introduction would not reduce the problem. The following comment by the Scotch Whisky Association is representative of the whole industry's viewpoint:

"... attempts to dictate drinking habits by legislation and taxation would be an infringement of personal liberty and... would in any case create more and more difficult problems than those they were intending to solve." (House of Commons, 1977b, p471)

The industry's opposition to control policies is based in part upon a rejection of the consumption theory of alcohol problems, discussed in the previous chapter. It points out that the level of alcohol problems in the UK is lower than in many comparable countries, and that many countries with similar consumption levels experience differences in the degree of alcohol problems (see, for example, the comparative levels of consumption and abuse in Holland and Poland, in chapter three, table three).

The industry prefers instead to focus on the individual, rather than alcohol consumption, as the main source of the problem. The professed aim of the industry is to alter the harmful drinking habits of the 'minority' which abuse alcohol, leaving the rest of the population free from interference. The Brewer's Society identifies three main 'at risk' groups where it believes harmful drinking habits can develop. These are: the young; drinking drivers; and problem drinkers at work. (Brewers' Society, 1983) The brewers suggest that the drinking habits of these groups can be altered in three main ways: by educating about alcohol - encouraging moderate drinking habits; through the development of early identification procedures - under which problem drinkers could be discovered and helped; and finally through a programme of research - which could establish the links between individual habits and drinking problems.

The industry has already begun to promote such a strategy. In 1977 the Brewers' Society collaborated with the British Retail Association (BRA) and other retailers in the alcohol field to produce publicity aimed at discouraging under-age drinking. The drinks industry has also provided funds for research into the causes of alcohol problems and the effectiveness of preventive measures. Between 1980 and 1985, the Brewers' Society alone donated around £2.5m to research projects in this area.[10] Individual drinks companies have also given money, mainly for medical research, in the past.

It is also worth noting that until 1984, the Medical Council on Alcoholism (MCA) received approximately 40% of its income from the industry. Since the reorganisation of the national voluntary organisations in the field of alcohol misuse in 1984 (see chapter two), it has been entirely dependent on contributions from the drink producers. It is perhaps significant that the MCA has not been a strong supporter of control policies, and has in the past focused mainly on education, training and treatment strategies. Its approach has therefore been highly compatible with the industry's perspective, and this is partly why the industry has been willing to fund the MCA.

But why, one may ask, is the industry bothering to show any concern at all about alcohol problems? After all, other industries have strenuously denied that their products are associated with ill-health or other social and environmental problems. The tobacco industry for example has never conceded publicly that smoking causes lung cancer, despite the wealth of statistical evidence suggesting such a link. (Taylor, 1984) Similarly the food industry denies that some of its products contain additives and other substances in such quantities that may be harmful to health. (Millstone, 1984)

The alcohol industry has realised the advantages of taking up a responsible position. If alcohol became widely associated with ill-health, the product's image would suffer and sales would almost certainly begin to fall. But by appearing concerned about the problem, and by giving support to an alternative strategy which is less damaging to its interests, the industry can maintain the product's image and resist any decline in sales. Furthermore, if as a result of this strategy the level of alcohol problems did not rise further, the industry would benefit directly in the long run. As some within the industry have acknowledged, 'dead customers ring no tills.' (Ambler, 1984) In other words the long term potential of the market would be secure if the physical and financial well-being of consumers could be protected.

Another reason why the drinks industry has decided to adopt a responsible position lies in the fact that alcohol is not always harmful. Unlike the tobacco industry, the drinks industry is able to argue that its product when taken in moderation causes no harm. The drinks producers have developed this line of argument further in recent years by marketing low and non-alcoholic drinks. This strategy, which is examined more closely in the next chapter, is commercially sound because in general these drinks are highly profitable. Yet at the same time (though the industry would not admit this) the growth in the market share of low alcohol drinks may lead to a reduction in the overall level of alcohol consumed and thereby, according to the consumption theorists, cause a fall in the incidence of alcohol-related problems.

So far we have considered the view of the industry as presented by the main producer associations. Individual firms have tended to leave the task of responding on issues of collective interest, such as alcohol misuse, to these associations. There have been exceptions however. A number of individual Scotch Whisky companies have in the past given money towards research into alcohol problems. Independent commercial concern was also reflected in a confidential document produced by Grand Metropolitan a few years ago. The document indicated that the company was dissatisfied with the response of the industry as a whole on the issue. It went on to declare that the company itself would in future be taking the initiative to establish a major programme of education about alcohol in an attempt to alter drinking habits. (Ambler, 1984) Independent statements such as this, however, rarely come into the public domain.

The producer trade associations have shouldered the burden of responsibility for responding to the growth in alcohol problems. The retail organisations broadly agree with the position taken by the producers; they oppose control policies and believe that alcohol misuse is best tackled by a strategy of education, early identification, research and treatment. There are however a few tensions within the industry, which need to be noted. One disagreement emerges out of the position taken by the pub landlords' association, the National Union of Licensed Victuallers (NULV) on the question of restricting licensed outlets. The NULV believes that the licensing system ought to be used to restrict the number of outlets selling alcohol. Its main interest here is to preserve the business of its members and to protect them from competition, particularly from the off-licence sector which has grown dramatically in recent years. Even so, the NULV has publicly agreed with parts of the alcohol misuse lobby, that the expansion of outlets has increased the availability of alcohol, and that this has been partly responsible for the rise in the level of alcohol consumption and misuse. This goes against the line taken by the rest of the industry, which is generally against any further restrictions on the availability of alcohol.

For the most part though the drinks industry appears to form a cohesive lobby on the issue of alcohol misuse. The producer and retailer organsiations take similar approach to alcohol problems and internal disagreements, where they exist, are rarely publicised. Moreover, the lobby is on the whole well-coordinated by the producer associations. These considerations, coupled with the economic leverage of the industry noted earlier, suggest that the industry is well equipped to articulate its viewpoint to policy makers. In the next section we shall see if this is in fact the case.

Presenting the Industry's View

The consultative process

It is perhaps best to begin by looking at what is generally regarded as the most influential channel for presenting views: contact with government departments through the consultative process. The drinks industry is consulted by a wide range of government departments. But most of its contact is with the Ministry of Agriculture, Fisheries and Food (MAFF), which is the industry's 'sponsoring department'. Every industry has a sponsoring department, which generally supervises the industry, advises it, listens to its views, an in some cases regulates its conduct. Usually this sponsorship role is performed by the Department of Trade and Industry (DTI). But there are significant exceptions. The pharmaceutical industry is sponsored by the Department of Health and Social Security (DHSS), whilst the construction industry is the responsibility of the Department of the Environment (DoE). The alcoholic drinks industry is sponsored by MAFF in view the department's overall responsibility for food and drink matters.

Contact with MAFF is both formal and informal. Formal contact takes the form of committees established under the auspices of the National Economic Development Office (NEDO). These committees, which are called Sector Working Groups (SWGs), examine a particular area of industry and make recommendations on how economic performance might be improved in future. In the alcoholic drinks sector there are three SWGs: the first examines the brewing industry; the second, the Scotch Whisky industry; the third, gin and vodka. Each committee contains representatives from the drinks companies, the trade associations, the trade unions, and the government. The Brewing SWG for example has 15 members: two representatives from the National Economic Development Office; two from MAFF, including the Assistant Secretary who heads the department's Alcoholic Drinks Division; two from the Brewers Society (one of whom is the SWG chairman); three from brewing companies; and six trade union representatives. The two other SWGs are organised on similar lines.

The SWG framework enables both sides of the industry, along with government, to examine issues affecting the industry. It also provides a channel through which the industry can present its views to government. Although most of the issues examined by the SWGs have been rather technical - a recent report from the Brewing SWG for example looked at the application of microelectronics in the industry - opportunities have arisen for the industry to argue its case on the issue of alcohol misuse. For example in one of its reports the Brewing SWG restated the industry's position on alcohol misuse and made a thinly veiled criticism of control policies, such as taxation, licensing, and advertising controls. (National Economic Development Office, 1983) Similarly, reports from the Gin and Vodka and Scotch Whisky SWGs, have opposed the use of taxation as a means of regulating alcohol consumption. (NEDO, 1982, 1985)

Unlike the brewing and distilling industries, the wine industry does not have a SWG to convey its views. The main reason for this is that SWGs are designed to promote domestic industry; yet the wine industry is dominated by foreign producers, as we saw earlier. There is however a non-governmental body which exists to promote the wine industry. This is the Wine Development Board, which was set up in 1967 with a general brief to promote wine drinking in Britain. It also makes representations to government on matters affecting the wine industry. The Board is funded jointly by the wine importers and by countries who export wine to this country; and is governed by representatives of the major drinks companies.

Despite the existence of formal channels, most of the contact between MAFF and the industry is informal and takes place outside the NEDO structure. This takes the form of telephone conversations and 'ad hoc' meetings between representatives of the main producer associations - the Brewers' Society, the Wines and Spirits Association, and the Scotch Whisky Association - and Ministry officials. This informal contact ensures that the dialogue between MAFF and the industry is close and continuous. Within MAFF the civil servants in the Alcoholic Drinks Division have most contact with the industry, though other divisions - such as Food Science, Food Standards, Cereals and the Horticultural Division - are also in touch with the industry from time to time.

According to civil servants at the Ministry, ministers have not in the past taken a great interest in the drinks industry and as a result most decisions have fallen by default to the civil servants. This state of affairs has howvever changed markedly in recent years, with ministerial interest being aroused by two things in particular. First of all, the threats posed to the industry by the alcohol misuse lobby's support for control policies. Second, the particular economic problems of the Scotch Whisky industry. Since these developments the producer associations, particularly the SWA, have had much more contact with Agriculture Ministers than before. For example in reply to a Parliamentary Question in 1981, the then Minister of Agriculture, Peter Walker was able to tell the House that he was 'in constant touch with the Scotch Whisky Association about various issues of concern to the industry.'[11]

MAFF then is the focal point for the industry's lobbying within Whitehall. Although the Ministry does not respond passively to the industry's demands, and should not therefore be regarded in any way as a creature of the industry, it nevertheless shares the view of the industry on many issues. This convergence of views tends to occur especially when the industry is fairly unanimous on an issue, as in the case of alcohol misuse. On this particular issue, the Ministry supports the industry's view, that control policies should not be adopted. It sees such a approach as potentially damaging to the industry's economic welfare. and in view of its departmental responsibility for the industry, has opposed moves within government to implement policies along these lines.

But MAFF is not the only department to be in touch with the industry. Indeed, regular contact is maintained with at least seven other departments, each of which has responsibilities connected in some way to the industry's activities. The Department of Trade and Industry has a general responsibility for consumer welfare, competition and fair trading, advertising, and exports. It has been in contact with the drinks industry on all of these issues at some time in the past. In 1983 for example arguments about wine measures led to discussions between the department and the Brewers Society, the NULV, and the BHRCA.[12] The recent round of mergers and takeover bids in the industry, such as the Distillers and Guinness merger in 1986, has also brought this department in contact with the industry. A dialogue has also been maintained on the issue of advertising, in view of the DTIs responsibilities. But the relationship between the DTI and the industry is perhaps closest on export matters. The spirits industry, as a major exporter, is in regular contact with the DTI on this subject. The nature of this relationship is widely acknowledged and in 1981 the Secretary of State for Trade and Industry himself referred to his 'department's frequent and regular contacts with the Scotch Whisky Association.'[13]

The Treasury and Customs and Excise are also in touch with the industry. Customs and Excise has a continuous dialogue with the producer associations on technical questions regarding tax collection and in particular the collection of excise duties. The Wines and Spirits Association for example discusses such matters regularly with the department at Commissioner level. Whilst the Treasury is in contact with all these trade associations, in view of its overall responsibility for taxation policy. Aside from any informal contact, the producer organisations each send a delegation to the Treasury once a year, to plea for favourable treatment in the Budget (see chapter six below).

The Home Office has met the industry to discuss a variety of matters in the past. But the most popular subject in recent years has been the licensing laws - which in England and Wales is a Home Office responsibility. The department has received representations on this issue from many organisations in the industry, including retailers' organisations such as the NULV as well as the Brewers' Society. North of the border, the Scottish Office is responsible for licensing matters and has also in the past received delegations from the industry on this issue. We shall examine the effectiveness of this lobbying in chapter seven when we take a look at the issue of licensing law reform.

Finally, the industry has in recent years discussed the problem of alcohol misuse with both the DHSS and the Department of Transport (DoT). In discussions with the DHSS it has argued against control policies and in favour of its own strategy, outlined above. The Brewers' Society and the other two main producer assocations persuaded the DHSS to recognise the Alcohol Forum, mentioned in chapter three. The industry has also been particularly concerned about the problem of drinking and driving and this has brought it into contact with the Department of Transport. On several occasions in the last few years the Brewers' Society has been involved in discussions with this department concerning the industry's attempts to discourage drinking and driving.[14]

In general then the industry enjoys close, and in some cases continuous, contact with government departments. This is particularly true of the producer associations whose economic leverage has ensured their insider status. (Grant, 1985) The industry relies a great deal on these organisations to present its viewpoint. On some issues however the retail organisations have been actively involved in discussions with government departments. The British Retailers Association and its precursors have usually been able to present their views in this way when necessary. In contrast other retail organisations, such as the NULV, have had less access to these channels.

Although the industry has contact with government departments, this does not necessarily mean that it has directly influenced government policy. Indeed the industry's case has undoubtedly been helped by the general predisposition in Whitehall against control policies, noted in the last chapter. In short it has been pushing at an open door: the industry's representations on the issue of alcohol misuse did not convert government departments to supporting its viewpoint, but rather reinforced their opposition to control policies.

Direct links with government departments are generally regarded as being the most effective kind of political contact. But lobbies also operate on other fronts and the drink industry is no exception. In the next section we examine the degree of support which the industry has in Parliament, and the extent to which this complements its consultatative status.

Parliamentary connections

A considerable number of MPs have some kind of financial or political interest in the drinks industry. Estimates of the size of this interest are given in table seven. These figures are however only a rough guide to the actual magnitude of the drinks interest in the House. They include direct economic interests which have either been declared by MPs or which have been unearthed by political researchers. For example, Paul Dean is included in the 1983 and 1987 figures because he declared his interests as a director of the drinks company, Watney Mann.

Political interests are also declared by some MPs. Michael Colvin is included in the above figures because of his role as political advisor to the National Union of Licensed Victuallers. Several other MPs hold official posts with drink industry associations. Some, such as Neil Hamilton, are employed as political advisors or consultants -in his case the Brewers' Society. Robert Hicks is a further example, being the Parliamentary liaison officer of the restaurants and caterers' association, the BRHCA. Whilst Roger Sims is the Parliamentary advisor to the Scotch Whisky Association. Some MPs, on the other hand, are actually members of drink industry associations. For example, John Townend was formerly the chairman of the Wines and Spirits Association.

Table 7

Members of the House of Commons with Drink Interests

Parliamentary Sessions	Number of MPs with Drink Interests
1970-4	23 ‡
1974-9	19 †
1979-83	34 **
1983-7	53 *
1987-	47 *

Sources:
* *Action on Alcohol Abuse*
** *Daube (1981)*
‡ *Roth (1972)*
† *Roth (1975)*

Individual companies also retain MPs as political advisors and consultants in their own right. Bowen Wells is the Parliamentary Advisor to International Distillers and Vintners (IDV), the Grand Metropolitan subsidiary. Robert Rhodes-James MP is a consultant to Allied-Lyons, and Sir Dudley Smith and Roger Gale fulfil similar roles for Bass Ltd and Scottish and Newcastle Breweries respectively.

The size of the drink interest in Parliament could be larger than the above figures and examples suggest. This is because some MPs with interests in this area have been omitted from these estimates. There is considerable under-reporting of MPs' family and other personal connections with drink industry interests. For example, although Paul Channon's ties with the Guinness family are well known, Sir Nicholas Bonsor's connections with the Watney family is not common knowledge and this has led to his omission from the above estimates.

Other kinds of indirect interest are also omitted, such as those MPs with interests in farming for example. They have a vested interest in the welfare of the drinks industry because it is a major consumer of agricultural produce. Also of the 80 MPs with interests in advertising, it is likely that a fair proportion have an indirect interest in the drinks industry in view of the contribution of alcohol to advertising revenues. (Daube, 1981)

MPs having contacts with public relations and lobbying organisations are also excluded from the above estimates, even though they might have an indirect interest in the industry. These organisations are essentially political middlemen who retain MPs to campaign on their clients behalf. For example, George Gardiner MP is a director of T.A Cutbill PR Ltd, whose clients include the Wines and Spirits Association and the brewers, Whitbread Ltd.

The other main area of under-reporting of drink interests in the estimates is constituency interests. In 1983 there were 130 brewing plants and 119 distilleries in operation. These production plants tend to be concentrated in certain areas. The employment they provide represents a considerable constituency interest for the incumbent MPs in these areas. Hamish Watt, former MP for Banff, once declared to the House that his constituency contained approximately one third of all the malt whisky distilleries in Scotland.[15] Many other Scottish MPs have constituency interests in the Scotch Whisky industry. Brewing is less concentrated regionally. Nevertheless, some MPs have considerable constituency interests in brewing and recognise its importance to the locality. An example is Ivan Lawrence, MP for Burton on Trent, a major brewing centre (It should be noted that Lawrence was included in the above estimates in view of his appointment as chairman of Burton Breweries).

The problems of evaluating the size of the drinks lobby in Parliament is even greater when one looks at the House of Lords. Unlike the Commons, the Lords does not disclose details of members' interests. Also the exact number of active peers is unknown and this adds to the difficulties of establishing precisely the size of the lobby in the Upper House. But it is clear that a number of Lords have a significant interest in the industry. Lord Bancroft, a former senior civil servant, is now a director of Bass Ltd. Lord Davis of Penrhys also holds a directorship in the brewing industry. Lord Pritchard of West Hadden, a former chairman of Allied Breweries, is currently the Vice-President of the Wines and Spirits Association. Whilst Lord Ingrow is a member of the Brewers' Society Executive Committee.

In view of the above discussion it seems that the size of the drink industry lobby in Parliament may well be considerably larger than it at first appears. One must take care however not to equate an interest with political activity on an issue. It is worth noting that Patrick Jenkin, Secretary of State at the DHSS at the time when the department was pressing for strong action on alcohol abuse, was formerly an executive with Distillers Ltd. Even so, bearing this caveat in mind, there is much evidence to suggest that in general MPs have pursued their interests in this area.

These interests have been reflected in the tabling of Parliamentary Questions. Table eight presents an analysis of Parliamentary Questions tabled on the drink industry topics (excluding alcohol misuse - see chapter two) in the House of Commons over an eight year period. From the early sixties there was a sharp increase in the number of PQs, peaking in the seventies. There has since been a decline, though the number of PQs tabled is still considerable at fifty per annual session.

Table 8

Parliamentary Questions on the Drinks Industry

(a)Number of PQs over time.

Sessions	Number of PQs
1960/1-64/5	26
1965/6-69/70	116
1970/1-74/5	318
1975/6-79/80	273
1980/1-84/5	244

(b)Number of PQs by industry

Topic of PQs	75-6	76-7	77-8	78-9	79-80	80-1	81-2	82-3	TOTAL
Alcohol Industry in general	37	18	11	2	4	12	2	14	100
Scotch Whisky/ Spirits	15	19	27	8	12	6	8	5	100
Wine Industry	12	13	7	5	7	5	4	5	58
Brewing	13	32	17	3	11	1	3	4	84
Total									342

It will be seen in part (b) of table eight that the Scotch Whisky industry has been a major topic, accounting for 41% of the Parliamentary Questions concerning a specific sector of the drinks industry. The large number of PQs tabled on this industry was largely due to the effective organisation of the Scotch Whisky lobby in Parliament during the period under analysis. The backbone of this organisation is the all party backbench group (APG) on Scotch Whisky. APGs in general act mainly as a source of information for backbench MPs, but they also provide a platform for Parliamentary activity on a particular issue. (Richardson and Kimber, 1972; Morgan, 1979) In addition APGs often have close links with outside pressure groups. The secretary of the Scotch Whisky APG is Roger Sims MP, who is also the Parliamentary Adviser to the Scotch Whisky Association.

Other APGs also serve the industry. The associations representing drinking clubs established an APG in the early eighties. In addition the Retail Trade APG and the Tourism APG have also considered issues affecting the drinks industry in recent years. This may have been partly due to the fact that the groups' respective chairmen, Geoffrey Finsberg MP and Robert Adley MP, have both had some involvement with the drinks industry in the past. Finsberg was formerly the political adviser to the NULV, whilst Adley has financial interests in the licensed trade, being the director of a hotel chain and a member of the BHRCA. Other drink interests have also established their own Parliamentary committees, though these do not have the status of a Parliamentary APG. The Wines and Spirits Association and the

National Union of Licensed Victuallers are both known to have Parliamentary Liaison Committees, which liaise with MPs on matters regarding the industry.

In summary then, the drink industry has a fairly large number of MPs on which it can rely for support. In addition it maintains channels - in the form of political consultants and parliamentary committees or APGs - which can be used to mobilise support when an issue affecting the industry's welfare emerges. In subsequent chapters we examine specific instances where these channels have been utilised.

The drinks industry and the Conservative Party

Although the issues affecting the alcohol industry, and the question of alcohol misuse in particular, tend to cut across party lines, the industry is traditionally allied with the Conservative Party. The reasons for this are largely historical. (Baggott, 1986) In the last century the temperance movement, in its battle against the 'liquor traffic', became more party-political in outlook. This culminated in the affiliation of the movement to the Liberal Party in the latter half of the century. As the Liberals began to introduce measures to restrict the industry, the brewers, distillers, and the licensed trade moved closer to the Conservative Party. As a result the alcohol control issue became 'a political issue... a party political issue, with the Liberals on the side of temperance reform and the Tories opposing any measures which might embarrass the trade.' (Williams and Brake, 1980)

The decline of the drink question in the inter-war period and the concomitant decline of the Liberal Party changed the nature of the issue. It is no longer a party political issue. Even so the Conservative Party still favours the drinks industry. In the present Parliament, out of the 47 MPs who have visible interests in the industry, all but two are Conservatives. This represents an overwhelming proportion, even when one takes into account the large Conservative majority in the present House of Commons. Yet in spite of this apparent bias, some of the key figures in the alcohol misuse lobby - such as Sir Bernard Braine for example - have been Conservatives. Moreover, as we saw in the last chapter, important government initiatives on alcohol misuse have been backed by Conservative health ministers - Lord Joseph, Patrick Jenkin, and Sir George Young. The current review of alcohol policy by the government (see chapter three) also suggests that the Conservative Party is far from being a creature of the industry, as was apparently the case at the turn of the century.

But the drinks industry is nevertheless influential within the Party. In addition to its strong links with the Tory backbenchers, the industry may also carry weight with the leadership in view of the political contributions which it makes to the party funds. In 1983 for example, Allied-Lyons, which has considerable interests in brewing, was one of the biggest donors. Its contribution of £82,000 was accompanied by Distillers' donation of £50,000. (*The Economist* 6 October, 1984) In addition many other drinks companies have in recent years given smaller amounts, and these add up to a considerable sum. In 1981 for example twelve drinks firms gave a total of £96,000- approximately 5% of the Party's total income from company donations in that year. (Labour Party Research Department, 1981)

Organised Labour and Consumers

So far nothing has been said about two important groups that are closely linked with the industry, yet which do not have a commercial interest as such in the production or sale of alcohol. These are the employees of the industry and the consumers of alcoholic drinks. In this final section the focus is upon these groups and their stance in relation to alcohol misuse.

Labour

The labour force on the production side of the drinks industry is relatively well organised. Four unions have an interest in brewing and distilling: the General and Municipal Workers Union (GMWU), and the Transport and General Workers Union (TGWU) have a considerable interest; whilst the Association of Professional, Clerical and Computer Staff (APEX), and the Amalgamated Union of Engineering Workers (AUEW) have a much smaller representation. The GMWU is the main union in distilling, having around 15,000 members in this industry. The TGWU has around 2,000 members in distilling and together with the GMWU accounts for around 90% of the workforce in thiis sector. In brewing the situation is the reverse with the main union being the TGWU (roughly 28,000 members), whilst the GMWU has around 5,000 members in the industry. Unionisation in the brewing industry is around 80%.

In contrast unionisation in the retail sector is low. The only organisation of any substance here is the National Association of Licensed House Managers (NALHM), which represents the managers of brewery-owned public houses. This organisation has around 10,000 members, a high proportion of the potential membership. The only other Union involved in this sector is the Union of Shop, Distributive and Allied Workers (USDAW) which has around 3,000 members in the specialist off-licence trade.

Finally, it should be noted that for most of these unions the alcoholic drinks industry membership represents only a small proportion of total membership. There is therefore no reason why issues affecting this industry should take priority over other concerns. Only the NALHM draws its membership exclusively from the alcoholic drinks industry. Whereas the sector provides only 2% of the GMWU's total membership, and about the same proportion of the membership of the TGWU.

Even so the general unions are concerned about alcohol misuse, particularly within the alcohol industry itself. They have cooperated in the establishment of special workplace policies to help problem drinkers, and are keen to prevent alcohol problems through educational programmes for workers. The unions are however aware that the drinks industry is a major employer. They worry that control policies, particularly the regulation of alcoholic drink prices will lead to more job losses in this sector. On such issues therefore the unions tend to side with the drinks industry associations.

Consumers

Consumers are potentially powerful in two senses. Economically they are powerful in that without consumers there would be no market for alcohol. They can exert power by exercising choice in the marketplace. Politically, as voters, they can prevent alcohol policies from being introduced (or indeed support their introduction) through the ballot box.

There are however significant restrictions on consumer power in practice. Their ability to choose is limited by the lack of information about alcohol products. Advertising seeks to persuade not to inform, and this tends to undermine consumer rationality. As a result, consumers may not accurately perceive the problems associated with alcohol. Whilst consumers' political power is often inhibited by their inability to organise effectively. In particular, consumer organsations tend to be small and relatively weak.

There are two main types of consumer organisation. General consumer organisations, such as the National Consumer Council and the Consumers' Association, have taken up a fairly neutral stance on the issue of alcohol misuse. They have been concerned about the extent of the problem, but have not supported nor opposed control policies. Specialist consumer organisations, such as the Campaign for Real Ale (CAMRA) and the Society for the Preservation of Beer from the Wood (SPBW) have been less neutral, as we shall see in a moment.

CAMRA claims to have approximately 20,000 members and has over 150 local branches. The affairs of the association are governed by an elected National Executive, although its day to day operations are conducted by a small permanent staff. SPBW in contrast has been much less active in recent years, although it is the older of the two organisations. Its organisation is fairly informal, and it consists of around a dozen autonomous branches. It relies much less on centrally directed action and is altogether a less vigorous body than CAMRA.

The specialist organisations like SPBW and CAMRA have tended to side with the industry on the issue of alcohol misuse. This has contrasted with their criticism of the drinks industry on other issues. They have for example been strongly opposed to the closure of traditional public houses and to modern brewing technology. But more recently CAMRA has been particularly critical of the brewer's advertising policies and has gone as far as to call for a ban on drink advertising. Its position on this issue is shaped in part by concern that advertising by the larger brewers may reduce the sales of the smaller brewers which CAMRA seeks to preserve. It is worth noting, though, that CAMRA's support for an advertising ban is shared by many organisations within the alcohol misuse lobby, though for different reasons (see chapter five).

Conclusion

The size and potential power of the drinks industry in the UK is clearly considerable. As an industry it makes a considerable contribution to jobs, profits, output, taxation and overseas trade.

As a lobby it is coherent, well-organised, and effectively coordinate. It possesses a range of useful political contacts in Parliament, government and in the Conservative Party. The industry also has allies in farming and advertising, who themselves have considerable influence. Taken together, these political and economic resources suggest that the drinks industry is a formidable force, which policy-makers cannot ignore.

In the early development of the alcohol misuse issue, the drinks industry and its allies did not have to mobilise these resources. The fragmented alcohol misuse lobby was weak and, apart from the temperance organisations, was not directly challenging the commercial interests of the industry. But the arrival of control policies on the political agenda and the increasing coherence of the alcohol misuse lobby has changed the situation radically. The industry was forced to respond with policy initiatives of its own, coupled with an attack on control policies. It used its political contacts very effectively to ensure that policy-makers were aware of its viewpoint. The government's refusal to back control policies demonstrated that this effort was not in vain.

Notes

1. Company Reports (1987)
2. Information supplied by Mark Booth, former research fellow at the University of York
3. Information supplied by the Wines and Spirits Association
4. Information supplied by the Wines and Spirits Association
5. Infomation supplied by the Scotch Whisky Association
6. Home Office sources
7. Information supplied by Geoff Hardman, research fellow at the University of York
8. Central Statistical Office
9. Figures calculated from Ministry of Agriculture and Brewers' Society statistics
10. Information supplied by Brewers' Society
11. *House of Commons Official Report* Volume 996 Column 625w 16th January 1981
12. *House of Commons Official Report* Volume 375 Column 6w 28th April 1983
13. *House of Commons Official Report* Volume 999 Column 311w 24th February 1981
14. *Morning Advertiser* 25 May 1984 p2
15. *House of Commons Official Report* Volume 906 Column 541-2 25 February 1976

5 Preventing alcohol misuse: islands of consensus?

As we saw in the last chapter, the drinks industry has not attempted to ignore the problem of alcohol misuse. It agrees with government, and the alcohol misuse lobby, that the best way forward is to prevent alcohol problems at an early stage. The drinks industry supports certain preventive strategies, such as health education about alcohol, and programmes which offer help to problem drinkers at an early stage. It also publicly accepts that alcoholic drinks should be presented in a socially responsible manner in promotional campaigns and in the media generally. These approaches to the problem can therefore be seen as potential islands of consensus: policy areas where the conflict of interest between the alcoholic drinks industry, the government, and the alcohol misuse lobby may be resolved in a way acceptable to all parties.

This chapter considers these policy areas in an attempt to assess the scope for compromise on alcohol policy. We begin by examining early detection programmes for problem drinkers. The next section deals with the issue of health education. The last two sections examine the more contentious issues of alcohol promotion and its presentation in the media.

The Early Detection of Problem Drinkers

There are a variety of ways in which those experiencing drinking problems can be identified. But the common aim of these approaches is to single out those needing help at an early stage and refer them to the appropriate services. In this way one can prevent further harm by dealing with drinking problems before they reach a chronic stage.

Professional training

One way of detecting problem drinkers at an early stage is by training those in the caring professions to spot drinking problems in individuals within their client group. (see DHSS, 1979) This approach has attracted official support. The government's consultative document on alcohol misuse, *Drinking Sensibly*, backed 'training programmes to improve understanding amongst health service professionals and others in the caring professions of the extent to which drinking problems may underlie ill-health and social problems.' (DHSS, 1981b) Other professions too may have a role to play in this process of early identification. Teachers, the police, and magistrates are also in a position to detect drinking problems in their respective 'client groups'.

In principle, there is a great deal of consensus about the need to train professionals so as to improve their awareness of drink problems. Certainly the drinks industry has no objections to such a strategy. In practice though, the professions have been slow to incorporate alcohol awareness within their training programmes. The traditional autonomy of professions has been mainly to blame for this. Those responsible for profesional training jealously guard their independence and dislike being dictated to by government on any matter.

Despite this kind of resistance, a change in professional attitudes towards alcohol has begun to take place in recent years. As we saw in chapter three, many professional organisations now take a much greater interest in alcohol misuse. This in turn has begun to influence opinions, attitudes and awareness amongst practising professionals. There have also been some changes in professional education. For example, since 1980 the General Medical Council has insisted that medical students must be given at least a basic knowledge of alcohol-related problems.

Alcohol and work policies

The second major approach to the early identification of problem drinkers has been to attempt to detect alcohol problems in the workplace. Essentially such alcohol and work policies have four components. (McNeill, 1984) First, a statement of aims or a rationale concerning the reduction of alcohol problems in the workplace. This rationale may relate to such things as producing a healthier workforce, reducing absenteeism, or reducing alcohol-related accidents in the workplace. In connection with these last two points it is worth noting that at least eight million working days are lost each year to alcohol-related absenteeism (see chapter one), whilst 20% of accidents at work are in some way connected to alcohol (Emery, 1986) Secondly, an alcohol and work policy should contain clear procedures to identify problem drinkers, confront them, get them to recognise their problem, and to assess their needs, referring them to services if necessary. Third, a programme of educating employees is needed to inform them of drink problems, the procedures outlined above, and the need for such a policy. The final component of an alcohol and work policy is the training which needs to be given to those who will implement the policy, departmental and line managers, supervisors, foremen and so on.

The evidence on the effectiveness of such policies is mixed. On an individual level around 70% of those identified are successfully rehabilitated. But on a more general level it seems that many problem drinkers are not detected by the procedures established. (see Cyster and McNeill, 1985)

A further problem has been the limited take up of alcohol and work policies by British industry. The exception is the drinks industry, where companies have not been slow to introduce policies for their employees. Their response is not surprising given the fact that those who work in the drinks industry have a high risk of developing drink problems. (Royal College of Psychiatrists, 1986 p124) More recently the drinks industry has supported initiatives to encourage industry as a whole to develop alcohol and work policies. In 1987 for example the Wines and Spirits Association issued a booklet, *Alcohol Policy Guidelines for Companies* which gave advice on how to set up such a policy.

Attitudes may be beginning to change (see *The Independent* 29 October 1988), but industry generally has been resistant to initiatives on alcohol and work in the past. In the mid-seventies the National Council on Alcoholism established a special committee to examine the problems of alcohol at work. This committee recommended that the government's Health and Safety Executive should take a closer interest on alcohol problems at work. It also urged employers and unions to get together in order to develop a code of practice on developing alcohol and work policies in the future.

It appears that the employers organisations, like the Confederation of British Industry (CBI) were not a enthusiastic as the unions about these recommendations. In any event, it took the Health and Safety Executive four years to respond to the NCA report. The government eventually came down in favour of the report by backing alcohol and work policies. Both the general policy document *Drinking Sensibly* (DHSS, 1981b) and the Health and Safety Executive's (1981) statement *The Problem Drinker at Work* encouraged joint action by management and the unions to establish such policies. The latter document, which was drawn up in consultation with the DHSS and the Department of Employment, also gives advice to firms on how to establish an alcohol and work policy.

In general though, government is reluctant to interefere with industry and would not force companies to develop such policies. Much then depends on the employers and unions. It is perhaps worth noting that only 15% of Scottish firms purchased *The Problem Drinker at Work*. (Lucas, 1987) With this kind of take-up rate it seems that alcohol and work policies have not as yet grown sufficiently to prevent alcohol misuse on a large scale.

Health Education about Alcohol

According to the government, in its 1981 consultative document, future education programmes would help widen understanding among the general public of the health risks of alcohol misuse about: the social pressures which could lead to the adoption of harmful drinking habits; sensible levels of alcohol consumption; and the advantages for the young of healthy lifestyles during their school years and beyond. In addition it was envisaged that the government would continue to support publicity on the dangers of drinking and driving (see chapter eight).

Why did the government apparently respond in a positive manner to the calls for more health education ? First of all, it should be noted that the DHSS, the government department most concerned about alcohol misuse, was able to exert a strong influence over health education policy. Though health education was at this time administered by a quasi-governmental agency, the Health Educational Council (HEC), the independence of this body was limited. Its members were appointed by the DHSS in consultation with the Department of Education; and its budget was controlled by the DHSS. Indeed according to some, the HEC was 'run virtually like a department of the DHSS.' (House of Commons, 1977b p99) In contrast the DHSS was unable to exert the same degree of influence over the other potential instruments of alcohol policy (for example the licensing laws, taxation, and so on) which were the responsibility of other departments (see chapters six and seven).

The second reason for the government's positive stance on health education was, paradoxically, that the measures proposed were fairly limited. The education programme proposed was not expensive, and therefore could not criticised by the Treasury on financial grounds. Moreover, nowhere in its consultative document did the government commit itself to a significant expansion in health education. Indeed following the publication of *Drinking Sensibly* the amount spent on alcohol education by the HEC rose by only £100,000 per annum, to a total of £300,000 in 1982.[1] This amount was unlikely to finance much of an expansion in health education. Even so it was precisely this - the lack of resource implications, and the provision of alcohol education on a scale small enough to avoid being accused of 'preaching' - which minimised opposition to health education both within and outside government, allowing a positive (though limited) policy to emerge.

But the third and most significant reason behind the policy was the general consensus which existed on this issue. According to Adrian Pollitt, formerly of the HEC:

"What is remarkable... is that amid all this controversy is to be found one small island of consensus, upon which weary policy makers can be observed taking refuge in large numbers. This refuge is health education... There are not many problems of public policy that can attract such a degree of consensus of approach from so wide a range of interests." (Pollitt, 1984)

Superficially this analysis is correct. In recent years health education, as a means of preventing alcohol misuse, has been endorsed by organisations as hostile to each other as the Brewers' Society and the UK Alliance. Moreover, the alcohol misuse lobby and the industry have shown a willingness to work together to promote an expansion of education about alcohol. This was illustrated clearly by the events leading to the passage of the Licensing (Alcohol Education and Research) Act in 1981. This Act resulted in an extra £2m becoming available for projects connected with research into, and education about, alcohol misuse.

The Alcohol Education and Research Fund

The 1981 Act was a product of a series of initiatives from government, the alcohol misuse lobby, and the drinks industry itself. The original impetus came in 1972 from the Erroll Committee which had been appointed by the Home Secretary to review the liquor licensing system of England and Wales. (Home Office, 1972) The Erroll Committee has recommended amongst other things the abolition of the Licensing Compensation Authorities (LCAs). These bodies had powers under the Licensing Act of 1904 to levy the holders of liquor licences; the proceeds of this levy went into a Licensing Compensation Fund (LCF), administered by the LCAs. As originally envisaged, the LCF would compensate licencees whose premises had been closed down as part of a deliberate policy of reducing the number of licensed outlets, which had operated at the turn of the century.

In the post-war period however, the compensation bodies became largely dormant, with few claims being made upon them. Indeed licensed outlets began to increase in number during this period. By 1980 the LCF was worth around £4m. The Erroll Committee decided that the LCAs and the LCF were moribund and believed that the money could be put to better use. It accordingly recommended that the compensation funds should repay charges imposed on the licensed trade over the last five to ten years. In addition the committee urged that the balance be transferred into a national trust fund from which grants could be made for the purposes prescribed by the Home Secretary. It should perhaps be mentioned at this point that these recommendations owed much to the evidence given to the committee by two organisations in particular: the Justices' Clerks' Society (JCS) and the Brewers' Society.

In the short term, nothing came from this initiative. But in 1976 there was a further development, following approaches made to the Home Office by the Brewers' Society and the National Union of Licensed Victuallers (NULV). They proposed that the LCF be used for a variety of purposes, including the funding of programmes to prevent alcohol problems. There then followed a series of consultations between these organisations and the Home Office. Next, the voluntary organisations were consulted; the National Council on Alcoholism (NCA) was particularly interested in the industry's proposals and urged that the funds be released as quickly as possible.

In the light of this consensus, the government gave its backing to the Licensing (Alcohol Education and Research) Bill, introduced in 1980 by Robert Banks, MP for Harrogate. The bill provided for the abolition of the LCAs and the disposal of the LCF. It was proposed that the LCF be divided equally between the industry and a new trust to be called the Alcohol Education and Research Fund (AERF). The AERF would in turn be administered by a Council - the AERC - whose members would be appointed by the Home Secretary.

During the bill's passage, MPs connected with both lobbies made speeches in support of the measures proposed.[2] These included representatives of the drink industry, such as James Wellbeloved MP (then Parliamentary Adviser to the NULV), and Sir Dudley Smith MP (consultant to Bass Ltd); and those connected with the alcohol misuse lobby, such as Sir Bernard Braine MP (chairman of NCA), Clive Soley MP (chairman of the Alcohol Education Centre), and Tristan Garel-Jones MP (a member of the Parliamentary Temperance Group and the NCA). The Home Office took an active role in promoting the measure, even though it was a back-bench bill. This illustrates how government departments can use private members' time to obtain legislation on subjects not significant enough to be included in the government's own legislative programme.

The Licensing (Alcohol Education and Research) Act became law in 1981, and injected resources into an area which most agreed was short of funds. It had been the product of a consensus between the industry, the alcohol misuse lobby, and the government. Moreover it should be stressed that the industry did not take up a passive role on this issue. On the contrary it was at the forefront of the pressure for action, and was crucial in securing a response. Had it not taken the initiative, the money might well still be languishing in the LCF.

The limits of consensus on alcohol education

But the industry's support for alcohol education has its limits. In the last chapter we saw how it was clearly in the drink industry's interest to recognise the problem of alcohol misuse, and to support prevention policies like education. But certain types of education messages are unacceptable to the industry. For example, it would not be happy with an education programme which over-emphasised the social problems connected with drinking, or which stressed the social acceptability of abstaining from drink. The industry will only support the kind of health education which does not clash with its commercial objectives. It also seeks to ensure that this kind of education prevails, mainly by producing its own educational material about alcohol - which is then used by schools, youth clubs, employers, and so on. The industry also has three representatives on the AERC, enabling it to exert some influence over the kind of project receiving finance from the AERF. Finally, the industry exerts political pressure so as to ensure that national health education programmes do not undermine its commercial operations.

Many believe this latter point was clearly in evidence in 1987, when the government announced its decision to abolish the Health Education Council (HEC). The

79

HEC has since been replaced by the Health Education Authority (HEA), which has the status of a special health authority, and is subject to the direction of Health Ministers. Though, as earlier suggested the independence of the HEC was highly ambiguous, the abolition of the HEC has been seen by some as being inspired by the drinks industry.

Hard evidence of such a conspiracy is not surprisingly difficult to come by. But the industry had a clear motive to urge that the HEC be abolished. The HEC did begin to take a much tougher line on alcohol misuse during the early eighties, significantly at the same time as the government appeared to be washing its hands of responsibility (see chapter three). For example, the HEC wanted to support the newly-formed campaigning organisation, Action on Alcohol Abuse, (Smith, 1987 p74) but was discouraged by the DHSS. The former director of the HEC, Dr David Player has subsequently spoken on television about the harassment he received from government officials on this particular issue. Player clearly saw the drink industry as the main protagonist, acting behind the scenes to put pressure on the HEC.[3] His claims suggest a conspiracy theory aimed at removing him and his team by replacing the HEC with a new authority; significantly Player was not re-appointed to the new Health Education Authority.

It is too early perhaps to tell if the HEA will toe the line on alcohol policy. Moreover, as we saw in chapter three, alcohol has recently once again returned to the political agenda and this has forced government to pursue a more vigorous policy of late. It seems that in the present political climate the HEA is being given more licence than would have been the case a couple of years ago. There has also been an increase in the amount of resources given to alcohol education at a national level. Currently the HEA receives £500,000 from the Department of Health for alcohol education, much more than the HEC received, though this is still only a fraction of the £6 billion raised by the government in indirect taxes from alcohol.[4]

Earmarked taxes

A number of specific proposals concerning alcohol education have been opposed by the drinks industry and by government, and this also highlights the limits to consensus. In 1977, the House of Commons Expenditure Committee recommended that 'a higher proportion of the (then) £2,000m raised in duty and taxation on alcohol should be devoted to educating children and young adults in the dangers of alcoholic dependence.' Although the Scotch Whisky Association supported this proposal, it received a fairly cool reception from the other trade organisations. But the main opposition to earmarking tax revenues in this way came from within government itself. The Treasury in particular is known to be against this method of distributing tax revenue. Its opposition led to the Expenditure Committee's proposal being rejected on the grounds that ' such a proposal would.... represent a major departure from the principles which have governed the distribution of tax revenue in this country.' (Cmnd 7047, 1977)

Earmarking a certain proportion of alcohol taxes would have several advantages, and is supported by most organisations in the alcohol misuse lobby for the following reasons. First, it would tend to increase resources going towards health education. At present levels of taxation for example, a 5% health education levy on indirect taxes from alcohol would raise around £300m. This dwarfs the amounts currently spent on alcohol education by the HEA, the Department of Transport, the alcohol misuse lobby, health authorities and the drinks industry put together. Secondly, such a levy would raise revenues roughly in line with changes in the extent of the alcohol problem. Providing alcohol taxes and prices remained the same in real terms, a rise in consumption would produce a comparable increase in overall tax revenue. The levy on this overall revenue would in turn raise more money for health education to meet the problems associated with higher levels of consumption.

There are two further varieties of earmarked tax which have additional advantages from the viewpoint of the alcohol misuse lobby. First of all, the levy could be imposed on top of existing taxes on drink. In other words it would represent an entirely new tax on drink, in addition to VAT and excise duties, and would not simply be an earmarked proportion of revenues from these sources. Therefore, unless duties (or VAT) were reduced accordingly, the prices of alcoholic drinks prices would rise following the imposition of such a levy. This would not only raise money, but could through increased prices have an impact on the overall consumption of alcohol and thereby reduce the level of alcohol problems. The relationship between price, consumption and alcohol misuse is examined in greater detail in the following chapter.

A further variation on this theme is to levy the health education tax on alcohol advertising rather than on the price of alcoholic drink. This it could be argued helps to improve the balance between advertising and education, since an increase in advertising budgets would raise revenue for health education. Not surprisingly such a measure is opposed by the drinks industry and the advertising industry. It may also be ineffective if alternative forms of promotion not classified as advertising are used in an attempt to avoid paying the tax. A more effective way of dealing with the impact of advertising might therefore be to restrict it directly, an issue we consider in the next section.

Advertising: The Government Intervenes

During the seventies there was a definite increase in the pressure for further restrictions over the advertising of alcoholic drink. Most of this pressure came from a number of official committees. The Erroll Committee on licensing was particularly concerned about certain advertising images which it saw as being directed at children. As its report stated, 'we do not think that it is particularly responsible for the industry to suggest to young people that drinking is in some way a prerequisite of social success and acceptability - a suggestion which we think has been implicit in a number of recent television campaigns.' (Home Office, 1972 p45) Three years later, the House of Commons Select Committee on Violence in Marriage was also critical of the current standards of advertising. It recommended that 'the Government should now introduce a vigorous publicity campaign against the excessive consumption of alcohol, particularly by the young, and should formulate a positive policy on the advertising of alcohol.'

These sentiments were echoed in the late seventies by other official committees such as the House of Commons Expenditure Committee, the DHSS Advisory Committee on Alcoholism, and the Central Policy Staff (CPRS). The Expenditure Committee did not make any explicit recommendations about alcohol advertising; but it was worried about the 'constant depiction of alcohol in advertisements as essential to success in life.' (House of Commons, 1977a) The Advisory Committee noted that 'advertising, and the media in general, portray alcohol in a one-sided way.' (DHSS, 1978) The CPRS (1982) report however went further, recommending that alcohol advertising be prohibited from associating alcohol with 'desirable habits or lifestyles' and that government should actively ensure that advertising 'encourage moderation and sensible use of the product.'

The alcohol misuse lobby on the other hand was less active on this issue than on others, such as taxation and licensing law, during the seventies. Few within the lobby held the view that alcohol advertising increased consumption and thereby misuse. There was however some support for more restrictions on alcohol advertising, particularly with respect to children. The BMA wanted such restrictions as part of a general campaign on alcohol misuse. The NCA and the temperance movement were also broadly in favour of action along these lines. But none of these organisations really pressed hard for reform during this period.

One reason for the alcohol misuse lobby's relatively weak position on this issue was the general lack of evidence about the effect of advertising upon alcohol misuse. (Ogborne and Smart, 1980; Smart and Cutler, 1976; Treml, 1975) The inconclusive nature of this evidence has been summarised as follows:

"To adopt the phraseology of the foreperson of a Scottish jury the case against alcohol advertising remains not proven." (Plant and Ritson, 1983 p117)

Richard Smith, the editor of the *British Medical Journal*, also admits that there are serious difficulties involved in measuring the relationship between alcohol advertising and alcohol problems. Most agree with him that '...it is an extraordinarily difficult thing to prove statistically and a lot of the evidence that is available is kept locked up in the boardrooms of the drink manufacturers.' (Smith, 1985)

The drink manufacturers themselves, along with the advertising industry, are more certain about the relationship between advertising and alcohol misuse: they argue that no such relationship exists. This position is clear from a document produced by the advertising industry (Waterson, 1981) which states that 'the research evidence available... clearly suggests that advertising has little or no impact on mature alcohol markets, other than at the brand level. Alcohol advertising is directed at selling individual brands, and does not encourage people to drink ever larger quantities of the product.' The commercial interests in alcohol advertising do concede that certain sections of society - children in particular - might be affected by certain advertising practices. Though they believe that any problems arising from this can be avoided by responsible advertising. As Kenneth Dunjohn, a former chairman of the Brewers' Society, stated at a conference on alcohol advertising in 1981:

"the drinks producing industries willingly acknowledge that their products are capable of misuse and that this necessarily requires them to exercise restraint and awareness of the likely problems." (Dunjohn, 1981)

So in principle, the drinks and advertising industries have accepted the need for responsibility and restraint when advertising alcoholic drink. Furthermore, they have in practice been prepared to accept a number of informal restrictions on alcohol advertising. In a moment we shall take a look at these restrictions and how they came about. But before moving on it is necessary to place the restrictions in context by briefly describing the general system of advertising regulation in the UK.

The system of advertising control in the UK

Advertising control in the UK is based largely on two parallel systems of self-regulation. (Baggott and Harrison, 1986) Advertising in the broadcast media - radio and television - is regulated by the Independent Broadcasting Authority (IBA) and the television and radio companies. Whilst advertising in the non-broadcast media (that is press, poster and cinema advertising) is governed by the Advertising Standards Authority (ASA) and the Advertising Association (AA). These systems of control are labelled 'self-regulatory' because they rely heavily on the advertisers and the media to police themselves.

The IBA has a statutory duty under the Broadcasting Acts to draw up a code of practice on advertising standards; although the code itself does not have statutory force. The IBA Code was drawn up, and has been subsequently amended, on the basis of advice of an Advertising Advisory Committee (AAC), which contains representatives from industry, medicine and the general public. Any changes suggested by the AAC are then discussed by the IBA and the Home Office, the government department having overall responsibility for broadcasting. The IBA administers and enforces the Code, pre-checking and monitoring advertisements to ensure that they conform to the provisions laid out in the Code. In the case of television advertising the IBA's activities are augmented by a filter system operated by the Independent Television Companies Association (ITCA). ITCA processes all advertisements before they reach the IBA and seeks to ensure that they conform to a further set of guidelines issued by the IBA. These guidelines are a comprehensive set of rules which are more informal but also more detailed than the IBA Code. A similar filter system exists for radio advertisements, operated by the Association of Independent Radio Companies (AIRC).

Advertising in the press, cinema and posters is governed by another code of practice operated by the Advertising Standards Authority. ASA was originally created in the sixties by the advertising industry itself, as a means of pre-empting government legislation on advertising. It now has a greater degree of independence from the industry; since 1974 non-industry representatives have been in a majority on its governing body, the Council. Also the ASA has more financial independence than it had before. Although it is still funded by the industry, the money is now channelled through an independent board of finance.

Unlike the IBA, ASA does not generally pre-check advertisements. The exceptions being advertisements for cigarettes and contraceptives. Its main function is to monitor advertisements and to publicise breaches of the code. Also it should be noted that the ASA Code is drawn up by a special committee of the Advertising Association, the advertising industry's representative organisation. This committee is known as the CAP Committee. The CAP Committee, unlike the IBA Advertising Advisory Committee, does not have any lay members, but draws its membership exclusively from the advertising industry. It is generally regarded that the regulation of advertising in the non-broadcast media is less strict than the regime which governs television and radio advertising. Indeed a report during the seventies by the Office of Fair Trading (OFT), the official watchdog on competition and consumer affairs, cast doubt on the effectiveness of the advertising control system in the non-broadcast media in its present form. (OFT, 1978) Recently the regulation of advertisements in this sector has been tightened up. From 1989, the Office of Fair Trading will have reserve powers to prevent certain misleading advertisements. But the system will remain overwhelmingly self-regulatory.

Reforming the rules on alcohol advertising

As the pressure for restrictions on alcohol advertising intensified during the seventies, both the ASA and the IBA codes adopted special rules governing advertising standards in this area. The first round of changes came in 1974, in response to the demands made by the newly-elected Labour Government. In the broadcast media, restrictions on alcohol advertising, which had formerly been contained in the IBA guidelines, were incorporated in a special appendix of the IBA Code itself. These new rules prohibited advertisers from associating alcohol with driving and social success, amongst other things. The implicit and explicit encouragement of underage and excessive drinking in advertisements was also ruled out. The ASA Code was also modified at this time. It too has since contained a special appendix on alcohol advertising.

The reforms of 1974 were part of the Labour Government's general policy on advertising: alcohol advertising was just one of a range of issues which it decided to tackle in the interests of consumer protection. Indeed this is why the main responsibility for negotiating the above changes with the advertising industry was borne by the Department of Prices and Consumer Protection (DPCP) and the Office of Fair Trading (OFT), rather than the Department of Health and Social Security (DHSS).

In contrast the second round of changes, which took place five years later, was prompted mainly by the DHSS. It first became involved in 1978 when, in response to the reports of the Expenditure Committee and the Advisory Committee on Alcoholism, it approached the Home Office and the IBA in an attempt to persuade them to consider changes in the IBA Code. In particular the DHSS wanted the Code to ensure that advertisements did not encourage potentially harmful drinking habits. Following these discussions, the AAC (the IBA committee which considers changes in the Code), examined whether or not an amendment was justified. (IBA, 1978) In the event, the AAC recommended to the IBA that the Code be amended to prohibit the association of drink with acts of daring, toughness, and masculinity in advertisements. The AAC also advocated the incorporation of the existing rules on alcohol advertising within the main body of the Code - hitherto they had been part of a special appendix - this would give the rules a much higher profile than before. Following the AAC recommendation, the IBA discussed the proposed changes with the Home Office. There appear to have been no disagreements at this stage and the changes were duly incorporated in the revised IBA Code. (IBA, 1979)

During 1978 the DHSS also discussed the advertising of alcohol in the non-broadcast media with ASA and the Incorporated Society of British Advertisers (ISBA). ISBA is the trade association which caters for those companies who regularly advertise their products in the media. As the drinks companies are amongst the biggest advertisers - in 1984 no less than sixteen alcoholic drink companies were found amongst the top 250 advertising budgets - they clearly form an important group within this association.[5] After talking with the DHSS, ISBA convened a special meeting of its drink industry members. The aim of this was to put forward proposals to the Advertising Association's CAP Committee on how non-broadcast alcohol advertising could be further restricted. Following this meeting, ISBA then pledged that its members would in future ensure that drink advertisements were socially responsible. In particular ISBA recommended that they should not associate drink with sexual success or masculinity. The CAP Committee subsequently endorsed these recommendations and a revised ASA Code came into effect. (ASA, 1980)

The DHSS was also engaged in other 'behind the scenes activities' around this time. Health ministers were urging the industry to be more circumspect in advertising their products, according to a former minister. Also, in 1979 the DHSS brought together the Health Education Council (HEC) and the Brewers' Society to discuss alcohol advertising.[6] The HEC wanted the industry to commit itself to ensuring that drink advertisements emphasised the moderate use of alcohol. No explicit agreement came out of this particular dialogue, but the amendments to the IBA and the CAP Codes indicated that the industry might be prepared to make further concessions in the future.

The DHSS was keen that alcohol advertising be used as a positive instrument to counter alcohol misuse. This was clear from the following passage in *Drinking Sensibly* which called for 'action by the drinks and advertising industries (i) to improve understanding of the relative strength of alcoholic drinks; and (ii) to discourage harmful drinking habits.' (DHSS, 1981b)

But although the industry wanted, for reasons discussed in the previous chapter, to project a public image of responsibility, it was not prepared to forgo effective marketing techniques in view of the implications for sales and profitability. In short, it was reluctant to change the guiding principle underlying its advertising policy from sales maximisation to the reduction of alcohol misuse. As a result progress on this front was limited, and no real agreement was reached on the use of advertising to promote moderate drinking, though clearly some individual drinks companies were more in favour of moving in this direction than others. (Ambler, 1984)

More recently however there has been an interesting new development. Drinks companies have become more involved in the marketing of low alcohol and non-alcoholic drinks. In the beer market these drinks only account for just over 1% of total sales. Yet currently 20% of brewers' advertising budgets are being devoted to the promotion of these products. This can be seen as promoting moderation, not by getting people to drink less but by persuading them to consume drinks containing lower levels of alcohol. It remains to be seen whether or not these campaigns have an effect on individual drinking habits.[7]

An advertising ban ?

The government's approach to alcohol advertising has been to try and modify it. A total ban on alcohol advertising is thought in official circles to be counter-productive for two reasons. First of all, a ban precludes the use of advertising as an adjunct to health education, by promoting moderate drinking habits. Second, a ban may merely lead the industry into developing more subtle forms of promotion, such as sports and arts sponsorship, which lie outside the scope of the ban.

Even so, there are a number of precedents for imposing a ban on the advertising of alcoholic drinks. The ban on cigarette advertising on television, which was introduced in 1965, shows how far British government's have been prepared to go in discouraging products which have implications for public health. There are, however, significant differences between cigarettes and alcohol: cigarettes are believed to be generally harmful to health, whilst alcohol is only considered damaging when taken to excess, or when consumed in 'inappropriate' circumstances (for example, when driving). Hence the case for a ban on alcohol advertising is much weaker. But such considerations have not stopped a number of countries from banning drink advertisements. Finland, Sweden and Norway, all did so during the seventies. They have recently been joined by France which banned the advertising of alcoholic drinks on TV in 1987. As yet it is difficult to tell whether or not these measures have significantly contributed to a reduction in alcohol misuse in these countries. (Davies and Walsh, 1983)

Surprisingly, there is a more direct precedent for a ban on alcohol advertising in the UK. Since the introduction of commercial television in 1955, there has been a voluntary ban on the advertising of spirits on TV. This ban, which is policed by the Scotch Whisky Association and the TV companies association (ITCA), originated not out of any concern over the advertising of hard liquor but as a result of sound commercial judgement. British spirit producers, as we saw in the last chapter, are heavily export-oriented. In the fifties they collectively decided to refrain from advertising in the domestic market. The spirit firms did this in an attempt to cut costs, which they believed would enable them to reduce prices and compete more effectively abroad. Later ITCA formalised the agreement and it has remained in force, with a few minor exceptions.[8]

These precedents were useful to those who wanted a more general ban on alcohol advertising. Pressure for such a move has built up since the late seventies. In 1980, for example, the Churches Council on Alcohol and Drugs adopted a resolution urging its members to work for the banning of all advertising of alcohol products, except at the point of sale. Such a policy has also attracted support from other elements of the alcohol misuse lobby. In 1980 the BMA Representative Body voted for a ban on alcohol and tobacco advertising and called on the Council to press for such a policy. The BMA leadership were however reluctant to tackle the issue of alcohol advertising, wishing instead to concentrate on the campaign against cigarette advertising, which they regarded as the greater evil. But in spite of this reluctance, pressures from within the association continued. This culminated in the passage of a motion at the 1985 Annual Conference which called for an immediate ban on alcohol advertising. Once again this went against the advice of the leadership, who were keen that the BMA should not acquire a puritanical image. This division of opinion continued, and at the 1986 Conference the BMA leadership got the upper hand, obtaining a reversal of the previous year's decision. So whilst it is clear that support for a ban has been building up, the BMA is far from united on the advertising issue and this in turn undermines its case.

In contrast Action on Alcohol Abuse, the organisation formed in 1983 by the Royal Medical Colleges to campaign on alcohol misuse, has taken a more consistent line. In a strategy document of 1986, it called for a ban on alcohol advertising to be imposed by 1990. Action on Alcohol Abuse also called for an immediate ban on other promotional activities, such as sports sponsorship by drinks companies (this issue is discussed later on in the present chapter). More recently a ban on alcohol advertising has attracted support from the Campaign for Real Ale, though not primarily for public health reasons (see chapter four, above).

There has also been some Parliamentary support for an advertising ban. A number of Parliamentary Questions on this subject have been tabled since the late seventies. For example in July 1979, Dr Roger Thomas MP, a medical practitioner, asked the Minister for Health if he would ban alcohol advertising.[9] A number of peers also tabled Questions on the issue around this time. Lord Houghton of Sowerby and Lord Avebury, asked the Minister for Health if he would ban the advertising of alcohol on TV.[10] Ministers responded by rejecting the case for a ban, chiefly on the grounds that there was no evidence to support such a move. This is still the official position today.

There were a number of other reasons why a ban has been so unequivocally rejected. First of all, the lobby which opposes a ban is a powerful one, comprising three distinct groups: the drink industry, the advertising industry, and the media. The drink industry, as has already been mentioned, wishes to retain alcohol advertising - ostensibly because it enhances competition, but in reality because it is a powerful marketing tool which helps the industry sell its products. There are, however, circumstances where the industry may contemplate a ban on commercial grounds, as we have seen. The self-imposed ban on the advertisement of spirits on TV being the case in point. But the industry will not countenance a government-imposed ban which they see as an infringement of commercial liberty.

It was shown in the previous chapter that the drink industry is a major advertiser. Because of this it attracts a lot of support from the advertising agencies on this issue. A number of agencies have a considerable interest in alcohol advertising, and a ban would be very damaging to them. They are, as one might expect, amongst the most vociferous opponents of a such a policy. One agency, Allen, Brady and Marsh, which has handled Guinness' advertising account, has been particularly active on the issue in the past. In 1981 its chairman, Peter Marsh presented the case against a ban to the Conservative Party's Parliamentary Media Group. (Marsh, 1981)

But even those agencies which have little or no interest in alcohol advertising have been antagonistic to a ban on alcohol advertising. Indeed the advertising industry is generally hostile to bans of any kind. It tends to see a ban on one particular product as a dangerous precedent. According to the director-general of the Advertising Association:

"We have what is described as the domino theory: knock them all down one by one. In other words, first the advertising of one product regarded as harmful, then use that as precedent to try and restrict the advertising of other products."[11]

The media also has a considerable interest in alcohol advertising. Commercial television is particularly dependent on the revenues from drink advertisements. In 1984 the largest drink advertisers in the UK spent between 75% and 100% of their advertising budgets on TV advertising.[12] The independent TV companies themselves estimate that 7% of their revenue comes from alcohol advertising. (Henry, 1980)

These groups - the drinks industry, the advertising agencies and the media - have a common interest in opposing an advertising ban. Their efforts to defend alcohol advertising are coordinated by the Advertising Association (AA), the advertising industry's representative organisation. The TV companies' association, ITCA, the advertisers' association, ISBA, and the agencies' association, the Institute of Practioners in Advertising (IPA) are all affiliated to the AA. The level of coordination on the alcohol advertising issue increased in 1980 with the creation of a special sub-committee within the AA. The Alcohol Coordinating Committee (ACC) was established to ensure that the AA presented a coherent policy on this issue. Represented on this committee are ISBA, IPA, the Cinema Advertising Association, the Scotch Whisky Association, the Brewers Society, and the Gin Rectifiers and Distillers Association. Some drink, media, and advertising companies are also directly represented, including Bass, IPC Magazines, Scottish TV Ltd, and

Everett's Ltd.

The creation of the ACC illustrates the importance which the AA now attaches to matters affecting alcohol advertising. Indeed a 1983 poll of the AA Council showed that 62% believed that the fight against legislation on drink advertising was 'very important'. (Advertising Association, 1983) This was the highest level of support for any single trade defence issue: alcohol advertising is clearly a priority issue for the Advertising Association.

The well-organised opposition of these commercial groups is one reason why the government has refused to adopt a ban on alcohol advertising. Indeed the Advertising Association alone is a formidable opponent, having considerable political leverage. (Baggott and Harrison, 1986) But the government has also been divided internally over the question of a ban. The Ministry of Agriculture (MAFF), as the sponsor of the drinks industry is generally opposed to further restrictions on the industry's commercial liberty. The Department of Trade and Industry (DTI) sponsors the advertising industry and is against a ban for similar reasons. Whilst the Home Office, responsible for broadcasting, is not convinced of the need for such a policy. Neither is the DHSS in favour of a total ban on alcohol advertising. As we saw above, the department believes that responsible advertising could actually help reduce alcohol misuse by emphasising moderation; an outright ban could mean the loss of this opportunity. But even if the DHSS had wanted a ban it would still have had to persuade the departments responsible for the regulation of advertising - the DTI in the case of non-broadcast media and the Home Office in the case of the broadcast media - of the necessity for such a policy.

The third and final reason why a ban on alcohol advertising has not been adopted is that the measure has insufficient support. Although, as noted above, a number of Parliamentary Questions have been tabled on the subject, they constitute a trickle rather than a torrent. There is also an overall lack of support for a ban within the ranks of the alcohol misuse lobby. Of all the groups involved in this lobby (ie: excluding CAMRA) only the temperance-related organisations and Action on Alcohol Abuse now openly favour a complete ban.

There is also a general lack of support for an advertising ban amongst the general public. This has been indicated in a series of opinion polls conducted in recent years. For example in 1979 a NOP poll on behalf of the *New Statesman* found that only 21% of respondents believed that drink advertisements should be banned. On the other hand 76% were opposed to such a move. (Taylor, 1979) This was confirmed by a poll conducted on behalf of the National Consumer Council in 1981. This survey showed that 26% were in favour of a ban, whilst 70% disapproved. In addition only 10% of the respondents believed that a comprehensive ban on alcohol advertising would reduce alcohol misuse.

However, it should be noted that a MORI survey taken in 1980 suggested that public support for partial ban may be greater than these figures indicate. It revealed that whilst only 29% of the respondents supported a comprehensive ban, many more- 46% -approved of a ban on alcohol advertising on TV. Even so the MORI poll did not allow for a 'don't know' response, and therefore the actual support is likely to be lower than this.

Although most of these polls were taken some time ago, there is still no sign that public opinion is strongly against drink advertisements. But there has been more concern about alcohol advertisements of late, and in particular about the effect of drink advertisements on young people and children. Surveys have shown that advertisements for alcoholic drinks are extremely popular with children. (Greenberg et. al., 1986; Association of Market Survey Organisations, 1988) There is also further evidence that drink advertisements are occupying prominent positions in commercial breaks, and appear to increase around sports programmes and the early evening (peaking between 1800 and 1900 hours) when children are likely to be watching. (Barton et. al. 1988)

Concern about the effect of drink advertising on children and young people was recently articulated by the Home Office working party on young people and alcohol, which was set up in 1987. (see chapter three) This committee came down in favour of a ban on alcoholic drinks on TV and in the cinema. (Home Office, 1987) The government has since rejected this recommendation. Instead through the ministerial committee on alcohol abuse (see chapter three), it urged the IBA and the Advertising Standards Authority to tighten up their codes of practice.

Action has been swift. By the end of September new codes were in place incorporating new rules on the appeal of alcohol advertisements to the young. (IBA, 1989; ASA, 1988) These new rules involve restrictions on the use of humour in advertisements. Humorous advertisements had been used in the past to get around some of the other restrictions which had earlier been imposed. Also the revised codes set higher minimum age limits for characters in drink advertisements, and ban personalities likely to appeal to those under eighteen from appearing in drink advertisements. In addition the IBA has agreed to tighten up its detailed guidelines to advertisers: from now on alcohol advertisments are not to be shown around programmes which have a strong appeal primarily to teenagers.

Sports sponsorship: another case for restriction ?

Advertising is only one of a range of marketing techniques used by the drinks industry. Over the last decade other promotional forms have come to the fore. Of these sports sponsorship is by far the most significant. (Central Council on Physical Recreation, 1983) In the world of sports sponsorship the drinks industry is second only to the tobacco industry in terms of money spent on this form of promotion. (Grattan and Taylor, 1985) According to latest available figures the brewers alone spent £3m in 1983.

But as with advertising, sports sponsorship by the drinks industry has come in for increasing criticism. Some now believe that by associating alcohol with a healthy activity, it serves to obscure the public's perception of the relationship between drinking and ill-health. In this way sports sponsorship could inhibit the effectiveness of health education programmes, thereby impeding any movement towards moderate drinking habits.

Some organisations, such as Action on Alcohol Abuse and the Royal College of Physicians, have called for tough restrictions on this form of promotion. But the main problem for those who support such moves is one of evidence. The link between sponsorship and alcohol misuse is even more difficult to prove than the effects of advertising. As a result the demand for restrictions has been weak.

Opposition to controls on sponsorship, on the other hand, has been strong. The alcoholic drinks industry is against such measures. Moreover, sport and its followers would in the short term at least be the main losers from the withdrawal of sponsorship by drinks companies. The Central Council on Physical Recreation (CCPR), which represents the ruling bodies of most recognised sports in the UK, has consistently upheld the right of individual sports to take funds from whom they please. Whilst within government itself restrictions are opposed by the Department of the Environment (DoE), the department responsible for sport and its finance.

In view of the weakness of the demand for action in this area, the strength of the opposition, and the lack of evidence linking sports sponsorship by drinks companies to alcohol misuse, it is not surprising that this issue has failed to make an impact on the political agenda. As a result, the government has never seriously considered banning the sponsorship of sport by drinks companies.

Alcohol and the Broadcast Media: The Wider Context of Presentation

In this final section, the wider question of the presentation of alcohol in the media is considered. Advertising and sports sponsorship are only part of the overall picture of alcohol presented in the media. According to Anders Hansen, a researcher in the field of mass communications at Leicester University:

"...commercial advertising of alcohol accounts for a relatively small proportion of of the overall stream of alcohol images in television content." (Hansen 1985)

Certainly the drinking of alcohol is widely portrayed on television. According to Hansen's research two thirds of prime time TV programmes make reference to alcohol. Drinking scenes take up 14% of the programme time of British 'soap operas'. (Hansen, 1988)

The importance of non-advertising images in the media was also recognised by the DHSS Advisory Committee on Alcoholism in the seventies. (DHSS, 1978b) The committee went on to note that the media in general tends to portray a rather one-sided picture of alcohol, emphasising its pleasures and playing down its perils. The Advisory Committee also believed that television, as the most powerful medium, could be used more positively to educate the public about the dangers of alcohol. It suggested that 'long running radio and television serials, which already have a high informational content, could be especially useful in illustrating the dangers of alcohol misuse.' This was broadly supported by the House of Commons Expenditure Committee (1977a) in its report on alcohol abuse. It recommended that 'television should be more extensively used to put across the dangers of alcohol abuse.'

The DHSS agreed with these comments and recommendations. This was reflected in the government's discussion document *Drinking Sensibly*, which noted that 'it would not be surprising if the depiction of drinking during TV and Radio programmes, in plays, in books and films, were a stronger influence on people's behaviour than commercial advertising.' (DHSS, 1981b)

This could be interpreted as an excuse to avoid taking action on alcohol advertising. But this clearly was not so; the government has on several occasions taken steps to tighten up advertising standards, as we have already seen. Moreover, the DHSS did attempt to influence the presentation of alcohol in a wider sense by putting pressure on the broadcasting authorities during the early eighties. The department responsible for broadcasting, the Home Office was also involved in this process.

The BBC's director-general at the time, Sir Ian Trethowan, did not accept that the portrayal of alcohol was in any way one-sided or unbalanced. In subsequent discussions with the Home Office, the BBC made it clear that it would not be taking any action to modify the presentation of alcohol in its programmes. The IBA, on the other hand, had already drawn up guidelines on the presentation of alcohol for commercial stations. It too was involved in discussions with the Home Office and agreed to re-examine the existing guidelines. This led to a new set of stricter programme guidelines for independent television in 1984.

The government's pressure on broadcasters therefore had mixed results. More recently the Wakeham Committee (see chapter three) has called on the IBA and the BBC to re-examine the presentation of alcohol in programmes. As yet the outcome of this new initiative is unknown.

There is of course a limit to which government can press the broadcasting companies on matters of this kind. There are three main constraints at work. First of all the government can lay itself open to criticism that it is interfering with the freedom of the media. The government has often been accused of censorship or even dictatorship when trying to influence broadcasting policy in the past. Secondly, as in the case of advertising and sports sponsorship restrictions, the government is inhibited by lack of evidence. It has always been difficult to evaluate the effect of media messages on individual behaviour. But the evidence linking the portrayal of drinking in the broadcast media with alcohol misuse is particularly weak. (Hansen, 1985, 1988) The broadcasters often argue in their defence that the presentation of drinking habits merely reflects the practices which already exist in society. Some within the alcohol misuse lobby on the other hand claim that the media is damaging because it reinforces harmful drinking habits. It is difficult to prove or disprove either of these contentions. In the absence of such evidence, government action will always be limited.

Finally, in the particular case of commercial broadcasting, the television and radio companies might strongly resist further guidelines on presentation where measures begin to discourage alcohol consumption. This is because a fall in consumption would most probably reduce the amount of money available for drink advertising. This in turn would squeeze the commercial broadcasters' incomes. In addition it is also worth noting that a number of drinks companies have begun to develop direct financial interests in the media. Whitbread for example has a 20% stake in Television South (TVS).[13] If this trend continues in future on a larger scale, the drinks industry may be able to exert even more influence over broadcasting. It will therefore be in a very strong position to coordinate opposition to further restrictions on presentation.

Conclusion

During this chapter, a wide range of policy issues have been examined: professional training, alcohol and work policies, education, advertising and promotion, and the portrayal of drinking in television programmes. These issues have two things in common. First, they all involve information about preventing alcohol problems. Professional training and alcohol and work policies inform professionals and employers about the existence and diagnosis of alcohol problems. Such measures may also ultimately inform individual problem drinkers, helping them to come to terms with their problems. Health education, alcohol promotion, and the portrayal of alcohol in the media have the potential to inform the general public about the scale of alcohol problems, appropriate drinking habits, and the dangers of alcohol misuse.

The second thing that these policies have in common is that in many respects the government, chiefly through the DHSS and more recently through the Ministerial Committee on alcohol abuse, has been able to endorse limited strategies to prevent alcohol abuse. There are a number of reasons why such action has been possible in these specific areas of policy. The action taken in each area has been relatively uncontroversial. The drinks industry is reasonably happy with the early identification programmes, informal advertising restrictions and basic health education, mainly because such measures have reinforced the industry's responsible public image. In addition, there has been little public interest in these issues and therefore the government has not run the risk of courting unpopularity by its actions. Parliamentary and ministerial interest has also been fairly low, since these issues have generally been of marginal political significance. Also it should be noted that the measures taken (with the exception of the Alcohol Education and Research Act of 1981) have not required legislation and as a result the interdepartmental battles over legislative priorities, and Parliamentary conflicts over the content of legislation, have been largely bypassed.

Government action on these issues has also had the advantage of being high profile: the government has been seen to be doing something positive about alcohol misuse. This was done mainly to placate the alcohol misuse lobby, rather than the general public. The government, and the DHSS in particular, could not therefore be accused of doing nothing about the problems of alcohol abuse.

But above all, progress in these policy areas has been possible because of the degree of consensus and the considerable scope for compromise which existed.

There has been a great deal of agreement on the need for action on these issues between government, the alcohol misuse lobby, and the drinks industry. But this consensus was limited. The case for a ban on advertising was rejected, as were arguments for restrictions on sports sponsorship, and proposals to earmark taxation for health education purposes. These measures, it seems, did not come within the islands of consensus, and were not therefore adopted.

Notes

1. *House of Commons Official Report* Volume 62 Column 313 22 June 1984.
2. *House of Commons Official Report* Volume 1000 Column 563-82
   6 March 1981; Volume 4 Column 400-18 8 May 1981.
3. *The Guardian* 13 February 1987 p3
4. Correspondence with the Department of Health 21 November 1988
5. *Campaign* 7 June 1985
6. *House of Lords Official Report* Volume 402 Column 426 31 October 1979
7. Correspondence with G. Winstanley of the Brewers' Society 4 November, 1988
8. The exceptions to this rule are (1) the advertising of spirits in the context of supermarket or other retailers' advertisements; (2) spirits considered to be liqueurs (eg: Cointreau, Bailey's Irish Cream, but not gin or whisky)
9. *House of Commons Official Report* Volume 971 Column 89w 23 June 1979
10. *House of Lords Official Report* Volume 399 Column 1573 27 March 1979 and Volume 406 Column 1318 13 March 1980
11. *The Times* 25 April 1981 p2
12. *Campaign* 7 June 1985
13. *Morning Advertiser* 12 April 1984 p24

6 Price regulation: the ultimate disincentive?

In recent years the idea that alcohol misuse could be prevented to some extent by manipulating the price of drink has attracted considerable attention. Superficially, price regulation appears to be a powerful tool for reducing alcohol-related problems. Higher prices tend to reduce the consumption of most goods. By reducing the consumption of alcohol, alcohol-related problems may also decline. But is alcohol perhaps a special case? Would the ultimate disincentive of higher prices actually discourage excessive alcohol consumption and misuse? Perhaps even more importantly, why has government not been convinced of the need to regulate drink prices in the interests of public health?

This chapter focuses upon such questions. The opening section examines the price regulation debate, the evidence concerning the effects of manipulating drink prices, and the views of the various lobbies and government departments in relation to this issue. This is followed by an analysis of the approaches to alcohol pricing by recent British governments. First, we look at the record of the Labour Government in the seventies; then move on to examine the approach of the present Conservative Government. The third section is focused more specifically upon the actual process by which the government sets taxes on alcohol, since this has a major bearing on price levels. Finally, the issue is placed in a European context by looking at the implications for alcohol prices of the UK's membership of the EEC.

The Price Regulation Debate

There is much evidence to suggest that the price of drink has a significant influence on both alcohol consumption and misuse. One cross-national comparison for example has concluded that 'in general those countries which have higher taxes and prices tend to have lower alcohol consumption and liver cirrhosis deaths.' (Davies, 1983) The incidence of liver cirrhosis, as we have already mentioned, is a general indicator of the level of alcohol misuse. Other studies have confirmed the relationship between price, consumption, and misuse. (Bruun, 1975; Davies and Walsh, 1983; Popham, Schmidt, de Lindt, 1975) Furthermore recent evidence in a British context suggests that rising prices can significantly reduce consumption. (Kendall, de Roumanie, Ritson, 1983)

Although in recent years there has been a marginal increase in the price of beer in real terms, (Treasury, 1983; Godfrey, Hardman, Powell, 1986) the price of alcoholic drink in the UK has generally been falling since the sixties. Between 1969 and 1981 for example the price of beer fell by 2.5% in real terms; wines and spirits prices fell over the same period by 37%.[1] Other data confirms that during the seventies the price of alcoholic drink rose much less than the general price level (Central Statistical Office, 1988 p101). Again this was mainly due to a dramatic relative decline in the price of wines and spirits. (Godfrey, Hardman, Powell, 1986)

One reason for the fall in the real price of drink was the failure of successive governments to index the excise duties on alcoholic drink to the rate of inflation. Excise duties, unlike *ad valorem* taxes such as VAT, do not automatically rise with the price of the product. As a result drink prices have been lower than if the real value of duties been maintained. The relationship of excise duties to inflation in recent years is shown in table nine. This table clearly shows that since 1980 duty on beer has been uprated at least in line with inflation, but this has not been the case with wines and spirits. Possible explanations for these differences will be explored later in this chapter.

Table 9

Changes in Excise Duty relative to Inflation

Years	% Inflation rate	% Change in duty		
		Spirits	Wine	Beer
1976/7	16.5	11.5	12.6	15.8
1977/8	15.8	10.0	10.0	10
1978/9	8.3	nil	nil	nil
1979/80	13.4	nil	nil	nil
1980/1	18.0	13.7	13.9	22.5
1981/2	11.9	14.6	16.9	37.9

	%	% Change in duty		
Years	Inflation rate	Spirits	Wine	Beer
1982/3	8.6	6.4	12.2	13.3
1983/4	4.6	5.0	5.8	5.9
1984/5	5.0	1.9	-19.9	11.1
1985/6	6.0	1.9	8.3	7.5
1986/7	3.4	nil	nil	nil
1987/8	4.2	nil	nil	nil
1988/9	4.6	nil	4.5	4.7

Sources. *House of Commons Official Report Volume 110 Column 677w 18 February 1987; H.M. Treasury*

The price of drink relative to the prices of other goods, one would imagine, is likely to have some effect on demand. But one also has to take into account changes in personal incomes. Table ten illustrates how alcoholic drinks have become a relatively cheaper item in terms of earning power.

Table 10

Work Required by Male Manual Worker to Purchase Alcohol

Year	Pint of Beer (minutes)	Bottle of Whisky (hours)
1965	13.1	6.0
1970	11.3	4.8
1975	9.6	2.9
1980	9.9	2.1
1984	11.3	2.2

Source. *Godfrey, Hardman, Powell, 1986*

The need to prevent the price of alcohol from falling further was highlighted by the three official committees which examined the alcohol problem in the late seventies(see chapter three). The Expenditure Committee urged that 'the price of alcoholic drink should remain at the same level relative to average incomes as it now is and should not be allowed to become a relatively cheap item in the the shopping basket.' (House of Commons, 1977a) Whilst the DHSS Advisory Committee on Alcoholism recommended that taxation be specifically used to bring this about:

"alcohol should not be allowed to become cheaper in real terms and... when real income levels rise taxation levels on alcohol should be adjusted to counteract the increased bouyancy of consumer spending."

The Central Policy Review Staff (CPRS) also agreed that taxation was a key instrument which should be used in the prevention of alcohol misuse. According to its report 'alcohol duties should be one of the principal reflections of the government's strategy on alcohol. They are the single most important instrument the government has for influencing alcohol consumption.' The CPRS also recommended that duty levels should increase at least in line with the Retail Price Index. It saw this as a minimum requirement, to be followed up later with a commitment to use taxation as a means of reducing total consumption.

The three committees' unanimous endorsement of price regulation has since been matched by the degree of cohesion shown by the alcohol misuse lobby on this issue. Most of the organisations within this lobby believe that prices should be manipulated in an attempt to reduce alcohol misuse. Although, as we shall see later, some of the organisations involved have been more vociferous in demonstrating their support than others.

Most of the influential medical organisations mentioned in earlier chapters have favoured the use of fiscal policy to raise prices. The Royal College of Psychiatrists for example recommended in 1979 that 'public revenue policies of government should be intentionally employed in the interests of health so as to ensure that per capita alcohol consumption does not increase beyond the present level and is by stages brought back to an agreed lower level.' This advice was repeated in the Royal College's second report in 1986.

Other medical bodies have also endorsed action along these lines. The 1987 report on alcohol by the Royal College of Physicians called for price controls to raise drink prices over the next five years. Higher drinks prices were also supported in a joint statement of all the Royal Colleges in 1987. (*British Medical Journal* 14 November 1987) Whilst the BMA favours linking alcohol prices to the retail price index. (BMA, 1986)

Concern about the price of alcohol has also been voiced by the temperance societies and by the voluntary organisations in the alcohol field. During the seventies, the National Council on Alcoholism (NCA) strongly urged goverment to commit itself to higher drink prices. The NCA chairman, Sir Bernard Braine MP, tabled several Parliamentary Questions, drawing attention to the falling real price of alcoholic drink and its consequences. Other MPs connected with other voluntary groups also tabled Questions on this issue during this period. They included Frank Hooley MP, then the vice-president of the UK Alliance; and Clive Soley MP, the president of the Alcohol Education Centre.[2]

Since the reorganisation of the voluntary organisations in 1983 (see chapter two above), both Alcohol Concern and Action on Alcohol Abuse have continued to press the goverment on this issue. They have on several occasions in recent years met with Treasury officials to discuss the possibility of higher taxes on alcohol.

Within government, the alcohol misuse lobby has been supported by the Department of Health and Social Security, which broadly accepts the relationship between price and alcohol problems. Moreover, the DHSS has in the past tried to persuade the Treasury to maintain drink prices in real terms. This position reflects both the quality of the evidence linking price and alcohol misuse, and also the cohesion of the alcohol misuse lobby on this issue.

Opposition to price policies

Turning now to the case against pricing policies, there are three main arguments used by opponents of price regulation. These arguments relate to: the likely ineffectiveness of such a policy; the burdens imposed on consumers and the drinks industry; and the side-effects on the wider economy.

Although the quality of the empirical evidence linking price and alcohol consumption has not been seriously challenged, some have continued to believe that price regulation may not be as effective in reducing alcohol misuse as some suggest. Indeed it should be noted that one of the studies mentioned earlier, which has provided evidence in support of price regulation, makes the warning that 'alcohol consumption can and does develop independently of price.' (Davies, 1983)

The fact that consumption is affected by other variables, as well as price, does not necessarily undermine the case for price regulation. Indeed the alcohol misuse lobby has always accepted that price is one factor amongst many affecting consumption. Hence the lobby's emphasis on the need for a comprehensive package of measures to tackle alcohol misuse. More damaging to its case however is the existence of further evidence, which casts doubt on the likely impact of price regulation upon alcohol consumption. On the basis of such evidence one economist has concluded that 'studies of consumers behaviour in countries such as Britain tend to show that higher beer prices do not result in a marked drop in beer consumption. Higher spirit prices have a more pronounced effect on consumption but the results are still not dramatic.' (Plant and Ritson, 1983 p150)

Higher prices might not discourage some drinkers if they are addicted to or dependent on alcohol. Such people may be forced to obtain the money to pay for drink by other means, including crime, creating further social problems. Also, it should be noted that higher prices have less impact on the wealthy. It could therefore be argued that price increases mainly affect those on lower incomes and are unfair, as well as ineffective in reducing alcohol consumption.

A related point is that if drink prices were raised to an artificially high level, people may begin to produce their own alcohol, so as to avoid paying the high prices of commercially produced alcoholic drinks. Not only would this be counterproductive, but it would also raise yet another set of health and social problems. Home brewing is not of course illegal; but private distillation of spirits is. High drinks prices in the UK may also further encourage other criminal activity such as the smuggling of alcohol. Moreover the quality of products on the black market cannot be guaranteed and this may lead to the sale of drinks with a dangerously high alcohol content. As a result the level of alcohol-related health problems might actually increase.

These arguments about the ineffectiveness of pricing policy in tackling alcohol misuse are often, but not always, used in conjunction with a second set of arguments - that such a policy imposes unacceptably high costs upon both the drinks industry and consumers. The industry clearly sees price regulation as a burden. Direct price controls are disliked because they restrict the commercial freedom to set prices. Whilst higher taxes on drink are seen as perhaps even more damaging. The industry is able to point out that alcoholic drink is already heavily taxed. At present the incidence of taxation (that is the proportion of final price paid in taxation) on beer, wines and spirits is 40%, 45% and 65% respectively.

In recent years the brewers and distillers have argued strongly against higher taxes on drink. In 1983 the NEDO Brewing Sector Working Group (see chapter four above) recommended that 'the government should only increase excise duties for its own fiscal policies; it should not increase duties for health reasons as the great majority of people... drink beer and other drinks with no harm to themselves or other people.' An earlier report from this committee took pains to point out the possible effects of high taxation on investment. (NEDO, 1977) Similarly, reports from the Distilling Sector Working Groups have recommended that goverment should attach greater, not less, weight to the industry's economic welfare when setting excise duties. (NEDO, 1978; 1982; 1985)

Consumers also appear to be opposed to a policy of alcohol price regulation. Opinion polls indicate that such a policy would be highly unpopular. In a MORI poll of 1980, those respondents who opposed price regulation were in a three-to-one majority. This is consistent with the findings of a poll conducted on behalf of the National Consumer Council in 1981, in which only 14% of the respondents believed that raising prices would reduce excessive drinking. There is however no more recent evidence to suggest any change in public sentiment towards alcohol prices and taxes. (Leedham, 1987)

Despite the apparent hostility of consumer opinion towards price regulation, most consumer organisations have not opposed such a policy. The general consumer organisations, such as the Consumers Association and the National Consumers Council, have been well aware of the growth in alcohol misuse. They have never opposed a policy of price regulation in view of its potential to reduce the problem. In contrast the specialist consumer organisations, such as the Campaign for Real Ale (CAMRA), have strongly opposed price regulation and higher taxation. In 1982 for example, as part of a lobbying exercise, CAMRA presented the Chancellor of the Exchequer with a beer barrel containing 50,000 signatures in an attempt to dissuade him from increasing beer taxes.

A further manifestation of the consumer interest on this issue has been the number of Questions tabled in Parliament by backbench MPs. Drink taxes and prices have been a popular subject for Parliamentary Questions. Many of these appear to have been tabled in response to complaints from the general public. The balance of opinion is illustrated by a sample of PQs tabled on the specific subject of drink prices between 1975/6 and 1981/2. Of the 51 PQs tabled, approximately 80% expressed opposition to higher prices. Also, the lack of an identifiable link between the MPs involved and the drinks industry appears to indicate that it was a consumer-led, rather than an industry-led response.

This should not be taken to imply that the industry was refraining from Parliamentary lobbying on the price regulation issue during this period. On the contrary, an analysis of the PQs tabled on the specific subject of alcohol taxation in the same period indicates a higher proportion of MPs with an identifiable link with the industry. Furthermore the significance of pricing and taxation matters is illustrated by the fact that these subjects accounted for approximately half the PQs (165) tabled on the alcohol industry during this period and around a quarter of all the PQs on alcohol matters in general.

Although Parliament has shown opposition to higher taxation and prices, it has not been the main focal point for the industry's lobbying activities on this issue. Most emphasis it seems has been placed on trying to influence government departments through the consultation process. Two departments in particular are known to be especially sympathetic towards the industry's position on this issue, in view of their departmental interests and responsibilities. These are the Department of Trade and Industry (DTI), and the Ministry of Agriculture Fisheries and Food (MAFF). Both departments have opposed higher taxes and the use of price regulation in the past on the grounds that such a policy would be damaging to the industry.

Two other departments also oppose the use of taxation to regulate drink prices. The Treasury, along with Customs and Excise, have mobilised a third set of arguments against such a policy, stressing the wider economic implications of price regulation. They point out that alcohol provides a considerable proportion of government revenue. In 1987 taxes in alcohol raised £6,250m. This represented 14% of revenue from indirect tax and 4.7% of central government's total revenue. It should be noted, though, that government is less dependent on alcohol tax revenue now than it was in the past. A hundred years ago over 40% of its revenue came from this source. (Wilson, 1940) Even so alcohol taxation is still seen by the Treasury and Customs and Excise primarily as a means of obtaining revenue. As Joel Barnett, a former minister at the Treasury, once observed :

"When you are looking at the economy as a whole you can't be concerned with only one aspect of it, as serious as the health one is. The trouble is you are always looking at the short term in the Treasury - at how you can get the maximum amount of revenue." (*The Listener* 18-25 December 1980 p815-17)

Excise duties, moreover, are regarded by the Treasury as an extremely useful instrument for collecting revenue, in view of their flexibility. Unlike other indirect taxes, like VAT for example, excise duties can be easily adjusted. They are therefore particularly useful in making up an unexpected shortfall in revenue. This is one reason why the Treasury has opposed other moves to index duties to changes in retail prices. When in 1982 a Select Committee of MPs recommended indexation for all duties, including alcohol (House of Commons, 1982a) the Treasury rejected this on the grounds that:

"Although... it might be practical to move to formal indexation of indirect taxes, it is highly questionable whether there would be any advantage in policy terms of doing so. If indexation provides greater certainty of maintaining the real value of the duties, it must also imply a considerable constraint on the Chancellor's flexibility...

The variation in the size of the duty increase illustrates the frequent need to take account of not only the aims of fiscal policy but also social and industrial conditions." (House of Commons, 1982b)

In addition to their utility as a tool of economic management, excise duties have important implications for counter-inflation policy. It has been estimated that a 10% rise in excise duties through increased drink prices raises the Retail Price Index by around 0.1% [3] Counter-inflation policy is also primarily a Treasury responsibility. Though other departments have been involved in the implementation of this policy in the past, such as the Department of Employment, and the now-defunct Department of Prices and Consumer Protection (incorporated into the Department of Trade in 1979). These departments have also been opposed to a policy of higher alcohol prices on the grounds that it would cause inflation.

To summarise then, in spite of the apparently clear empirical link between alcohol prices, consumption, and misuse, the issue of price regulation is highly controversial. On the one side we have the alcohol misuse lobby, along with the DHSS, which has supported price regulation and higher drink prices. On the other is the drink industry, the balance of consumer and public opinion, the drink industry's sponsoring departments, and the departments responsible for taxation and economic management. But on its own this catalogue of arguments and interests cannot tell us which factors have been the most important. In the following sections we therefore take this a stage further by looking at the influences upon policy making in recent years.

Price Regulation in Practice

Price controls under Labour

The policy of the 1974-9 Labour Government on alcohol prices can only be fully understood in the context of its overall approach to the control of inflation. Central to this approach was a system of general price control. This basically consisted of a Price Code, which set out the criteria for price increases, and a procedure whereby firms had to notify intended price increases to a government agency called the Price Commission. The Price Commission enforced the Code and had the power to refuse permission to raise prices. But the overall responsibility for the price control system belonged to the Department of Prices and Consumer Protection (DPCP).

This system was designed to limit all price increases - and this included drink prices. It was therefore a formidable barrier to those who believed that drink prices should be raised to discourage alcohol consumption. In order to be successful, they had to convince the government that alcoholic drink was a special case. But the pressure on government to regulate the price of alcohol on health grounds did not fully materialise until the late seventies. By this time it had been firmly established that drink prices, like the price of any other good, had to be kept as low as possible.

The downward effect of the price control system on drink prices in this period was compounded by two other factors. First of all there was the desire of ministers to use excise duties as a counter-inflationary tool. Duties were deliberately kept low in attempt to limit rises in the Retail Price Index. (Barnett, 1982 p58) This had obvious implications for drink prices, given the high level of excise duty on these products: prices fell dramatically in real terms compared with those goods attracting low or zero rates of duty. Secondly, and most probably for electoral reasons, the government appeared particularly keen to limit increases in the prices of certain commodities, such as food, beverages, and energy. Alcoholic drink fell into this category of goods, and this further explains why its price declined.

But of all the alcoholic drinks it was the price of beer which the government seemed particularly keen to limit during this period. This was probably because beer is the most popular alcoholic beverage amongst the working class - the Labour Party's traditional voters. Indeed as the next election approached the government appeared to take an increasing interest in beer prices. In 1977 the government responded to public criticism about increases in beer prices and brewery profits, by ordering an enquiry into the industry. This enquiry was to be undertaken by the Price Commission, which had recently been given wider powers to investigate price increases. The 1977 Prices Commission Act, which conferred these new powers, established two types of enquiry: (1) investigations into price rises notified by individual firms, where the initiative lay with the Commission itself; and (2) broader investigations relating to price changes in an industrial sector, initiated by the Secretary of State for Prices and Consumer Protection. The 1977 enquiry was of the second kind, indicating the presence of a considerable degree of political concern.

The decision to investigate was not well received by the brewing industry. This led to Questions in the Commons from MPs sympathetic to the brewers, such as Robert Adley MP, who told the House that:

"many brewers have expressed to me their view that this recent announcement on prices will have substantial effects upon their investment plans."[4]

But the brewers were upset even more by the content of the Price Commission's report when it appeared in July 1977. The report was highly critical of the level of drink prices, which it attributed in part to the structure of the industry. The Commission believed that the degree of horizontal and vertical integration in the industry was inefficient, and was largely to blame for its relatively high prices. Predictably, the Brewers' Society contemptuously dismissed these criticisms. But the Department of Prices and Consumer Protection, decided to act on the report. Its resolve was no doubt hardened by an increase in Parliamentary activity on this issue. Between January 1977 and February 1978, 32 Parliamentary Questions were tabled in condemnation of the increases in beer prices (the majority being concentrated in three months: January and July 1977, and January 1978). Of the 21 MPs who were involved in tabling these PQs, all but one were Labour backbenchers. It was against this background that the DPCP invited the brewers to the department for discussions.

At a meeting on December 16th, 1977, the brewers' representatives met the

Secretary of State for Prices and Consumer Protection, Roy Hattersley. The Secretary of State for Agriculture, John Silkin, was also present. Hattersley wanted a price freeze over the next twelve months and greater competition within the industry. The brewers refused to hold prices; although they agreed in principle to reduce the frequency of price increases. They also consented to further talks about competition. The agreement on the frequency of price increases was however incredibly short-lived. Less than a month after the meeting, the larger brewers notified the Price Commission of their intention to raise prices.

Hattersley publicly condemned these prospective increases as 'unjustified' But there was little that he could do at this stage, except perhaps hope that the Price Commission would heed his comments and investigate the price increase. It is possible that the Secretary of State's public outburst over the price increase had some effect, for the Price Commission decided shortly afterwards to investigate Allied Breweries' proposed price increase. This investigation was of the first type, outlined earlier, and therefore was, ostensibly at least. conducted at the Commission's discretion. In the event, the Commission allowed Allied to increase its prices and subsequently the other brewers followed. (Price Commission, 1978)

Inflation fell dramatically during 1978, the annual inflation rate for this year being only half that of the previous year. This factor, perhaps more than a fear of incurring Hattersley's wrath, persuaded the brewers to hold prices stable until February the following year. But an attempt by two of the largest brewers, Bass and Whitbread, to raise prices in February 1979 was delayed by the Price Commission, pending an enquiry.

The appearance of the Commission's report only two days after the General Election, fuelled suspicion that the decision to investigate, and the subsequent delay, had been electorally motivated. Certainly the industry appeared to believe this. (*The Times* 17 February 1979) Although these comments appear to have been part of a general campaign by business to discredit Labour's price control system. (Confederation of British Industry, 1979)

Even so, one should note that the government did not know of the timing of the May election until its defeat in the Commons - on a motion of no confidence on the 28th of March 1979. Therefore, it could not have engineered the Price Commission investigation with the election date in mind. There was at least a month between the Price Commission's decision to investigate and the Government's defeat in the House. Yet one has to remember that once the Lib-Lab pact had broken down in August 1978, the minority Labour government was open to defeat in the House. An election looked imminent from this time onwards. Given that rising beer prices might have affected the Labour's popularity in the immediate period before the election, the government had a clear incentive to prevent such an increase, even before March 28th. It may not have actually initiated the investigation by the Price Commission; but it was almost certainly involved in delaying the report until after the election.

The general election brought to office a Conservative Government which had markedly different ideas about price control, as we shall see in a moment. Its predecessor had viewed alcoholic drink, and in particular beer, as a commodity whose price had to be restrained. Such intervention was justified not only because of the Labour Government's counter-inflation policy, but also in view of its sensitivity about public opinion on this issue. But this, as we saw, brought the government into conflict with the brewing industry, which at this time wanted to increase beer prices in order to finance its investment programme and to maintain its profitability.

During this period, the arguments for higher drink prices on public health grounds were almost totally obscured. Even so in its White Paper on Prevention and Health in 1977, the government did claim to recognise 'the importance of price in raising or moderating overall demand for drink' and appreciated that 'alcohol-related harm is more likely to increase when the total amount of alcohol being consumed is rising than when it is stable.'. But despite its pledge to give the matter careful consideration, the government never appeared to take this into account in practice. This was in part because of the weakness of the alcohol misuse lobby at this time and the fact that its demands went against the grain of the government's overall counter-inflation and fiscal policies.

The Conservative Government

Whilst the economic policies of the Labour Government tended to work against the demands of the alcohol misuse lobby, those of the incoming government at first appeared to operate in its favour. Under the Conservative Government drink prices began to rise in real terms, for two main reasons.

First of all, the new government's counter-inflation policy scrapped the system of price control operated by its predecessor. Instead, firms would be free to determine the prices of their products. Shortly after taking office the government announced that the Price Commission would be abolished, and that the Department of Prices and Consumer Protection would be integrated into the Department of Trade. As the machinery of price control had been aimed at limiting price increases, its abolition therefore removed one of the major obstacles to higher drink prices. Secondly, drink prices began to rise as a direct result of the government's intention to shift the burden of taxation from direct to indirect taxes. These price increases were largely due to the significant rise in excise duties on alcoholic drink, particularly in the 1980 and 1981 Budgets, as shown in table nine above.

These aspects of the Conservative Government's economic policy favoured the alcohol misuse lobby. For the most part this was fortuitous. But there were some indications that the decision to allow drink prices to rise had also been influenced to some extent by health and social policy considerations.

An article in *The Economist* on the 20 December 1980 referred to an unholy alliance between the Treasury and the DHSS on the price of drink. The DHSS made representations to the Treasury, urging it to take alcohol misuse into account when making decisions on drink taxes. This apparently met with some success. Treasury spokesmen, when questioned about the taxation of alcoholic drinks, began to refer to these factors. A ministerial statement in 1983 noted that when determining the level of taxation '...health factors are among those taken into account.'[5] This contrasts with earlier statements where such references were conspicuous by their absence. In 1978 for instance, in response to a PQ, the Financial Secretary to the Treasury stated simply that 'decisions on the taxation of alcoholic drinks depend on a variety of factors including revenue needs, effect on prices and the general economic situation.'[6]

But although the Conservative Government appears to have been more aware than its predecessor of the importance of alcohol misuse when setting tax levels, it has not allowed such considerations to dominate economic policy decisions. Indeed, the idea of using taxes primarily to promote health and social welfare was ruled out by the government's consultative document on alcohol misuse, *Drinking Sensibly* in 1981:

"...the Government cannot accept recommendations that have been made for the systematic use of tax rates as a means of regulating consumption. Health and social implications are, however, clearly of great importance and the government intends, within the context of its economic stategy, to continue to take these into account when changes in duty and wider taxation policy are considered." (DHSS, 1981b p59)

The main source of opposition within government to the use of fiscal policy as a means of regulating alcohol consumption, as we have already seen, is the Treasury itself. The voice of the Treasury is clearly heard throughout the chapter in *Drinking Sensibly* which deals with this issue. Its viewpoint is particularly clear in the following extract:

"a further consideration in setting alcohol duties primarily to serve health and social ends is that this would reduce their value to the government as flexible instruments for obtaining revenue and for wider economic policy." (DHSS, 1981b p56)

The principal demand of the alcohol misuse lobby - that taxation should be explicitly used to manipulate drink prices and consumption, has therefore been comprehensively rejected by the Treasury. But why, one might ask, has the Treasury bothered to make references to health and social considerations when setting taxes? One possible explanation is that by mentioning these reasons, it hopes to minimise criticism of higher taxation on consumer goods. Perhaps it is no coincidence that when imposing high taxation on tobacco in recent years the Chancellor of the Exchequer has openly referred to the health consequences of smoking. (see Baggott, 1987)

The implication then is that the influence of the alcohol misuse lobby on this issue has been fairly marginal. Drink taxes and hence prices have risen as a consequence of the government's overall economic strategy, rather than as a result of the lobbying from this quarter. Moreover, references to health and social factors in connection with the setting of taxes appear to have been grounded in political expedience rather than a genuine, overriding concern for the problem of alcohol misuse. Generally the alcohol misuse lobby has failed to convince the Treasury of the need to set drink taxes primarily on public health grounds. This was confirmed in the 1986 and 1987 Budgets when the duty on alcohol was frozen in real terms, much to the consternation of the alcohol misuse lobby. Though perhaps the proximity of a general election, as in 1978/9, was the key factor at work once again.

More recently there have been further developments on the alcohol taxation front. In the 1988 Budget the Chancellor of the Exchequer reduced the rate of taxes on low alcohol drinks. This was the result of strong pressure from the alcohol misuse lobby and the DHSS. A tax differential between drinks having a low and high alcohol content was also broadly supported by the Home Office working party on young people and alcohol in 1987, and subsequently by the Wakeham Committee on alcohol misuse (see chapter three). Significantly, the drinks industry was not opposed to these proposals in view of their attempts to expand the sale of low alcohol drinks. (see chapters four and five)

The Tax-setting Process

In this section we look in more detail at the making of taxation policy in relation to alcoholic drinks. This process is dominated by an inner circle of departments - comprising the Treasury, the Inland Revenue, and Customs and Excise. An outer circle, which includes all the other central government departments having an interest in taxation can also exert some influence. (Sandford and Robinson, 1983) The inner circle controls the initiation and development of policy in this area. Whilst the outer circle, although occasionally influential, has a much more peripheral role and is only brought into the decision-making process at the discretion of the inner circle.

This distinction is reflected in the process by which alcohol excise duties are determined. Once a year, a few months before the Budget, there is a special meeting of civil servants drawn from the Treasury, Customs and Excise, MAFF, DTI, and the DHSS. Out of this meeting comes a recommendation to the Chancellor of the Exchequer on the level of drink duties for the next budget. The DHSS representative will usually request that the level of duty be increased at least in line with inflation, on health and social grounds. Whilst the DTI and MAFF will point out the consequences of such a move for investment, exports, and employment in the drinks industry, and argue for a low or zero increase in duty. But whatever arguments are employed, the preferences of the Treasury and Customs and Excise - based primarily on the needs for revenue - usually prevail.

The decision of this meeting is not final, as the Chancellor himself will ultimately decide the level of duty. He may also discuss the issue with other ministers, if he wishes to do so. Whether or not the other departments can influence the Chancellor at this later stage will depend on how he anticipates the political reaction to the recommended duty level. For this reason, pressure groups wishing to influence the level of duty will not only lobby departments sympathetic to their case, but also send delegations direct to the Treasury in an attempt to persuade the Chancellor to take account of their preferences in the Budget. They will point out the possible economic, social, and political consequences of adopting levels of duty which are unacceptable to them. This gives the Chancellor some idea of the reaction to the level of duty which he has in mind.

How influential are these delegations? The process of determining the Budget is traditionally a closed affair. Though it is much more open now than it used to be. (Sandford and Robinson, 1983 p228) Even the less powerful pressure groups within the alcohol misuse lobby have obtained access to the Treasury in recent years, including the voluntary organisations, Alcohol Concern, Action on Alcohol Abuse, and formerly, the National Council on Alcoholism. But although the Treasury will see such delegations, it does not always appear to hear them. More surprisingly perhaps, this is often the fate of the industrial pressure groups too. Of the major trade associations, the Brewers' Society in particular has not achieved a great deal of success in recent years through their annual pre-budget meeting at the the Treasury.

The general failure of these meetings to produce a change in policy has been confirmed by Joel Barnett, who has claimed that:

"The pressure groups for individual industries such as drinks, tobacco, and motoring would always be received politely but mainly ignored. We would either be convinced by the facts provided by our officials, or not as the case may be, but we were unable to be convinced by an obviously biased group lobbying in their own interests." (Barnett, 1982)

Taken in isolation, these meetings are no doubt of limited effectiveness. But in conjunction with other forms of pressure, and when the general circumstances are favourable, they can be useful in putting points across. Moreover, a well-organised campaign can succeed in persuading the Treasury that the case being made is a sound one. This is clearly illustrated by the recent success of the Scotch Whisky industry in its campaign for favourable treatment in the Budget.

The special case of Scotch Whisky?

Like the other main trade associations in the alcohol field, the Scotch Whisky Association tries to persuade the Treasury that its members constitute a special case, and should therefore be treated leniently when changes in excise duties are being considered. The annual delegation to the Treasury has in recent years tried to dissuade the Chancellor from raising duties on Scotch Whisky by pointing out the likely consequences of such action for employment and exports in particular. The industry employs around 20,000 workers, most of these in areas where unemployment is already high. It is also an export-oriented industry, with only 20% of output being produced for domestic consumption. But in recent years the industry has faced a number of difficulties - in particular competition from overseas, as other countries have become involved in the production and blending of whisky. Such developments, whilst threatening the industry's contribution to jobs and exports, have added weight to its case for special treatment.

The government appears to have taken these arguments on board. On only two occasions in the last thirteen Budgets has the duty on Scotch Whisky been raised above or in line with inflation. Whilst duties on wine and beer have been raised to this extent on four and seven occasions respectively (see table nine). This special treatment was made more even explicit in the 1985 Budget. Here the Chancellor, during the course of his Budget speech, cited the special problems of the Scotch whisky industry as the main reason for imposing a small increase in duty:

"In recognition of the current difficulties of the Scotch Whisky industry... I propose to increase the duty on spirits by only 10p a bottle, well below the amount needed to keep pace with inflation."[7]

These concessions were secured following a sustained campaign by the industry. The annual delegation to the Treasury played a part, providing a platform for its arguments. But the industry appeared to place considerable weight on its discussions with MAFF, its sponsoring department. In 1980 MAFF committed itself to implementing a report by the Distilling Sector Working Group, referred to briefly earlier in this chapter. (NEDO, 1978) This report contained a recommendation that the government attach greater weight in future to the industry's welfare when setting duty levels. Within government, MAFF, supported by the DTI, argued that this report should be heeded. Together they managed to persuade the Treasury to limit increases in duty.

This interdepartmental pressure was coupled with a well-organised campaign in Parliament. Between 1975/6 and 1982/3 no less than 100 Parliamentary Questions were tabled on the matters specifically concerning the Scotch Whisky industry, more than any other single alcoholic drink sector (see chapter four). Most of this activity was organised by the all-party group of MPs on Scotch Whisky in a deliberate attempt to put pressure on the government. Most of the members of this group had constituency interests in the industry. One such example was Hamish Watt, the MP for Banff whose constituency contained around a third of the malt whisky distilleries in Scotland. In 1976, Watt initiated a debate on the industry in an attempt to make government more aware of its problems.[8] There was also an attempt to promote activity in the Lords on this issue. In 1978 Lord Kinnoull introduced a debate on the Scotch Whisky industry,[9] whilst several peers have tabled Parliamentary Questions, drawing attention to its problems, in recent years.[10] By emphasising these problems, and in particular those associated with the relatively high level of tax on Scotch Whisky, Parliamentary pressure has made it much more difficult for the government to justify large increases in duty.

Finally, it is worth pointing out that the Scotch Whisky industry's arguments may have been given a sharper edge by certain electoral considerations. Both major parties feared the inroads which the Scottish National Party appeared to be making in the Scottish vote during the seventies. The Conservative Party in particularly was depressed about the prospect of becoming the 'third party' in Scotland. In this context the Scotch Whisky industry is a highly sensitive political issue. The industry's history is bound up with Scottish tradition and national pride.

Blows seemingly dealt to the industry by central government, such as large duty increases, suggest the possibility of even more serious electoral consequences for the party in power. The comparatively favourable treatment of the industry in recent years may at least in part reflect such considerations.

Tax Harmonisation: The European Dimension

The case of the Scotch Whisky industry illustrates that the inner circle of decision makers on taxation matters, though powerful, can occasionally be moved. This is confirmed by a second case where a drinks industry campaign, this time with the European Court in support, managed to force the Treasury into a favourable decision. As the decision went against the wishes of the alcohol misuse lobby, the case also illustrates the relative weakness of this lobby.

The story begins with an EEC Recommendation in December 1975, which called on the UK Government to alter the structure of duties on drink on the grounds that the present system discriminated against wine. (European Commission, 1975) The European Commission believed that the UK was protecting its brewing industry by levying a disproportionate level of tax on imported wines, thus violating Article 95 of the EEC Treaty. The UK Government denied that it was protecting domestic brewers, claiming that the two products were not substitutes for each other, and refused either to reduce wine duty or to increase beer duty as required. Talks between the Treasury and the Commission followed, but no agreement was reached. In 1978, the Commission responded to this impasse by starting proceedings against the UK Government at the European Court.

Eventually, almost five years later, the European Court came to a decision in favour of the Commission. This was supported at home by the Wines and Spirits Association, which called on the government to alter the structure of duties in wine's favour, as soon as possible. The Treasury did however have some room for manoeuvre. Neither the Court nor the Commission had specified how the changes should be implemented. The Chancellor of the Exchequer had three main options. First of all he could ignore the ruling, which raised the possibility of further political repercussions within the European Community. Second, he could satisfy Europe, and the wine industry, by increasing the duty on beer by 2p per pint whilst cutting 20p off the duty on a bottle of wine. Third, he could again satisfy Europe by leaving wine duty unchanged and imposing an increase in duty of 7p per pint on beer.

The brewers and the licensed trade were opposed to any response which produced a rise in beer duty above rate of inflation, and were therefore hostile to the third option. An increase of 2p would have kept beer duties in line with inflation. The brewers in their pre-budget meeting with the Treasury argued for a 2p rise in beer duty, to be phased in over two years (ie: a 1p increase in each year) combined with drop in wine duty as necessary. The pub landlords association, the National Union of Licensed Victuallers, also preferred a cut in wine duty, rather than a disproportionate rise in beer duty. This was the main message of their delegation to the Chancellor in February 1984. Further opposition to increasing beer duty in real terms came from the unions which had members in brewing, such as the TGWU, and from farmers who believed that the brewers' demand for barley would be seriously affected by such an increase.

Pressure group lobbying against this option was augmented by the activities of some MPs in Parliament. Prior to the Budget, MPs from both parties mobilised to oppose option three. A major feature of this was the tabling of two early-day motions (EDMs), both of which called on the Chancellor satisfy Europe by cutting wine duty and limiting the increase in beer duty (the second option, above) One EDM was put down by two Tory backbenchers - Michael Colvin MP (NULV's Parliamentary Adviser), and James Couchman MP, who had financial interests in the licensed trade. This was supported by 30 other Tory MPs. (House of Commons, 1984a) A second EDM, initiated by Labour MPs, was supported by a further 53 signatures. (House of Commons, 1984b)

The combination of these pressures had the desired effect. In the March Budget, the Chancellor increased beer duty by 2p per pint, and reduced wine duty by 18p per bottle, slightly less than expected. The full adjustment in the structure of duties was to be completed in the next Budget. This decision pleased all but the alcohol misuse lobby. They feared that a rise in overall consumption would result from the net fall in duties, but were unable to prevent this from happening. The lobby's weakness was mainly due, in this particular case at least, to a failure to get its act together. It did not engage in lobbying to the same degree as the brewers and the licensed trade. Indeed by the time the alcohol misuse lobby realised the full implications of the proposed changes for alcohol prices in general, it was far too late.

This specific decision, however, is only the thin end of the wedge. The European dimension is likely to become even more important in future in view of the creation of a single European market. A commitment by EEC member states to the free movement of goods in Europe from 1992 will require further harmonisation of taxes. As excise duties on alcohol in the UK are higher than the average imposed by other states in the community, the implication is that domestic duties will have to fall in line with a lower standard rate. The required reduction in UK alcohol duties is substantial. In terms of the original proposals put forward by the European Commission, the duties on spirits, beer and wine would be cut by 49%, 72%, and 89% respectively. (see *The Economist* 9 July 1988 pS20) This has obvious implications for price, and thereby alcohol consumption and misuse. One analysis has estimated that alcohol consumption could rise as a result by as much as 39% (Lee, Pearson, Smith, 1988)

It remains to be seen whether or not the reduction in UK duties will be scaled down. Certainly many of the Commissions proposals on tax harmonisation (including the specific proposals on duties) are being resisted by the UK government and other member states. It is also worth noting that Mrs Thatcher's Government has in the past successfully upheld the national interest in negotiations with other member states. So it is possible that some compromise could be reached on alcohol duties.

Some fall in the level of alcohol duty looks inevitable, however, and as a result a potential instrument of public health policy could be rendered useless.

Conclusions

In connection with this last point it could be argued that the potential of price regulation has never been fully exploited anyway by UK governments. As this chapter has clearly shown the price of alcoholic drink in the UK has been largely determined by the government's overall economic strategy, its counter-inflation and fiscal policy, and its need for revenue.

Electoral considerations it seems have also played a part in this. Governments have only been prepared to raise drink prices, so long as this does not conflict with these overriding economic and political objectives. The value of alcohol duties as a flexible instrument of economic policy has underpinned the government's reluctance to use it primarily as a means of promoting public health and social welfare through the manipulation of drink prices.

Within government the Treasury and Customs and Excise have been the main opponents to an explicit policy of alcohol price regulation. These departments have successfully resisted pressure from the health departments and the alcohol misuse lobby in recent years, largely because of their powerful role in the making of tax policy. The predictable opposition of MAFF and DTI within government has added even more steel to this resistance.

But opposition from within government departments cannot be held entirely responsible for the failure to adopt price regulation. Neither the Labour nor the Conservative Party, in or out of office, has cherished such a policy. On the contrary, as we have seen, politicians have responded to political campaigns working in the opposite direction. Had government been subjected to the same degree of pressure to increase drink prices in line with inflation, then perhaps price regulation might not have been such a remote possibility.

Although there has been considerable pressure from the alcohol misuse lobby in favour of such a policy, particularly in recent years, these activities hardly constitute a vigorous campaign. True enough, the lobby has engineered Questions in the House, has put forward its view in meetings with government officials, and has published authoritative reports backing up its case - some of which have attracted wide media coverage. Furthermore the alcohol misuse lobby has exhibited a relatively high degree of unity and coherence on this issue. But this pressure has not been coordinated on a scale comparable to the two campaigns undertaken by the industry, examined in the final two sections of this chapter. In both of these cases the industry achieved considerable success at the expense of the alcohol misuse lobby, because it campaigned far more effectively.

Taken together these factors explain why, in spite of the weight of empirical evidence linking the price of alcohol with the level of consumption and harm, the ultimate disincentive available for the prevention of alcohol misuse has not been

112

adopted. Moreover, as we saw in the final section, a shift in the balance of decision making on this issue from Whitehall to Brussels may make such a policy even less of a possibility in the future.

Notes

1. *House of Commons Official Report* Volume 31 Column 15w
    8 November 1982
2. *House of Commons Official Report* Volume 955 Column 78w 31 July 1978;
    Volume 958 Column 727w 23 November 1978; Volume 985 Column 336w
    22 May 1980
3. *House of Commons Official Report* Volume 37 Column 280 18 February
    1983
4. *House of Commons Official Report* Volume 931 Column 29 2 May 1977
5   *House of Commons Official Report* Volume 51 Column 557 22 December
    1983
6. *House of Commons Official Report* Volume 949 Column 585-6
    11 May 1978
7. *House of Commons Official Report* Volume 175 Column 795 19 March 1985
8. *House of Commons Official Report* Volume 906 Column 541-50
    25 Feb. 1976
9. *House of Lords Official Report* Volume 436 Column 944-64 24 November
    1982
10. See for example *House of Lords Official Report* Volume 436 Column 462-4
    21 January 1976; Volume 367 Column 1197-8 4 February 1981; Volume 436
    Column 233-4 14 December 1983

7 Licensing law reform: the boot on the other foot?

In the UK, the sale of alcoholic drink is regulated by the licensing laws. (Martin, 1988) Given the level of concern about alcohol problems in recent years, one might have expected pressure on government to impose further restrictions on the sale of alcohol. But in fact the boot has been very much on the other foot. The main proponent of licensing law reform has been the alcoholic drinks industry, pursing its desire for a more relaxed system of regulation. The alcohol misuse lobby meanwhile has been mainly involved in trying to prevent the laws from being liberalised, rather than in pressing for further restrictions.

In this chapter we examine in some detail the political battles which have been fought over the licensing laws. We begin by looking at the origins and purpose of these laws. Then we move on to consider the gradual liberalisation of the licensing laws in the post-war period . The final section looks at more recent developments which led up to the passage of a new Licensing Act in 1988.

The Origins and Purpose of Liquor Licensing

Basically the licensing laws restrict the availability of alcoholic drink, whilst at the same time regulating the environment of public drinking. There are three aspects of control embodied within the law. First, a licensing system, which in principle regulates the quantity and quality of retail outlets selling drink. This is reflected in the process of granting (or refusing) licences, which retailers of alcoholic drink have to possess. Several different types of licence exist, the main distinction being between off-licences - where alcohol sold has to be consumed off the premises - and on-licences, where this requirement is not necessary. Secondly, the licensing laws restrict the times during which alcoholic drinks can be sold. These are known as the permitted hours of licensed premises. In certain cases, though, special extensions to permitted hours can be obtained. Thirdly, the law seeks to limit the availability of alcohol to certain people, particularly children and young people. Perhaps the best known of these restrictions are the rules on under-age drinking and the prohibition of children in the bars of licensed premises.

Although the licensing sytem extends well back into the Middle Ages, the present laws date back to the First World War, when the government of the day imposed strict controls on alcohol drink as part of its emergency restrictions. (see Baggott, 1986) The government was persuaded partly by the campaigns of the temperance movement to restrict the liquor traffic, but mainly by the deleterious effects of alcohol consumption on the war effort. The widespread drunkenness of the time led Lloyd George to comment:

"We are fighting Germany, Austria, and the drink and, as far as I can see, the greatest of these deadly foes is the drink" (Williams and Brake, 1980 p47)

The emergency restrictions appeared to have a dramatic impact upon alcohol consumption, and the level of alcohol abuse, in wartime. This experience persuaded the authorities to retain most of the controls after the war.

It is clear that the present restrictions were introduced with a definite purpose in mind. But as time went by confusion arose about the role of the licensing laws. This confusion can be attributed to three factors in particular. First, the original rationale behind the present law has been undermined by the passage of time. Because the laws emerged out of a period of national emergency, they have been open to the criticism that they are not relevant to modern circumstances. Furthermore the dramatic social changes which have taken place since the laws were introduced makes them appear even more anachronistic.

Second, there is little contemporary evidence which shows unambiguously that licensing controls reduce alcohol abuse. (see section three below) There is some evidence that the controls imposed during the First World War were effective, as we have already suggested. (see Smart, 1974) Though one should not forget the presence of other factors likely to reduce alcohol consumption and misuse - such as the effect of the war on the size of the drinking population. The lack of conclusive evidence is not really surprising. The licensing laws attempt to control the availability of alcohol in a number of ways and it is difficult to separate the impact of these measures in practice. Also these measures interact with the culture of the nation in a complex manner, a point recognised by the Central Policy Review Staff (CPRS) in their report on alcohol policy in the seventies:

"the precise effect of these controls on existing customs and habits is uncertain and licensing is so deeply embedded as not to be easily capable of separate analysis." (CPRS, 1982)

A third source of confusion lies in the nature of the licensing system itself. The granting of permission to sell alcoholic drink is a highly decentralised procedure. Central government does not issue any guidelines to local licensing authorities and cannot direct them in accordance with any national policy. This has produced a considerable degree of inconsistency in the application of the law. Often neighbouring localities will have different approaches to the granting of licences and extensions to permitted hours, with little apparent justification. Local differentiation is also compounded at a national level by the existence of different laws covering Nortern Ireland, Scotland and England and Wales.

Licensing Law Reform in the Post-War Period

According to one cross-national study, 'the UK has one of the most developed and restrictive systems for the sale and serving of alcoholic beverages in Europe.' (Davies and Walsh, 1983 p259)

Even so, the lack of a clear underlying purpose has fostered a gradual relaxation in the law during the post-war period, and particularly since the sixties. This liberalisation process has taken place both on a formal level, as a result of changes in the law; and on an informal level, in the way the law has been enforced and interpreted.

Many aspects of licensing law are under-enforced. Under-age drinking has been a classic case in this respect. Survey evidence indicates a large disparity between offences committed and actual convictions. (Hawker, 1978; OPCS, 1986c; Justices' Clerks' Society, 1983). In 1984 only 314 individuals were proceeded against for selling alcohol to persons under eighteen.[1]

There is also evidence that many licensing authorities have adopted a more relaxed position on the granting of licences. This has been partly responsible for the massive increase in licensed outlets over the last thirty or so years. Between 1950 and 1983 the number of licensed outlets in England and Wales rose by 41% (Home Office, 1984) Licensing authorities in many areas do not have a policy on the granting of new licences. Indeed many seem to assume that the application for a licence is itself sufficient evidence of the community's need for yet another outlet selling alcoholic drink.

But to be fair it has to be pointed out that the powers of the local licensing authorities have been reduced by formal legislative changes during the post-war period. Since 1945 there have been three major reforms in this area, beginning with the Licensing Act of 1961.

The Licensing Act of 1961 relaxed the law in England and Wales in three main ways. First of all, the absolute discretion of local licensing authorities to grant and refuse licences was restricted by the introduction of a new category of licence for hotels and restaurants. The licences were different in that the licensing authorities could only refuse them on special grounds laid down in the Act. Furthermore the licensing authority's power was undermined by the establishment of the right to appeal against their decisions on all categories of licence. This gave the applicant an automatic second chance of obtaining a licence if at first refused. Finally, the 1961 Act extended the permitted hours of off-licensed premises. Formerly these hours were the same as those for on-licensed premises. The consequences of this change were not recognised at the time. But once off-licence hours corresponded to normal shopping hours, the larger multiple stores began to show a greater interest in selling alcoholic drink. This change in the law, coupled with the abolition of resale price maintenance in 1965, made it both convenient and profitable for them to do so. This was a further reason behind the expansion of licensed outlets in the sixties and seventies.

The changes introduced by the 1961 Act were not considered significant or controversial at the time. (Lee, 1961) Indeed, the government deliberately tried to avoid controversy by going back on an earlier commitment to extend the permitted hours of on-licensed premises. This issue had raised significant opposition from temperance and licensee interests. Finally, it should be pointed out that the 1961 Act did tighten up the law in a number of areas. For example, the under-eighteen rules on purchasing drink were extended to off-licensed premises, where they had not previously applied.

The review of licensing law in the seventies

By the end of the sixties most agreed that the whole area of licensing law was in need of an overhaul. Within government itself, the Department of Trade and Industry appeared to favour a more relaxed licensing system. The DTI had accepted the report of the Monopolies Commission in 1969 on the brewing industry. This report recommended a relaxation in the law so as to promote greater competition and efficiency within the industry. The Home Office, responsible for the enforcement of licensing law, was also keen to initiate reform.

The election of a Conservative Government in 1970 added weight to the case for reform. The Conservatives had considered the possibility of introducing licensing reform whilst in opposition. Reginald Maudling, the new Home Secretary, was clearly in favour of a more relaxed licensing system. He commented, not long after taking up his new post:

"I have long thought that the law on liquor licensing in England and Wales was archaic and in need of a thorough overhaul to meet modern conditions."[2]

It is also worth pointing out that the Conservative Party received £225,000 in political contributions (approximately £1m at todays prices) from the brewers in the three years prior to the election.[3] The brewers, who have traditionally had a good relationship with the Tory party (see chapter four), were broadly in favour of a more relaxed licensing regime. They represented a strong pressure group in favour of change. Other elements within the licensed trade were, however, less happy at the prospect of reform, as we shall see later.

The other main pressure group in favour of a more relaxed licensing regime at this time was the tourist industry. It believed that tourism would benefit if the licensing laws, particularly licensing hours, were liberalised. The tourist industry had tried unsuccessfully in 1961 to persuade the government to retain its original proposals to extend the hours of on-licensed premises in the licensing bill of that year. But during the sixties the industry's position had become stronger. This was reflected in the creation of the British Tourist Authority, along with the national tourist boards, in 1969. These bodies, which had a statutory duty to advise ministers on matters affecting tourism, were a useful channel through which the industry could present its view to government.

The final source of pressure was much more nebulous, compared with the others mentioned so far. This was the general climate of opinion in the late sixties and early seventies, which was highly conducive to liberal reforms of this kind. This was demonstrated by the successful passage of liberal measures on moral issues such as abortion and homosexuality during this period. The government believed that in view of this climate of opinion, liberal licensing reforms would also be supported by the general public.

The government's review of liquor licensing was undertaken by two separate departmental committees. The Home Secretary, responsible for licensing in England and Wales, appointed Lord Erroll of Hale as the chiarman of the first committee; whilst the Secretary of State for Scotland, responsible for licensing north of the border, appointed Dr Christopher Clayson to chair the second. The committees began taking evidence in April 1971. The Erroll report was published in December 1972. (Home Office, 1972) Whilst the Clayson report emerged eight months later. (Scottish Office, 1973) Both committees argued for a relaxation in the licensing laws. More specifically, they were in agreement on the following points.

First, that the local licensing authorities' 'absolute discretion' over the granting of licences should be replaced with judgements made on limited, specified grounds. Only on such grounds could a licence could be refused. Second, that permitted hours should be extended for on-licensed premises, and that the statutory afternoon break be abolished. Third, that children under fourteen years of age should under certain conditions be allowed in the bar of licensed premises.

The two reports differed however in a number of respects. Some of these differences originated from the dissimilarities of the two licensing systems. Yet this cannot explain why the Clayson report recommended the transfer of the licensing function from the existing licensing courts to local councillors, whilst the Erroll Committee proposed that this function should remain with local magistrates. Neither does it help us to understand why the Clayson Committee supported the current age limit for purchasing and drinking alcohol, whilst Erroll recommended a reduction in the age limit from 18 to 17 years.

The contrasting fates of Erroll and Clayson

The Clayson Report was accepted as a basis for legislation by the government. Though Parliamentary time for the Scottish licensing reforms was not found until the 1975/6 session, by which time there had been a change of government. Erroll's recommendations were largely ignored, although one or two minor points were taken up - such as the abolition of the Licensing Compensation Fund, discussed in chapter five.

There were four main reasons why the reports were treated differently. First of all, Clayson Report provoked a much less hostile response from the medical lobby, whilst the Erroll Report was strongly attacked in the medical press. For example, an editorial in the *British Medical Journal* pointed out that the Committee had failed to attach sufficient weight to public health considerations:

"The impression given is that the Committee is set on policies of relaxation for reasons other than those concerning public health. From a public health point of view the Report's main recommendations must be considered as untimely." (Anonymous, 1972 p626)

The Erroll report was also considered by the Standing Medical Advisory Committee (SMAC). This body, which provides expert advice to government on a wide range of health and medical matters, expressed its concern about the public health implications of the report and urged Health Ministers to oppose reform on these grounds.

The Clayson report, on the other hand, managed to sidestep much of this criticism. This is because it justified its recommendations not on consumer or trade grounds, as Erroll had done, but on public health grounds. The Scottish committee actually claimed that relaxed licensing laws would reduce the problem of alcohol misuse, by for example reducing the pressure to drink within a restrictive time period - a practice known as drinking against the clock. Finally, medical opinion may have been placated to some extent by the fact that Clayson was himself a doctor. In contrast Lord Erroll was a businessman and had served as a minister for trade in previous Conservative administration.

A second factor behind the acceptance of the Clayson report was the reception it received from the licensed trade. The Scottish licencees were at the time facing a much more restrictive regime than their counterparts in the south. Through their representative body, the Scottish Licensed Trade Association (SLTA), they welcomed and supported most of Clayson's recommendations. Licensees in England and Wales however were generally satisfied with the existing regime, and were generally against reform. Most English and Welsh licensees believed that Errolls' proposals would lead to increased competition and longer working hours. Their representatives - the National Union of Licensed Victuallers (which organises free landlords and tenants), and the National Association of Licensed House Managers (which represents salaried public house managers) - came out against change on these grounds. Though it should be mentioned that within the NULV, a growing number of publicans supported of some of Erroll's more controversial recommendations.

The support of Scottish licensees, and the lower degree of opposition from the medical lobby, meant that in Scotland the only real opponent to reform at this time was the temperance movement, in view of its traditional committment to strict licensing laws. The temperance organisations throughout the UK realised that in the current climate of opinion, further restrictions on the availability of alcohol were unlikely to emerge. But they believed that any liberalisation of the law was a step in the wrong direction, and would lead to an increase in alcohol consumption and misuse. Yet, even in Scotland where temperance has traditionally been strong, these groups could not mobilise sufficient opposition to Clayson. Indeed public opinion in Scotland was much more in favour of change than in England and Wales. Surveys conducted on behalf of the Clayson Committee showed that less than half of those questioned (48%) felt that the present laws were about right. A similar survey for the Erroll Committee showed support for the current regime at over 61%

This helps to explain why the official response to the two reports was so different. Not all Clayson's recommendations were taken up however. Indeed the government emphasised that the reform they had in mind was marginal and accordingly rejected a number of Clayson's more controversial recommendations. It did not for example accept the recommendation that children under fourteen years of age should be allowed in the bar of licensed premises. Neither did it support the case for Sunday opening of public houses, outlawed in Scotland under the existing legislation. Whilst on the question of permitted hours the government decided that the statutory afternoon break should be retained after all, though special extensions could be granted by licensing authorities. The only slightly controversial element in the government's bill was the provision for a later closing time in the evening. But since closing time was called an hour earlier in Scotland than in the rest of the country, this measure only brought the hours into line with England and Wales.

But in effect the 1976 Licensing Act relaxed the law much more than the government appeared to intend. Following a backbench amendment to the bill during its committee stage in the Commons, the government was forced to allow public houses the right to open on Sundays. Another unforeseen consequence occurred after the Act had been passed. It became clear that the powers conferred on the local licensing authorities - which enabled them to grant extensions to normal permitted hours - were being used more frequently than had been originally envisaged. A consequence of this was that the so called statutory afternoon break in many areas began to disappear, with some licensed premises remaining open all day. (Laurance, 1984)

So the Scottish reforms, rather than bringing Scotland into line with the rest of Britain, actually created a further disparity between the two systems. This in turn gave an added impetus to those wanting liberal reforms in England and Wales, who could now claim in turn that they wished to be brought into line with Scotland.

Reform through the back door?

Once it had become obvious that the government was not prepared to implement the Erroll report, a number of backbench MPs began to show an interest in promoting their own legislation along these lines. The first serious attempt to introduce

120

reform was made by Kenneth Clarke MP in 1976. His Licensing Amendment Bill contained two proposals: the first provided for an extension in permitted hours for on-licensed premises; the second sought to allow children under fourteen into the bar of licensed premises, under certain conditions.

The government officially adopted a neutral stance on the bill, although some departments were in favour of reform. The Home Office, for example, supported the bill and assisted in its drafting. Moreover, since the government as a whole took pains to provide adequate Parliamentary time for the discussion of the bill, its neutrality was rather benign.

Despite this assistance, the bill failed. It was defeated by a resurgence of the opposition to the Erroll Committee's original proposals. Parts of the licensed trade were still against liberalisation. The NALHM continued to oppose reform, along with the Union of Shop, Distributive and Allied Workers (USDAW) - which also had members in the licensed trade. But NULV had by this time moved away from its earlier position, outlined above. It now broadly favoured a relaxation in the law, and therefore supported Clarke's bill.

The anti-liberalisation lobby was well-organised in Parliament. A number of MPs connected with this lobby had formed an *ad hoc* all party group in Parliament to fight Erroll's original proposals. This organisation was the rallying point for those who opposed the Clarke's bill. Two MPs in particular masterminded the campaign against the bill: Ron Lewis MP, the Treasurer of the UK Alliance (temperance); and Sir Bernard Braine MP, the chairman of the National Council on Alcoholism. These two MPs kept up a constant attack on the bill during its various stages, and their efforts were largely responsible for its defeat.[4]

Following the failure of the Clarke bill, the chances of reform in England and Wales appeared slim. Indeed, any optimism which those wanting reform might have had was dispersed during the late seventies, by the reports on alcohol misuse, mentioned in earlier chapters (see chapter three). Each of these reports warned against the relaxing the licensing laws in the present circumstances. The House of Commons Expenditure Committee report (1977a) urged that 'extreme caution... be exercised in respect of any variation in the licensing laws.' Whilst the DHSS Advisory Committee on Alcoholism (1978b) recommended that 'licensing hours should not be extended until sufficient evidence exists that to do so would not aggravate the problem.' The CPRS (1982) called on government to resist pressures to make the licensing laws in different parts of the UK more consistent with each other.

Although still officially neutral on the question of licensing law reform, the government's attitude towards reform hardened following these reports. The Department of Health and Social Security (DHSS) in view of its responsibilities for public health, became strongly opposed to relaxing the law. Also the Home Office appeared to have accepted that licensing reform was off the political agenda, for the time being at least. This was clearly an unfavourable climate in which to attempt to promote reform. Nevertheless, Sir Nicholas Bonsor MP (whose father had been a director of Watney breweries and who himself had taken an interest in licensing matters as vice-chairman of the Conservative backbench tourism committee) introduced a further private members bill on the subject in 1979.

Bonsor's proposals were much milder than those contained in the Clarke bill three years earlier. The second bill provided for the same number of permitted hours as at present and retained an afternoon break. But it also sought to introduce greater flexibility in the opening hours of on-licensed premises by giving licensees the freedom to select their opening and closing times according to demand. Also, like the Clarke bill, it contained a clause permitting children under 14 years of age into the bar of licensed premises under certain conditions.

Even though the Bonsor bill was more modest than its predecessor, it had little chance of success. The anti-liberalisation lobby mobilised once again, this time armed with the above-mentioned official reports to support its case. The countervailing pressure during the second reading of the bill in the House of Commons was irresistable. After this the government refused it any more Parliamentary time.

The Resurgence of Pressures for Reform

The anti-liberalisation lobby's successful defeat of the two private members bills did not however produce an unambiguous response from government. On the one hand it appeared to be convinced that further reform should not be attempted as long as alcohol misuse remained a serious problem. According to the consultative document, *Drinking Sensibly*:

"The present government has made it clear that it has no plans to amend the licensing laws of England and Wales in the light of the more controversial recommendations of the Erroll Committee report." (1981b, p45)

But the government would not commit itself to a ban on further reform, as recommended for example by the Royal College of Psychiatrists in its 1979 report on alcohol problems. This was revealed by a Home Office Minister less than eighteen months after the publication of *Drinking Sensibly*:

"...we have not closed the door on the possibility of longer licensing hours, but we would wish to be assured that opening it wider will not lead to an increase in the problem."[5]

The difference in emphasis revealed by these statements reflects the balance of pressure within government itself on this issue. As mentioned earlier, the DHSS opposed change in view of the implications for alcohol misuse. But apart from the Home Office, two other departments continued to favour reform, namely the Department of Trade and Industry (DTI) and the Ministry of Agriculture Fisheries and Food (MAFF). DTI supported liberalisation chiefly on the grounds that it might encourage tourism (though tourism is now the responsibility of the Employment Department) Whilst MAFF, as the sponsor of the drinks industry is broadly in favour of any measures likely to improve the commercial position of the industry. These departments opposed the adoption of a moratarium on liquor licensing and were active in pressing for further reform.

The Home Office, as the department responsible for licensing law in England and Wales, was at the centre of these conflicting pressures. The department discussed the possibility of reform with officials and ministers in other departments on several occasions during this period. For example, in 1983 Leon Brittan, the then Home Secretary had several meetings with Norman Lamont, Minister of State at the DTI, on the possibility of future reforms. In addition, the other departments having an interest in licensing were frequently in touch with the Home Office through the usual civil service networks.

In an attempt to reach a compromise solution on this issue, the Home Office in the early eighties adopted a cautious attitude to reform (to satisfy the DHSS), whilst not ruling out the possibility of change (to placate DTI and MAFF).

The balance once again appeared to shift in favour of the anti-liberalisation lobby when in the first part of 1985 a great deal of media attention was focused on the link between alcohol and public disorder, and in particular crowd violence at soccer matches. Public concern about the problem of soccer violence reached a peak in May 1985, following a riot at the European Cup Final in Brussels. Many people were killed and injured during this horrific incident, for which British soccer hooligans were held mainly responsible. This was highly embarrassing for the Conservative Government, which has always tried to project an image of being tough on law and order. Ministers were therefore obliged to act to protect this image under strong pressure from the Prime Minister.

Following consultations with the police associations and the soccer authorities, the government appeared to accept that alcohol was a major causal factor in crowd violence. Accordingly measures to regulate the sale and consumption of alcohol, at and on the way to sporting events, were incorporated in the Sporting Events (Alcohol Control Etc) Act of 1985. The problem of soccer violence thus forced the government, and also the general public, to consider the role of legal restrictions in the prevention of alcohol-related disorder. It should be noted that there had previously been little enthusiasm to implement controls over alcohol at sporting events in England and Wales, despite the success of similar measures introduced in Scotland during 1980.

The events of 1985 also placed in jeopardy any intention to liberalise the licensing hours. Even so by May 1986 further developments had taken place. The Home Office, following an internal review, decided to back the case for licensing law reform. The following announcement was made by the Home Secretary, Douglas Hurd:

"After carefully studying all the relevant facts and in particular the evidence to emerge from the Scottish experience of longer opening hours the Government believe there is a strong case for considering some relaxation of the restrictions on licensing hours in England and Wales. There is no obvious consensus however on the precise nature of the changes which should be made. We believe it is important that any relaxation should maintain adequate and effective controls on licensed outlets given the concern which exists over alcohol misuse and the need to provide some protection for the public against added noise and nuisance. Any change will require legislation and I cannot give any indication at this stage of when this might be introduced but we support the case for reform in principle."[6]

This statement represented a considerable departure from the statement in *Drinking Sensibly* quoted earlier. After all, the reform of permitted hours was one of Erroll's most controversial recommendations. It also seemed highly inconsistent with the recent decision to restrict alcohol sales at sporting events. How can this shift in policy be explained?

The government's endorsement of the case for changing licensing hours was shaped by a number of factors. First of all, it can be seen as a response to the persistence of the pro-liberalisation campaign. One might have expected that in the aftermath of the reports on alcohol misuse, the proponents of reform would have abandoned their cause. But on the contrary, the brewing, tourism and leisure industries continued to press for change. There were two aspects to this renewed campaign.

On the one hand, the pro-liberalisation lobby made use of its consultative status to restate the case for relaxing the laws. The brewing industry continued to press its views through the Brewing Sector Working Group (SWG). In a report in 1983 the Brewing SWG urged the adoption of a system of longer and more flexible licensing hours to assist the development of the on-licensed trade. (NEDO, 1983 p27) The infrastructure committee of the British Tourist Authority (BTA) was another channel through which these views were conveyed. This committee includes representatives from the Brewers' Society, and the British Hotels Restaurants and Caterers Association (BHRCA), along with government representatives from the Home Office. Over the years the subject of licensing reform has been discussed by the committee on many occasions.

The other aspect of the campaign was the formation of a lobbying organisation to persuade public opinion and Parliament of the need for reform. Following discussions between the supporters of reform, the campaign for flexible hours - FLAG - was officially launched in 1984. A subsidiary (and undisclosed) aim of this new pressure group was to present a united front on the issue of reform. The brewing, leisure and tourism industries were well aware of the damage done to earlier campaigns by the opposition of parts of the licensed trade to reform. For this reason they were particularly keen to get both the NULV and the NALHM to support FLAG. Also, in an attempt to pre-empt any public opposition to liberal reforms, the proponents of FLAG invited the consumer group CAMRA to join the campaign.

The formation of FLAG was therefore part of a strategy to split the opposition to reform, whilst at the same time uniting the pro-liberalisation lobby. Such considerations also lay behind the specific demands of FLAG. The brewing, leisure and tourism industries all wanted longer hours. Yet they knew that flexible hours (ie: the same number of permitted hours but more licensee discretion over actual opening and closing times) was more in line with the wishes of both licensees and consumers. Ihe notion of flexibility was particularly attractive to the NALHM, the major opponents within the trade to longer hours.

The concept of flexible hours also confused the other groups which had former-ly opposed reform. Only the temperance societies now came out unambiguously against reform. Moreover, some elements within the alcohol misuse lobby began to support flexible hours, providing that such changes were accompanied by safe-guards, to prevent them being abused. Such a position was taken by Action on Alcohol Abuse. The BMA were also unclear about whether to oppose flexibility. This undermined the cohesion of the anti-liberalistion lobby and further streng-thened the case for reform.

The resurgence of the pro-liberalisation campaign, and the weakening of its opponents, was also reflected in growing Parliamentary pressure for reform, fol-lowing the creation of FLAG. At first this pressure was fairly low level, being reflected in the tabling of a handful of Parliamentary Questions and several debates. But early in 1986 a dramatic change took place. An Early Day Motion tabled by Roger Gale MP, the Parliamentary advisor to the Scottish and Newcastle drinks company, attracted over 200 signatures by the end of April. (House of Commons, 1986) This number included approximately half of the Conservative Parliamentary Party. At the same time an all-party group of MPs was formed to press for action on the licensing laws. The founder of this group was Michael Colvin MP, the Parliamentary Advisor to the NULV.

The impact of this was compounded by a third factor - the changing attitudes within government itself toward reform. To a large extent this was independent of the pressures discussed so far. Instead the main influence was the Thatcher Government's emphasis upon privatisation and deregulation. The licensing laws were one of a number of regulatory laws examined as part of a general review. The outcome of this review was published in a White Paper during 1985. (Cmnd 9571, 1985) In this document that the government made clear its intention to make a decision on licensing reform in the near future:

"Decisions on whether the opening hours of premises licensed to sell alcoholic drinks should be relaxed will be taken in the light of all relevant considerations.' (p532)

A likely reason for delaying the decision was that a study by the Office of Population Censuses and Surveys (OPCS), of the changes in drinking habits in Scotland since the licensing reforms of 1976, had not yet been published. Ministers felt that a decision could not be made before until this report was publicly avail-able. Although it should be pointed out that there are indications that the govern-ment deliberately delayed the publication of the report so as not to look too incon-sistent with the spirit of the alcohol ban at sports grounds.

The OPCS report was eventually published in February 1986 (OPCS, 1986d) and gave the green light to the government's plans for reform. The government interpreted the report as confirming that licensing reform had been popular in Scotland, and that alcohol consumption had only increased marginally since the changes. The latter point was in fact widely misrepresented: the report showed that consumption since the 1976 Act had risen considerably by 13%, mostly due to a massive increase amongst women drinkers - but this was not attributed to the changes in the law. Moreover, the OPCS report did not examine the effect of the Scottish reforms upon the specific indicators of alcohol misuse, such as the level of liver cirrhosis, and drink-driving and drunkenness offences.

A number of other studies have, however, tried to measure the effect of the law on alcohol abuse levels. Taken together these studies are rather inconclusive: some conclude that no harm has resulted from the legislative changes (Plant and Duffy, 1986; Eagles and Besson, 1985) Whilst others come to the opposite conclusion. (Saunders, 1985) The main reason why these studies have been unable to agree is that the complex relationship between licensing law, drinking, and harm, noted earlier, increases the scope for a wide variety of statistical interpretations.

The inconclusive nature of the evidence on the effect of the Scottish experience was the fourth and final factor behind the government's decision to endorse licensing reform. Moreover, the Scottish public's approval of the changes, indicated by the OPCS report, convinced ministers that similar measures in England and Wales would not be damaging to the government. Indeed there was a strong possibility that the government's endorsement of reform would improve its popularity.

Recent Developments: The 1988 Licensing Act

Following the Home Secretary's announcement of May 1986, the question was no longer whether licensing reform would be introduced, but when. The failure of government to introduce its own bill in the 1986/7 session of Parliament, in view of the crowded legislative timetable, led once again to backbench MPs introducing their own measures. Though this time they proceeded in the knowledge that the government would covertly support their action, by providing adequate Parliamentary time for debate.

Two bills were introduced, both supported by the government and the drinks industry. The first, introduced by Lord Montgomery, sought to abolish the afternoon break in permitted hours in licensed restaurants. The second, which attempted to extend the licensing hours of public houses, was promoted by Allan Stewart MP. Lord Montgomery's bill was successful: the Licensing (Restaurant Meals Act) became law in 1987, much to the joy of the catering industry, with whom Lord Montgomery was closely associated. Stewart's bill was however more controversial. It failed despite passing the committee stage in the House of Commons, where bills are given detailed consideration. As before, the anti-liberalisation lobby had used clever tactics in Parliament to wreck the bill - in particular by tabling amendments which made the legislation unworkable. This lobby also successfully drew media attention to the fact that three of the MPs on the standing committee which considered the bill (Jim Couchman, Michael Colvin and Roger Gale) had vested interests in the drink industry.

But the battle was far from over and the final blow to the anti- liberalisation lobby was soon to come. This was the inclusion of a clause in the Conservative Manifesto of 1987 'to liberalise liquor licensing hours' (Conservative Party, 1987)

Following the party's success at the polls in June, legislation looked inevitable. Indeed there was little delay. On the 4th of August, the Home Office issued a consultative document setting out in detail its plans for reform. (Home Office, 1987c) Subsequently the licensing bill was announced in the Queen's speech and introduced before the Christmas recess.

The passage of the Act

The main feature of the bill was the provision for all day drinking from 11am to 11pm, abolishing the afternoon break in on-licensed premises. However, as a safeguard, the afternoon break could be re-imposed by licensing authorities if they received complaints from the police, schools, or people living or working in the neighbourhood. The bill also contained a number of streamlining clauses to simplify the administrative process of issuing licences. For example, licences would now last for three years instead of one. Though licences could be revoked at any time within this period, if the licensing authorities thought necessary.

Despite the inclusion of safeguards, the government's bill prompted howls of protest from the anti-liberalisation groups. The Royal Colleges of Medicine, the Institute for Alcohol Studies, and Alcohol Concern were particularly vociferous. Their main concern was that the safeguards did not go far enough and that the whole issue of alcohol abuse has been totally ignored by the bill's provisions. They also pointed out that the general public did not support reform along the lines proposed by government. Independent opinion polls taken from 1970 onwards confirm this. The most recent poll in July 1988 showed that 54% opposed longer licensing hours. (*Observer* 24 July 1988)

To coordinate their activities the anti-liberalisation groups formed an organisation called 'Keep Alcohol Safeguards' in 1987. Although the main aim of this body appeared to be to persuade government to drop its plans, the true objective was to secure amendments to the bill introducing new safeguards. It attempted to do this by lobbying ministers, MPs, and peers. Labour MPs were fairly receptive to this pressure, including the Opposition spokeswoman on Home Affairs - Mrs Ann Taylor. MPs associated with the all-party group on alcohol policy also responded to this pressure, including Dr. Lewis Moonie, the chairman of this committee. The anti-liberalisation lobby also sought to mobilise public opinion on the issue, by writing letters to the major newspapers and appearing on television.

But this campaign faced an uphill struggle. Most Conservative MPs supported the bill, with the notable exception of Sir Bernard Braine, who had fought against reform on many occasions in the past. Around 40 Labour MPs supported longer licensing hours. Also the measure had support from many newspapers. Editorials in papers ranging from *The Independent* to the *Sunday People* came out in favour of the proposed reforms. (see *The Independent* 5 August 1987; the *Sunday People* 1 May 1988) It almost goes without saying that the brewers and the licensed trade backed the bill, though it should be noted that the pub managers were still rather lukewarm about the prospect of reform. Their organisation (NALHM) wanted clearer assurances about safeguards to protect their members, many of whom still feared that longer hours would lead to more work for less pay.

Unlike previous campaigns, the NALHM did not work closely with the alcohol misuse groups to combat the legislation and this weakened the anti-liberalisation lobby's cause. But more damaging was the support given to the government's bill by the British Medical Association, in spite of its position on alcohol misuse. In the past the BMA had warned against any relaxation in the licensing laws. But now it appeared to accept the government's view that the Scottish experience had been a success. This was extremely damaging to the anti-liberalisation lobby's case.

Despite facing such difficulties, the anti-liberalisation lobby did have a number of factors operating in its favour. First, the Home Office working party on young people and alcohol (the Masham Committee) had reported in November 1987, backing further restrictions on sales to under-age drinkers. (Home Office 1987b) Second, the government had shown its awareness of the alcohol problem by establishing the ministerial committee on alcohol abuse (the Wakeham Committee) in September 1987. These developments suggested that the government might be persuaded to introduce further safeguards alongside the provisions to extend hours.

A further issue may have also helped the anti-liberalisation lobby. During the first part of 1988, as the licensing bill was passing through its final stages, media attention was focused on the growing incidence of alcohol-related violence and riots. (see for example *The Times* 25 April 1988) Much of this disorder took place in rural towns and villages rather than inner cities, normally the venue for such disturbances. (see ACPO, 1988) This activity, though perhaps sensationalised by the media, nevertheless caused much public concern. The police were in the front line on this issue, and as a matter of urgency convened talks with the Home Office. But this concern, which peaked during June and July 1988, came too late to have much impact upon the Parliamentary debates on the Licensing Bill. Though significantly, the government was persuaded to delay the implementation of the new provisions concerning longer hours until later in the year. By which time public anxiety on this issue had become less intense.

In view of the growing concern over alcohol abuse, which accompanied the introduction of the bill, the anti-liberalisation lobby were able to secure a number of amendments. These went some way towards ameliorating the problem of alcohol misuse. Two main amendments were accepted by the government: one concerned under-age drinking, the other related to the loopholes in the existing law which allowed garages to sell alcohol.

In response to pressure from the Labour members on the standing committee which considered the bill, the Home Office minister, Douglas Hogg, agreed to tighten up the law on sales to under-age drinkers. He accepted in principle that the existing clause governing under-age drinking was inadequate. It was pointed out to him that because the licensee could claim in court that he or she was unaware of the true age of the drinker, prosecutions were unlikely to succeed. The Masham Committee and the Justices' Clerks' Society, amongst others, claimed that this defence effectively protected the licensee from prosecution, and called for the offence to be made absolute. This would mean that even if the under-age drinker appeared to look over eighteen, the licensee could still be prosecuted. Not surprisingly such a move was opposed by brewers and licensees, who feared a dramatic rise in prosecutions against the trade.

In view of this opposition, Hogg shifted his ground. Instead of proposing that the offence be made absolute, he introduced a new amendment at report stage which would enable licensees to defend themselves against prosecution if they could prove that they had exercised all due diligence when serving alcohol, and had no reason to suspect that the person in question was under-age. This went a long way towards satisfying the licensed trade's fears, and was roundly criticised by the anti-liberalisation lobby. Sir Bernard Braine commented:

"It is difficult to escape the conclusion that the Government have bowed to pressure from the Brewers' Society and other drinks industry representations on this matter"[7]

The anti-liberalisation lobby also tried to amend the bill in the Commons in an attempt to prevent garages from selling alcohol. They were also supported on this matter by the police and anti-drink driving groups. Though unsuccessful at this stage, a further attempt was made as the bill passed through the House of Lords. This amendment, tabled by Viscount Falkland - the vice chairman of the all-party group on alcohol policy - and Lady Ewart-Biggs, was successful. The government agreed to alter the bill, providing that existing licences were not affected. So whilst the new Act prevents any new application for a licence by garages, those currently selling alcohol will be allowed to continue doing so.

But the anti-liberalisation lobby were not alone in tabling amendments. The drinks industry too obtained a number of changes to the bill, the most important being the addition of an extra hour of drinking time on Sundays. Originally, despite pressure from the industry, the government made no provision to change licensing hours on Sunday. This was largely in view of the power of the anti-Sunday trading lobby, which had in 1986 spectacularly defeated the government's Shops bill. Ministers were not prepared to take on the lobby once again, and believed that the entire bill might be jeopardised if it sought to extend permitted hours on Sundays. Clearly backdoor methods had to be used, and the way in which the industry secured its objectives made a mockery of Parliamentary procedures.

During the Commons stages of the bill the Home Office ministers consistently objected to attempts to insert a clause on Sunday hours by MPs connected with the drinks industry. But when the bill reached the Lords a further amendment to increase Sunday hours was put forward by Lord Harmar-Nichols (who, incidentally, declared his financial interests in the hotel trade). What happened next bordered on the farcical. The Home Office spokesman in the Lords, Lord Ferrers, allowed the amendment to pass by mistake. This apparent 'cock-up' was later shown to be more of a conspiracy. For when the bill returned to the Commons, the amendment was accepted in spite of ministers' earlier assurances. As a result, the Licensing Act extended permitted hours on Sunday lunchtime by one hour, though an afternoon break was still retained.

Other developments

It could be argued that the reform of the licensing laws paradoxically assisted the case of the alcohol misuse lobby by highlighting the apparent inconsistency in government policy on alcohol. The media, though broadly supporting the relaxation in licensing hours, could not resist spotlighting the possible implications of deregulation in the light of what appeared to be a deterioration in the alcohol problem. Even so, the 1988 Act was a mainly a liberalising measure, and it remains to be seen whether or not it will make matters worse.

Many in the alcohol industry are aware that they are on trial, in the sense that any future deterioration in the problem will be blamed on the Act for which they lobbied so strongly. The industry feels particularly vulnerable on the question of under-age drinking, and in an effort to reduce this problem have launched a series of initiatives to put their own house in order before anyone else (ie: government) does. The Brewers' Society has therefore launched a campaign called 'Agewatch' to alert licencees of their responsibilities with respect to under-age drinking. The National Union of Licensed Victuallers meanwhile has drawn up plans to persuade its members to operate identity card systems, so that drinkers on the borderline of the drinking age can be identified more easily.

The government has announced that it does not want to become involved directly in the administration of these activities, though it broadly supports the industry's 'voluntary' attempts to tackle the problem of under-age drinking. The alcohol misuse lobby also applauds the industry's response, but would nevertheless prefer the government to take a more interventionist role.

On the issue of drinking in public places, however, the government has taken a more positive stance. This particular issue attracted public and ministerial interest in 1988 against the backcloth of drink-related public disorder. Coventry City Council, following pressure from local business in the main, decided to draw up a draft by-law banning drinking in public places. It asked the Home Office for the necessary approval and this was granted in July 1988. The Coventry by-law is clearly being seen in official circles as a pilot scheme, and other areas, including a number of seaside resorts - traditional hotspots for drink-related mayhem - are set to adopt similar rules in the light of the Coventry experience.

Another issue, which has not really been touched on in recent debates, is the question of outlet proliferation. Yet this widely believed by many in both the drinks industry and the alcohol misuse lobby to be a major factor in the growth of Britain's drink problem. The number of outlets selling drink, particularly off-licences, has increased dramatically in recent years as we earlier noted. One reason for the proliferation of outlets has been that many licensing authorities have either been unable or unwilling to restrict the number of licences granted. Although, as mentioned in the first section of this chapter, licensing authorities have in principle absolute discretion in granting licences, in practice they are hamstrung. Hotel and

Restaurant licences cannot be refused if the establishment is fulfilling its stated purpose. Licensing authority decisions are subject to appeal and their decisions can be overturned by the courts. Many licensing authorities do not have a policy on restricting the total number of outlets in their locality. Taken together these factors undermine the regulatory function of the licensing authorities and account for the dramatic growth in outlets.

A number of organisations have called upon licensing authorities to reassert their role in tackling alcohol misuse by restricting the growth in licences. These include bodies as diverse as Action on Alcohol Abuse and the National Union of Licensed Victuallers. But what is really needed it seems is a lead from central government to try and coordinate policy in this area. There are signs that this is beginning to happen. In recent months both the Home Secretary and the Secretary of State for Scotland have urged licensing authorities to take into account the problems of alcohol misuse when exercising their functions.

Finally, a brief word about another piece of legislation which became law in 1988. The Licensing (Retail Sales) Act began as a backbench bill, sponsored by Andrew Mackay MP. Supported by the government, the drinks industry, and the alcohol misuse lobby, this measure tightens up the law on the wholesaling of alcoholic drink. More specifically, it prohibits wholesalers from selling alcohol from the back of lorries at outdoor events at carnivals and other outdoor events. It is worth noting that the wholesale trade is not subject to the same restrictions as retailers, and that this had been causing concern for many years amongst both the industry and the alcohol misuse lobby.

Conclusion

The alcohol misuse lobby has been mainly, though not wholly, on the defensive on the issue of licensing law reform. This contrasts with its promotional stance on most other policy issues, such as taxation, advertising controls and so on. In view of this difference, two important questions need to be asked. First, has the alcohol misuse lobby achieved a greater degree of success on the licensing issue, than on others? Second, if it has, can this be attributed to the different role which the lobby has found itself playing?

When examining the policy making process it is never easy to establish whether one party or another has been successful. The present chapter illustrates this well. On the one hand it could be said that the alcohol misuse lobby has failed to prevent liberalisation of the licensing laws in the post-war period. But such a conclusion does not give adequate weight to the undoubted success of the lobby in opposing liberalisation in England and Wales in the seventies and early eighties. Also, it should be remembered that several licensing reform issues - the question of allowing children in public bars, and the reduction of the drinking age limit, for example - were effectively removed from the political agenda, as a result of the lobby's efforts. More recently the alcohol misuse lobby has been engaged in damage limitation, tabling amendments with some success to the governments licensing legislation; and using the issue of reform to re-open debates about the misuse of alcohol and the role of the state in relation to this problem.

But then again it could be argued that the drink industry got its own way in the end, once it had patched up the major divisions within its ranks. Once it had achieved this perhaps reform was only a matter of time. Its influence pervaded all key decision makers and opinion formers in Government, Parliament and the media. Above all the inclusion of licensing reform on the Conservative Manifesto reveals much about the extent of the industry's power and influence today.

But maybe one should not go overboard about the power of the industry. To a large extent the industry's desire for relaxed licensing hours of late fitted in with the government's own ideological stance, and the interests of a number of government departments. As with most of the other alcohol issues examined, the development of policy has been greatly influenced by broader political undercurrents. Liberal licensing reforms in England and Wales were possible because of the government's overall policy on deregulation. Had the public order problems associated with alcohol become more of an issue earlier than they did, it seems likely that the legislation would have been at least postponed. Such issues as deregulation and hooliganism lie outside the control of both lobbies and this once again illustrates how alcohol policy has been shaped by broader concerns and issues.

Notes

1. *House of Commons Official Report* Volume 102 Column 155w 22 July 1986
2. *House of Commons Official Report* Volume 808 Column 98w 8 December 1970
3. *House of Commons Official Report* Volume 800 Column 1247-50 29 April 1970; and Volume 877 Column 8 15 July 1974
4. *House of Commons Official Report* Volume 906 Column 820-69 27 February 1976; Volume 913 Column 75-1059 18 June 1976; Volume 915 Column 1144-235 16 July 1976.
5. *House of Lords Official Report* Volume 442 Column 411 9 May 1983
6. *House of Commons Official Report* Volume 98 Column 16-17w 19 May 1986
7. *House of Commons Official Report* Volume 126 Column 1016 3 February 1988

8 Drinking and driving: a successful campaign?

As we have seen, successive British Governments have refused to adopt policies which have the potential to regulate the overall consumption of alcohol. But they have been prepared to impose restrictions on certain sections of the community deemed to be particularly at risk from alcohol problems. The recent changes to the licensing laws (see chapter seven) on the subject of under-age drinking, for example, represented an attempt to restrict consumption amongst young people. The drink driving laws, the subject of this chapter, also restrict the drinking habits of a section of the community whose drinking habits have serious implications for public health and safety: motorists.

During the last thirty years or so, a number of legislative measures have been introduced with the intention of reducing the level of alcohol-related road accidents. Over time considerable resources have also been allocated to publicity programmes which warn of the dangers of drinking and driving. In 1987 the Department of Transport spent £2.5m on its anti-drink driving campaign, a figure which dwarfs the Health Education Authority's budget on alcohol education (£500,000 in the same year).[1] Why then has the government been prepared to back action on the specific problem of drinking and driving, whilst at the same time rejecting a general policy of controlling alcohol consumption? By examining the development of drinking and driving policy during the post-war period, it may be possible to identify those factors which have promoted such a positive response from government on this issue.

The development of drink driving policy in the UK is best seen in five distinct phases; each of these phases will be examined in turn. First, we look at how the issue arrived on the political agenda during the late fifties and sixties, and the minor changes in the law which were made in response to this. Second, the background to the introduction of the Road Safety Act of 1967, which amongst other things introduced the breathalyser and a legal limit of alcohol for drivers, will be examined. The third section deals with the period following the passage of this Act and the subsequent appointment of a committee of inquiry to look into the operation of the drink driving laws. Next, we look at the fate of this committee's report and the genesis of the 1981 Transport Act, which incorporated some of its recommendations. Finally, we examine some recent developments, inin particular the growing strength of the campaign for random breath testing, a measure which some argue is the only way in which the problem of drinking driving will ever be effectively curbed.

Drink Driving on the Agenda

During the fifties, public concern about road safety began to mount in line with a dramatic growth in road accidents and casualties. Between 1950 and 1960 the annual number of accidents in Great Britain increased by over 60%; casualties by 70%. By the end of this decade almost 350,000 people were killed or injured on Britain's roads evey year. (Ministry of Transport, 1960) There were several suggestions put forward to account for this alarming trend: the greater number of motor cars on the road, the increased use of roads by freight traffic, and drinking and driving.

Although it had been an offence since 1925 'to be drunk while in charge... of any mechanically controlled vehicle'[2] the law was under-enforced. Even so, in 1955 almost 5,000 offences of driving under the influence of drink or drugs were recorded by the police. These statistics, along with the growing recognition that they represented ontly the tip of the iceberg, highlighted the link between drinking, driving, and road accidents.

In addition to general atmosphere of public concern, reinforced to an extent by the press, a number of pressure groups also began to stress the implications of drinking and driving for road safety. The British Medical Association and the Pedestrian's Association were very active on this issue, calling for better enforcement of the existing law. The police were also generally sympathetic to these demands, as were the Ministry of Transport (MoT) and the Home Office, though they claimed that little could be done within the present legal framework.

In response to these pressures, the Transport Minister set up a special committee in 1956, comprising officials from his ministry alongside representatives of the police associations. The committee was to review the law on drink driving, particularly the problems involved in proving the offences in court under the existing law - which many saw as the main obstacle to securing more convictions.

The question of proof was also crucial in another sense. Not only was enforcement difficult in the absence of a legally valid and objective test that would prove conclusively that an offence had been committed: it was also difficult to alter the law in order to provide for such a test in the absence of hard evidence that drinking and driving was a direct cause of road accidents. The lack of evidence in the latter sense lay behind the government's subequent refusal to change the law on drinking and driving in any significant way during the fifties. The only concession it felt confident enough to make at this time was a minor amendment to the 1956 Road Traffic Act which reduced penalties for drunken drivers who were in charge of a vehicle but who were not driving or attempting to drive. The thinking behind this was that it would dissuade such motorists from continuing their journey, thus removing a potential hazard from the road.

This move revealed that the government believed that drinking and driving had implications for road safety. Indeed as early as 1953 the Minister of Transport had broadcast messages on the BBC about the dangers of drinking and driving. But the government made it clear that further legislative changes could only be made in the light of more evidence about the relationship between drinking and driving and road accidents.

In actual fact the MoT was itself actively involved in trying to produce further evidence, in conjuction with the medical profession. In 1953, a joint initiative by the Medical Research Council (MRC) and the MoT's research body, the Transport and Road Research Laboratory (TRRL) led to a programme of research into the effects of alcohol on motorists. One of the most significant of these early studies was the Drew report which was completed in 1958. (MRC, 1958) This report catalogued the effect of drink on the individual's capacity to judge speed, distance and movement. Its findings confirmed that the motorist's consumption of alcohol impaired those functions necessary for safe driving. In the following year TRRL examined the effect of drinking on road accidents over the Christmas period. Its report showed that alcohol was the main factor in road accidents over the festive season. (TRRL, 1960) The availability of stronger evidence improved the prospects of a change in the law. By late 1960 the MoT appeared to be convinced of the need for new legislation. But this was not entirely due to the fresh evidence. Other factors were also at work.

First of all, the two main groups in favour of legislative change, the BMA and the Pedestrian's Association, had begun to articulate their demands more effectively. The BMA published an authoritative report in 1960 which concluded that 'the police must be given power to stop cars and require drivers to submit to chemical tests.' (BMA, 1960) The BMA was now therefore recommending not only better enforcement but specific changes in the law to achieve this. It believed that chemical tests, by giving an indication of the amount of alcohol present in the motorist's body, would go a long way to solving the problem of proving offences in court. As a result, the BMA argued, the law would also be more effective in deterring drinking drivers.

Whilst the BMA used its professional status to obtain access to officials, and was able to present the case for reform through these channels, the Pedestrian's Association was mainly concerned with trying to influence Parliamentary opinion. In 1959, Graham Page MP - the chairman of the Pedestrian's Association - introduced a private members bill which sought to tighten up the law on drinking and driving by, amongst other things, introducing roadside tests and a legal limit for motorists. Although the bill failed, it nevertheless indicated to the government that such a measure attracted considerable support from MPs. This was important since it demonstrated that legislation could be introduced on this cross-party issue without prompting an embarrassing backbench revolt.

It is worth pointing out that apart from Page's bill, and others introduced in subsequent sessions, Parliament did not play a great role in forcing the issue on to the political agenda. Instead Parliamentary activities, such as debates and PQs are best interpreted as being supportive of government intervention rather than promotional. This is perhaps confirmed by the fact that the average annual number of PQs tabled on the issue of drinking and driving rose significantly after the 1961/2 session of Parliament, by which time the government was already actively considering further legislation. The annual average of PQs during the years 1951-1961 was 4.7 PQs per session; this increased to 7.4 per session between 1961 and 1966. Even so, such Parliamentary activities played an important part in maintaining the issue on the political agenda, by demonstrating a considerable level of support for action on drinking and driving.

In addition to pressure group and Parliamentary activity, public opinion also appeared to favour further legislation. According to an opinion poll conducted by Gallup in March 1955, 75% of the public believed that motorists involved in road accidents should be subjected to a roadside test for alcohol. (Gallup, 1975) Although such polls only provide a rough guide to the state of public opinion, the evidence of such a large majority in favour convinced ministers that the issue was unlikely to be a vote loser.

The third factor which encouraged the government to initiate reform was the experience of other countries in testing motorists for alcohol. In February 1960 the Minister for Transport, Ernest Marples, sent a working party to Scandanavia to examine the operation of the drink driving laws there. Under Swedish law it was an offence to drive a motor vehicle with an amount of alcohol in the body over and above a specified legal limit. Swedish police also had strong enforcement powers and were able to stop and test motorists at their discretion.

Following the working party's report, the Minister of Transport, along with the Home Secretary (who has responsible for law enforcement) agreed that reform was necessary. Subsequently, in the Queen's Speech at the beginning of the 1960/1 session of Parliament, the government committed itself to legislation. Later in the session the Road Traffic Bill was introduced into the House of Lords. The bill sought to improve the enforcement of the law on drink driving, by clarifying the existing offence of 'unfit to drive' and requiring the courts to consider chemical evidence relating to the level of alcohol in the motorists' body. It also gave ministers the power to introduce breath testing machines (breathalysers) at a future date if they so wished. These machines, which were used in Scandanavia, could be used as a screening test, indicating whether or not a further chemical test (on a sample of the motorists' blood or urine) was necessary.

In the event however the bill was lost. The lack of Parliamentary time was the official explanation given, and this appeared to reflect the relatively low priority of road safety in the government's overall legislative programme. This prompted an angry response from road safety groups, though they were placated by the government's assurances that the bill would be reintroduced shortly. It was indeed enacted in the following session, becoming law in 1962.

It should be noted that the new legislation did not go as far as the systems operating in the Scandanavian countries. It did not introduce a legal limit, nor did it give the police the power to automatically check motorists at their discretion: a motorist could only be subjected to a breath test if involved in an accident. So the 1962 Road Traffic Act was in fact a compromise. On the one hand it tried to satisfy the demands of the road safety lobby; whilst at the same time seeking to placate those who opposed the change in law.

The idea of a legal limit, and the extension of police powers to test motorists for alcohol, attracted opposition from two main sources. First of all, the motoring organisations - the Automobile Association (AA), the Royal Automobile Club (RAC), and its Scottish counterpart, the SRAC- were not convinced that such changes in the law would be in the interests of the motorist. The MoT regarded these organisations as the representatives of motoring opinion and listened carefully to their views. Moreover it realised that the motoring organisations often played a key role in implementing policy - by publicising changes in the law - and therefore it was important to secure their cooperation, as far as possible.

The opposition of these organisations appears to have been a significant factor in the government's rejection of both the legal limit and the extension of police powers at this time. But a second source of opposition was also relevant. This was the Law Society, which argued that many of the changes proposed by the road safety lobby were unwarranted. In view of its status as a respected professional body, ministers attached considerable weight to the Society's views. This was perhaps a further reason why some of the more radical measures were not adopted.

Despite having to compromise in 1962, the MoT and the Home Office recognised that further reform would be necessary. They also realised that stronger measures would require the consent of the dissenting groups, especially the motoring organisations. The MoT believed that this could be brought about in two ways. First, through a high profile publicity programme about drinking and driving. This began in June 1964, and was intended not just to promote sensible attitudes amongst motorists, but also to convince motoring opinion (and hopefully the motoring organisations which claimed to represent their interests) less resistant to further legislative change. Secondly, the Ministry had the TRRL conduct further studies of the effects of drinking and driving in an attempt to establish the kind of evidence that might persuade the motoring organisations to change their position.

A further report from the TRRL - which appeared in 1964 - in conjunction with the publicity programme, began to weaken the resistance of the motoring organisations. They gradually began to accept in principle the need for further changes in the law. Two other developments around this time also appear to have been significant in this respect. In addition they appeared to be convinced by a new research report from the United States which also emerged in 1964. This was the so-called 'Grand Rapids' study, which provided conclusive evidence that the actual amount of alcohol in the body was strongly correlated with the probability of having an accident. Moreover, beyond a certain level this risk factor worsened significantly. (Borkenstein, 1964) This is illustrated by the following example. A driver with a concentration of 80mg of alcohol per 100ml of blood in his body (the present legal limit) was shown to be twice as likely to have an accident than a motorist who has not been drinking at all; when the blood-alcohol concentration increases to 150mg/100ml (twice the current legal limit) the driver is ten times more likely to be involved in an accident compared to a sober motorist.

The mounting evidence about the dangers of drinking and driving, continued pressure from the medical profession and road safety organisations, and the willingness of the motoring organisations to countenance further restrictions increased the prospectd for further reform. The appointment of a new Transport Minister, Tom Fraser MP, by the incoming Labour Government of 1964 was also a significant development. Fraser was believed to be particularly sympathetic towards the case for a stronger law on drinking and driving. With his backing the MoT along with the Home Office undertook a joint review of the law towards the end of 1964.

The MoT-Home Office review focused on the question of a legal limit. The consensus was that driving skills became seriously impaired beyond a level of 80mg of alcohol per 100ml of blood. The BMA in a further report, and in discussions with the two departments, was the main proponent of this limit. (see BMA, 1965) The government decided to accept this advice and on the 14 April 1965, the Minister for Transport made the following statement in the House of Commons:

"The government accepts in principle that it should be made an offence to drive with more than a prescribed amount of alcohol in the blood."[3]

The actual level of the legal limit was to remain unknown outside government circles until the publication of the government's White Paper later in the year. Meanwhile the other main issue - concerning police powers to conduct alcohol tests at the roadside - still had to be resolved. A Home Office working party was established in an attempt to settle this particular matter, and we shall consider its findings in the next section.

The Road Safety Act 1967

By 1965 the issue of drinking and driving was firmly lodged on the political agenda, and had been for a number of years. The government's response to the pressures which had been building up during this time was the Road Safety Act of 1965, the subject of this section. The government heralded its legislation with a

White Paper on Road Safety, published in December 1965. (Cmnd 2859, 1965)

Although there was by now a general consensus that further legislation was needed to tackle the problem of drinking and driving, the government's proposals nevertheless aroused much controversy. (see *The Times* 22 December 1965) The main area of disagreement concerned the extension of police powers to test motorists. Although the need for a legal limit was widely accepted, some still had reservations about how this should be enforced.

The government, following the recommendations of the Home Office working party set up to examine testing procedures, opted for 'random testing'. This meant that the police would not have to justify their decision to test motorists; such tests would instead be conducted at their discretion. The alternative procedure was to restrict police discretion by allowing them to test motorists only in certain circumstances: for example, when they had been involved in an accident, or if the police had strong reasons to believe that the motorist had been drinking.

The government's support for random testing was hotly contested. The motoring organisations, despite their support for further legislation, were incensed at the decision. The RAC and the AA announced their determination to fight the proposals and made clear their refusal to cooperate with the MoT in publicising the new measures to their members. The opposition of the motoring organisations should not have come as a surprise to MoT as they were in touch with the AA and the RAC before the White Paper was published and were well aware of their views. But the motoring organisations lacked influence at the Home Office, and since it appeared that the decision to adopt random testing was initiated by the Home Office rather than the MoT, this was a point of some significance.

The motoring organisations now had to try an alternative strategy if they were to defeat the government's intentions. They realised that the measure could now only be defeated in Parliament. But they were not without their allies in the House. The Conservative Parliamentary Committee on Transport was also opposed to random testing, on the grounds that it infringed individual liberties. Their pledge to fight the measure introduced party politics into what was essentially a cross-party issue. This worried the Labour Government, which believed that if the Conservative Opposition mobilised against the measure, then voting in Parliament would be close. The possibility of an embarrassing defeat for the government was very real indeed, as at this time it had a tiny majority of four in the House of Commons.

A further source of opposition to random testing was the licensed trade. The publican's associations were particularly concerned that random testing would discourage customers and damage their business. But in general the response from this quarter was fairly low-key. This was because at this time the issue of drinking and driving was seen as primarily a road safety issue with libertarian implications, rather than an alcohol control issue. Another reason for the muted response of the drinks industry during this period was that sections of it stood to gain if drinking and driving was further restricted. The off-licence trade in particular could expect its sales to increase if people decided to drink at home instead of driving to the pub.

Finally, some of the police associations, particularly the Police Federation (which represents ranks up to inspector), had reservations about random testing. They were mainly concerned about the manpower implications of this procedure, believing that it would place upon them an obligation which could not be met in the light of present resource constraints. Their unease was highly damaging to the government's case, since the police were broadly on its side; they supported new legislation on drinking and driving in principle. The government was thus alienating one of its strongest supporters by pursing random testing. But above all, the co-operation of the police was essential if the new law was to operate effectively.

So despite the widespread agreement in principle about the need for a stronger law on drink driving, serious divisions began to emerge on matters of procedure. Even so the government persisted with its original proposals as set out in the White Paper. In January 1966 the Road Safety Bill was introduced by the newly-appointed Transport Minister, Barbara Castle - who like her predecessor was committed to reform. But it was during the bill's second reading in the Commons, a month later, the controversy over random testing came to a head. Seven MPs spoke out in favour of the measure; nine against. As expected, most of the opposition came from MPs connected with the Conservative Transport Committee. Significantly one of the most vociferous of this group was also the RAC's Parliamentary adviser, Sir Richard Nugent MP.[4]

Despite a rough ride the bill passed through its second reading stage, and was subsequently considered by a standing committee. But the committees' deliberations were interrupted by the calling of a general election in March and the bill was lost. The return of a Labour Government, and the return of Castle as Secretary of State for Transport, led to anticipation that the bill would be automatically re-introduced. Indeed it was, but only after a heated argument within cabinet, which Castle won with the assistance of the Prime Minister, Harold Wilson. (Castle, 1976) Yet it soon became clear that this represented not an outright victory but a compromise. For when the new bill was published in November 1966, the commitment to random testing had been dropped. Instead, police discretion was to be restricted; they would only be allowed to test motorists if they appeared to be under the influence of drink, if they had committed a moving traffic offence, or if they had been involved in an accident.

Castle denied that the decision to drop random testing had been the result of organised lobbying against the proposal. She claimed that the changes were made in response to public opinion:

"Though the opposition to this proposal totally failed to convince me that our plans were wrong it did convince me that enough people thought that we would in some sense unjustly persecute completely innocent motorists to make me think again."[5]

But evidence from opinion polls suggested that a majority of the public was actually in favour of random testing. In a Gallup Poll taken in January 1966, 59% of the respondents supported such a move. (Gallup, 1975 p849) The state of public opinion on this issue was further revealed by a poll conducted in early 1967, which indicated that 71% of the public believed that the government's measures were not strict enough. (Gallup, 1975 p909)

Even so, Castle was particularly keen to deny that the decision to drop random testing had been due in any way to the opposition of the motoring organisations. She pointed out that on other issues, such as the decision in 1965 to impose a 70 MPH speed limit on previously unrestricted roads, the opposition of these groups had not prevented the goverment from legislating. There was however a great deal of difference between these two issues. On the issue of random testing, the motoring organisations could rely on the support of other groups, such as the Police Federation and the Conservative Commmittee on Transport, and parts of the licensed trade. Together these groups formed a strong coalition. Indeed, as Galbraith, the chairman of the Conservative Parliamentary Committee on Transport, suggested, Castle had seen the red light on the issue of random testing.[6]

The critics of the bill won a significant victory here. The Conservative Transport Committee continued to try to dilute it further. Awdry, the committee's vice-chairman, tried to alter the bill so as to make the twelve month ban on conviction of a drink driving offence a discretionary rather than, as it stood, an automatic sentence. He was not succesful. The government also opposed amendments which were aimed at strengthening the law. For example, when Alex Lyon MP and Frank Hooley MP, both of whom were Labour MPs having connections with the temperance movement, tried to reintroduce random testing during the bill's passage, the government forced them to drop their amendments.

But even after the Road Safety Act became law in 1967, the issue of random testing was still salient. The Home Office, it appeared, was still in favour of this procedure. This was revealed by its advice to chief constables just before the new Act came into operation in October. A circular was issued which emphasised that motorists could still be breathalysed for any moving traffic offence, even those not directly related to the ability to drive, such as faulty brakes, lights and so on. (Home Office, 1967) The motoring organisations saw this as a way of introducing random testing 'through the back door'. They believed that the Home Office was encouraging the police to use the law in a way contrary to the intentions of Parliament. As we shall see later on in this chapter the controversy surrounding random testing is still with us.

The Aftermath... Then Blennerhasset

Despite the controversy surrounding its introduction, the Road Safety Act of 1967 was subsequently hailed as a great success. Accidents during Christmas 1967 were 37% down on the previous year.[7] Significantly the proportion of drivers killed in road accidents having a blood alcohol level over the legal limit fell dramatically after the introduction of the Act. In the ten months before October 1967, a quarter of these drivers had a blood alcohol level of 80mg/100ml and over. Twelve months later this proportion had fallen to 15%. This indicated that the Act was having a marked impact on the drinking habits of motorists. It was subsequently estimated that between 1967 and 1974 5,000 lives were saved, and 200,000 injuries prevented, by the Road Safety Act of 1967. (Birch, 1985) More recently the total number of lives saved since the Act has been put at around 13,000. (Action on Drinking and Driving, 1987)

Despite these considerable achievements, the problems of drinking and driving continued to grow as time passed. By 1971, the proportion of drivers killed in road accidents who were over the legal limit had risen to 20%. By 1972, it had returned to its 1967 level. Road accidents in turn continued to rise dramatically from this time.

One reason why the old trend began to re-establish itself was that motorists gradually realised that the actual chances of being caught and prosecuted for drink driving offences were relatively low. This was in spite of the fact that the proportion of positive breath tests actually rose between 1969 and 1973. The chances of being caught were low partly because of the limited resources of the police, and partly because of the restrictions on breath testing placed on them by the 1967 Act.

Although the Home Office, as we saw earlier, had been accused of introducing random testing by the back door, the police kept well within the law. Indeed it became increasingly evident that their powers were too restricted and that this hampered the enforcement of the legal limit. As a result there was a growing constituency of support for giving the police wider discretion to test motorists.

Road safety organisations such as the Pedestrian's Association and the Royal Society for the Prevention of Accidents (RoSPA) had favoured such an approach for quite a time. But by the mid-seventies even the motoring organisations and police associations - which had been opposed to random testing in the sixties - supported what they now preferred to call 'discretionary testing'. In point of fact there was little difference between random testing, as defined in the 1965 White Paper, and discretionary testing. Both implied that the police would no longer have to justify tests on specific grounds. But the motoring organisations and the police associations nevertheless maintained that the two were not the same. They believed that random testing implied the use of roadside checkpoints to stop and test motorists 'at random'. Whilst accepting the need for discretionary testing, they therefore still remained opposed to random testing.

There was also much concern about the number of motorists who managed to escape prosecution by exploiting loopholes in the law. The existence of such loopholes also served to reduce the law's effect as a deterrent to drinking and driving. Since 1967, defence lawyers had proved resourceful in securing acquittals on technical grounds. Many of these acquittals were clearly against the spirit of the 1967 legislation - in one celebrated case the accused was acquitted simply because the police officer who had administered the breath test was not wearing his hat! (the 1967 Act specifies clearly that a breath test must be administered by a police officer in uniform; the defence claimed successfully that a policeman without a hat was not 'in uniform'). Incidents of this kind led to demands that the law be clarified from a range of bodies including the Law Society, the Bar Council, the police associations, the Magistrates Association, the road safety organisations, and the motoring organisations.

Other groups also supported a tightening up of the law at this time. These included the BMA, the National Council on Alcoholism, and the temperance organsations. But these groups blamed the increase in road accidents not just on deficiences in the law but on the overall level of alcohol consumption, which was increasing dramatically during the early seventies. In essence they saw drinking driving as yet another symptom of the general problem of alcohol misuse, rather than a special problem in itself. This is not to say that the other anti-drink driving groups were ignorant of the general problem of alcohol misuse. Indeed a number of these organisations suspected that many drunken drivers were in fact addicted to alcohol and that different procedures would have to be formulated to deal with these people. This broader perception was displayed particularly by RoSPA and the Automobile Association both of which have called for more restrictions on drivers suffering from drink problems.

The government too began to recognise that the increase in overall alcohol consumption was a factor behind the rising toll of drink-related accidents, though it rarely admitted this publicly. The following statement in 1974 by Lord Elwyn Jones, then Lord Chancellor, reveals much about the government's thinking at this time:

"...the consumption of alcohol in the community has increased rapidly in the last few years with inevitable repercussions on our roads."[8]

Dissatisfaction with the operation of the 1967 Act, coupled with the concern about alcohol misuse in general led to a review of the drink driving laws. This took the form of a departmental committee of enquiry established in 1974 by the Department of the Environment (DoE). This department had been responsible for road safety matters since 1970, when it absorbed the MoT. But the issue of drink driving still cut across departmental lines, and other departments were closely involved with the review. For example, the DHSS, Home Office, and the Scottish and Welsh Offices, all appointed assessors to oversee the committee's work. The actual membership of the committee though reflected the government's emphasis that the main issue was law enforcement, rather than public health. Three of the twelve members practised law, including the committee chairman, Frank Blennerhasset QC. A further two were chief constables. Other specialists were also included: a representative from TRRL, a Home Office Forensic Scientist, a medical officer with a background in transport, and an expert in alcohol addiction. The other three are lay members.

The Blennerhasset Committee presented its report to the DoE in December 1975. It made six main recommendations, as follows:

1.   That the present legal limit remain at 80mg of alcohol per 100ml of blood.
2.   That wherever possible in future admissible evidence of excess alcohol levels be established by breath samples, rather than blood or urine tests.
3.   That proof of offence be less dependent on technical procedures set out in the law.

4. Continued publicity on the dangers of drinking and driving.
5. That police be given wider powers of discretion to test motorists.
6. The need to a establish a 'high risk offender' procedure, whereby persistent offenders and drivers who drank heavily would not have their licences returned until they could prove that they were no longer suffering from drinking problems.

The Genesis of the Transport Act 1981

Nine months passed before the government accepted the Blennerhasset report as a basis for legislation. This delay was mainly the result of disagreements within government over the committee's recommendations on discretionary testing and the high risk offender (recommendations 5 and 6 above). Eventually a temporary compromise was reached. In its statement on the 4th of August 1976 the government accepted the principle of a high risk offender procedure. But the question of discretionary testing was not mentioned, indicating that it still had to be resolved.

It was the government's failure to resolve the discretionary testing issue which was chiefly responsible for the delay in reforming the drink driving laws. Even though the Blennerhasset Report had been accepted by the government, legislation was not introduced until 1981. Yet the Department of Transport (DoT) - which now once again a department in its own right having split from the DoE - wanted to implement Blennerhasset much earlier and was particularly keen to introduce discretionary testing. The Secretary of State for Transport during the late seventies, William Rodgers, was clearly in favour of giving the police wider discretion. The Home Sectretary, as far as can be established did not oppose this personally, though there are indications that Home Office civil servants advised caution, having had their fingers bitten in the late sixties on this issue.

Other cabinet colleagues were less enthusiastic about putting legislation before Parliament. At this time the Labour Government had a very small majority in the Commons and the government feared an embarrassing defeat in the House. So although public support for reform was still running quite high, even amongst motorists (see Gallup Political Index, 1986), the introduction of legislation at this time was nevertheless seen as a considerable political risk.

There were also a number of technical, rather than political, reasons why legislation could not be introduced immediately. The high risk offender procedure for example raised a number of complex issues. A major sticking point concerned the criteria needed to establish whether or not it was safe to return the offender's licence after his period of suspension. Some way of proving that the individual in question was no longer a risk would have to be found. Yet in practice it was difficult to determine this conclusively. In order to resolve this issue, the government opened discussions with the National Council on Alcoholism (NCA).

Another technical delay related to the second recommendation of the Blennerhasset Report, noted above - evidential breath testing. Since 1967 the police had used the breathalyser as a screening test for motorists. If the test proved positive, the motorist then had to give a sample of blood or urine, which provided evidence for the prosecution. The Blennerhasset Committee believed that the accuracy of breath-testing machines had improved sufficiently enough to be used as direct evidence. Although the government accepted this recommendation, it pointed out that a new generation of breath testing machines would be required, and that these would have to be rigorously tested. This would obviously take some time to complete.

As a result of these practical and political factors, the Labour Government never legislated on drink driving. But in 1979, following the election of the Conservative Government, it seemed that the period of delay was coming to an end. In August 1979 the new Secretary of State for Transport, Norman Fowler, announced that a Green Paper on drinking and driving was being prepared. This sudden burst of activity, after five years of delay, can be explained by three developments.

First of all, Fowler himself was strongly in favour of implementing the Blennerhasset recommendations as quickly as possible. He had raised the issue in Parliament several times whilst in opposition. Secondly, the Conservative Government had a large majority in Parliament. So the chances that its legislation could be overturned by a backbench revolt were considerably less than its predecessor. Third, most of the technical problems which had played a part in preventing the early implementation of Blennerhasset, had by this time been fully examined. The government could no longer argue with credibility that technical factors were still responsible for the delay.

When the government's Green Paper was published in December 1979, it bore a remarkable similarity to the Labour Government's statement on the Blennerhasset report in August 1976. The recommendations on the legal limit, evidential breath testing, loopholes in the law, and publicity, were all accepted; but the government reserved judgement on the high risk offender procedure, and expressed its opposition to discretionary testing.

It appears that the refusal to endorse the high risk offender procedure was largely based on practical difficulties of the kind noted earlier. Also within the Department of Transport there was believed to be considerable opposition to this proposal from the Driver Vehicle Licensing Centre (DVLC). According to one source the DVLC expected that the adoption of such a procedure would create a lot of extra work at a time when the Government was committed to reducing civil service manpower.

The rejection of discretionary testing is more difficult to explain. There was now a strong body of opinion in favour of adopting such an approach. The police and motoring associations no longer opposed it; they now beleved that the problem was so bad that it justified discretionary testing. Meanwhile other organisations, such as the BMA, the NCA and the Justices' Clerk's Society were arguing more strongly in favour of its adoption. Their case was strengthened by the report of the CPRS on alcohol policies in 1979 which recommended that all Blennerhasset's recommendation, including discretionary testing, be introduced. (CPRS, 1982)

Furthermore, public opinion was now overwhelmingly in favour of discretionary testing. According to opinion poll evidence, a significant majority of motorists now accepted it. (MORI, 1980)

Despite this evidence, the government continued to maintain that discretionary testing did not have enough public support to justify its introduction. There we, however other reasons for their reluctance. First of all, the Conservative leadership believed that it could face problems convincing some of its own supporters of the necessity for discretionary testing. One Conservative MP in particular, Anthony Beaumont-Dark, was particularly active in voicing his opposition to discretionary testing in the press, and on the backbenches. Many of those on the right of the party shared his view.

A second factor which may also have had a bearing on the government's decision was the considerable opposition within the drink industry to discretionary testing. It was not that the industry was unconcerned about drink driving or the scale of alcohol-related road accidents. For example, in 1980 the Brewers Society, in conjunction with the NULV, launched an educational campaign against drivers who drank to excess. But it was nevertheless true that certain sections of the industry - the on licensed trade - stood to lose out if measures such as discretionary testing were adopted. For reasons mentioned earlier the off-licensed trade was less concerned about this issue. Indeed they could benefit if drivers decided to drink at home. This could perhaps explain why the Scotch Whisky Association, which has no direct interest in the on licensed trade, has not opposed discretionary testing in recent years.

Opposition by parts of the drinks industry to discretionary testing was also reflected in the Parliamentary debates on the 1980 Transport Bill. This bill sought to enact the proposals outlined in the Green Paper a year earlier. During the debates a number of MPs sympathetic to the brewers opposed attempts by other backbenchers to widen the discretionary powers of the police.

In the event, the attempts to persuade the government to introduce discretionary testing were defeated. Moves to reduce the legal limit, a policy equally disliked by the government and the brewers, and which had also been rejected by the Blennerhassset Committee, were similarly thwarted. Five of Blennerhasset's main recommendations eventually became law. The high risk offender procedure, though not included in the 1981 Transport Act, was subsequently incorporated under existing legislation which allowed Transport ministers to with hold licences on medical grounds, following pressure from the NCA and medical opinion. This new procedure, introduced in 1983, automatically withdraws the licence of any individual who had been convicted twice for drinking and driving with a blood alcohol level over two-and-a-half times the legal limit within a ten year period. The licence can only be returned when the offender has been medically certified as fit to drive.

Recent Developments

Drinking and driving, despite the deterrent of legislation and the government's publicity campaigns, is still a serious social problem. Around 120,000 drivers each year are convicted of drinking and driving offences. Though the annual number of people killed and injured in road accidents has fallen since the early seventies, there are no grounds for complacency. Six thousand people are killed every year on the roads, and according to some recent research as many as a quarter of these are involved in accidents attributable in part to alcohol. (Foster, Dunbar, Whittet, Fernando, 1988) In 1984 the proportion of drivers killed in road accidents with a blood alcohol level above the legal limit was 25% - the same proportion as in 1967, before the Road Safety Act came into operation. (Harrison, 1987) Currently the government is considering new ways in which to tackle this persistent problem. As part of the governments new plans, the high-risk offender scheme is to be expanded. All drivers found guilty of drinking and driving offences twice in any ten year period, or caught once with a blood alcohol level is two-and-a-half times the legal limit, will be covered by the new measures. It is expected that as many as 40,000 motorists could have their licences suspended as a result. As with the original scheme outlined in the previous section the high risk offender wil have to pass a medical examination before the licence can be returned.

The government is also currently considering a number of measures proposed by the Department of Transport's road traffic review, published in 1988. (DoT, 1988) The review, also known as the North report, called for a new offence of causing death by driving under the influence of drink or drugs, to be created. The effect of this would be to make it easier for the prosecution to secure a conviction than under the present law. It also proposed that all individuals convicted of drinking and driving should have to pass a driving profficiency test before being allowed back on the road. Another of North's recommendations relevant to drinking and driving was that the licensing authorities (see chapter seven) should not renew liquor licenses to those who have persistently served alcohol to motorists committing drinking and driving offences.

In part the new initiatives on drinking and driving have emerged out of the growing concern about the alcohol problem in general which led to the creation of the Wakeham Committee (see chapter three). But within government circles much credit must also be attributed to the junior minister at the Department of Transport since 1985, Peter Bottomley, who has done much to keep drinking and driving on the government's agenda. Bottomley seems to have taken a personal interest in the issue. He has been active within government in supporting further measures, as well as spearheading the public campaign against drinking and driving.

Government has been under strong pressure from the anti-drink driving lobby to take further action. New groups have been formed to fight alongside existing pressure groups on this issue. In 1985, the Campaign Against Drinking and Driving (CADD) was formed by parents who have had children killed by drunken drivers. This organisation not only provides support for victims, but has campaigned strongly for further government intervention to prevent drinking and driving. Another group, also formed in 1985, has been involved in a similar campaign. Action on Drinking Driving (ADD) is an umbrella organisation incorporating a number of organisations which have for many years been concerned about drinking and driving. Its members include Alcohol concern and the Institute of Alcohol Studies. Its main function is to coordinate this lobby more effectively so as to secure changes in the law.

The strength of the anti-drink driving lobby has also been reflected in Parliament. Action in Parliament on this issue has been coordinated by the Parliamentary Advisory Council for Transport Safety (PACTS). This body has cross-party support and has pressured government to tighten up the drink driving laws in recent years by introducing Private Member's Bills, initiating debates, and tabling PQs and motions. It also has a fairly good relationship with the DoT, and is highly respected by ministers and officials in the department.

But although the pressure for more action on drink driving is producing some results, there is one area of policy that it is still regarded as highly contentious. This is the issue of allowing the police further powers to stop and test motorists which, as we have already seen, has caused a great deal of controversy over the last thirty years. At present the government still refuses to back discretionary or random testing of motorists, though the pressure for such a move is now very strong indeed. It is now supported by the following organisations, amongst others: the Association of Chief Police Officers, the Association of Police Surgeons, the British Medical Association, the Institute of Alcohol Studies, Alcohol Concern, Action on Drinking and Driving, the Campaign Against Drinking and Driving, and the environmentalists, Friends of the Earth. There is also evidence of strong public support, with one opinion poll showing that 93% of the general public are in favour of giving the police the power to test motorists at random. (*The Independent* 7 December 1988 p3) There is also Parliamentary support for random testing, exemplified by the backing given to such a move by PACTS. More recently the National Audit Office, the Parliamentary watchdog on cost-efficiency in government has called on the government to look again at the issue of random testing. (National Audit Office, 1988)

Many other countries have also adopted random testing. Finland, canada, New Zealand, France, the Scandanavian countries, Holland, West Germany, most of the United States, and some of the Australian States. Evidence from these countries appears to support the case for random testing. In Finland, for example, the introduction of random testing helped to bring about a substantial reduction in road accidents. (Dunbar, 1987) Why is the government still apparently opposed to random testing? There are now it seems four main reasons. First, the DoT's road traffic review did not not back random breath testing. It would appear inconsistent perhaps to reject this advice. Secondly, the Prime Minister, and many MPs on the right of the Conservative Party, are against it. Third, it is believed that the Home Office, which as we have seen as an important role in the formation of policy in this area, does not support the idea either (despite its support for such a move in the sixties). Finally, the brewers and the on-licensed trade continue to oppose random testing.

It should be stressed once again that in no way do the brewers want to see a rise in drinking and driving. They deplore the harm caused by drunk drivers as much as anyone else. Furthermore, the persistence of this problem could be damaging for their public image and may lead to even stronger pressure for further restrictions on alcohol generally. But they do feel random testing would damage their trade, as the Brewers' Society's own advice to licensees makes clear:

"Every day people die and others are maimed for life in accidents involveing motorists who have drunk too much. This causes some to argue that only draconian measures - like random testing, a lower or zero blood alcohol level, or long prison sentences will cure the problem. Steps like that would stop many motorists from venturing near a pub."[9]

As with the general problem of alcohol misuse the brewers see education as the answer. In recent years they have increased their efforts in this direction. Last year the brewers launched their 'Wheelwatch' campaign. This encouraged drivers to drink low and non-alcoholic drinks, and attempted to make landlords aware of the need to provide these drinks. In this way the drinks companies can maintain their profitability and their public image whilst making a contribution to solving the problems of drinking and driving. One brewer, Courage, sponsored a £1m TV campaign to warn of the dangers of drinking and driving; other individual companies have provided public transport for drinkers over the Christmas season. Though these moves are to be applauded one should be aware that, as *The Economist* (26 December, 1987) has noted, 'such campaigns are based on self-preservation as much as altruism.' In other words such voluntary action is not taken, then government may be forced to act, with even more damaging consequences for the trade.

Conclusion

Even after taking note of the failure of certain proposals put forward by the anti-drinking and driving lobby - such as random or discretionary testing - one cannot deny that the campaign for legislation on drinking and driving has been fairly successful. Certainly to date it has been relatively more successful than the wider campaign to promote action on alcohol misuse generally. The government has legislated in attempt to limit motorists' consumption of alcohol whilst at the same time refusing to adopt policies which have the potential to regulate overall alcohol consumption. This clearly requires some explanation.

One reason why government has taken a more active stance on this issue lies in the availability of clear empirical evidence linking alcohol consumption with road accidents. This contrasts with the policy issues examined in previous chapters. With the possible exception of price regulation, the empirical evidence to support government intervention has been either ambiguous or of poor quality.

149

Second, public opinion has been more supportive of action on drink driving than advertising bans on alcohol or price regulation. In recent years even motorists, who are at the sharp end of the drink driving laws, have been broadly in favour of further restrictions.

But favourable public opinion rarely promotes action. The stimulus for government intervention has come from elsewhere. Pressure groups have played an important part in this. Since the early sixties action on drink driving has been promoted by a strong lobby which has included the police associations, medical organisations, the motoring organisations, and road safety groups. In the seventies these groups were joined by the temperance movement and the voluntary alcohol organisations. In the eighties even more groups have joined in the campaign, such as CADD and Friends of the Earth. There is also much more coordination of the lobby's activities, with the formation of bodies like ADD and PACTS.

The anti-drink driving lobby has sought to influence policy through the media, Parliamentary contacts, and through its relationships with one of three government departments: the Department of Transport, the Home Office, and the DHSS, all of whom have an official concern with the problem. Department of Transport ministers and officials, in particular, have played a major role in promoting the issue within government circles and securing government support for anti-drink driving laws and larger publicity campaigns.

Fourthly, there has been little organised opposition to action on drink driving. Although, as we have seen, specific proposals - such as random testing - have encountered strong opposition from the drinks industry, the motoring organisitions, and right-wing MPs, and have been defeated as a result. But even the drinks industry, which is generally opposed to control policies, has accepted the need for legislation. Moreover, even when the industry has mobilised against certain proposals it has been visibly divided.

Finally, government intervention to restrict drinking and driving can be explained in terms of the development of the issue. The government's initiative on drink driving began in earnest during the early sixties. At this time the question of regulating drink driving was a road safety rather than an alcohol control issue. In other words the original emphasis of the legislation was to prevent accidents, not to prevent alcohol consumption. Since the seventies the issue has changed. Although road safety was still an important consideration, the general issue of preventing alcohol misuse was now also relevant.

The fact that the initial legislation on drink driving emerged before control policies entered the agenda was therefore extremely important. Had the pressure for this legislation arrived a decade later, it would have been seen as an alcohol control policy issue. The chances are that as a result the government initiatives would have faced a greater degree of opposition - particularly from the drinks industry - and, who knows, may not have emerged in their present form.

Notes

1. Figures supplied by the Department of Transport and the Department of Health
2. Criminal Justice Act 1925 Part III Section 40(1)
3. *House of Commons Official Report* Volume 710 Column 202w 14 April 1965
4. *House of Commons Official Report* Volume 724 Column 655-756 10 Feb. 1966
5. *House of Commons Official Report* Volume 735 Column 985 7 November 1966
6. *House of Commons Official Report* Volume 735 Column 998 7 November 1966
7. Department of Transport statistics
8. *House of Lords Official Report* Volume 352 Column 456 11 June 1974
9. Brewers' Society *Wheelwatch: A Briefing for Licensees*

9 Conclusion: alcohol, politics and social policy

The Politics of Alcohol

The regulation of alcohol is now clearly a political issue. As we have seen, government has over the years faced increasing pressure from a range of groups urging strong action against alcohol abuse. At the same time there have been powerful counter-pressures and constraints upon government, which have prevented the emergence of strategies aimed at controlling and reducing the overall consumption of alcohol. But we should not forget that politics is about compromise as well as conflict. Despite the apparent conflict between those who argue for alcohol control policies and those who oppose such a strategy, there has been considerable scope for compromise on a number of issues. The broad range of agreement on alcohol education, the early identification of problem drinkers, and the need for effective drink-driving laws, and so on, illustrates that the politics of alcohol need not always be a zero sum game.

This leads us back to the two specific questions identified at the outset. First, why has government not adopted control policies? Second, why has government responded at all to the growth in alcohol problems?(see chapter one). We shall now consider these questions in some detail in the light of our analysis.

The refusal to adopt control policies

Although alcohol is subject to regulation, by the licensing system, through taxation, and so on, successive British governments have refused to explicitly adopt a policy of reducing alcohol consumption by these and other means. The most obvious explanation for this reluctance appears to be the opposition of the drinks industry to such a strategy. As we have seen the industry represents a powerful lobby. It has organised effectively against control policies, using its formidable political contacts with Parliament and government, and its economic leverage.

Although the power of the industry is significant, we must take care to avoid simplistic conspiracy theories. After all, it cannot be said that the industry is unconcerned about alcohol misuse. Also, it is difficult to see how any government could tackle alcohol misuse without initially at least trying to secure the cooperation of the industry. The industry is wealthy and has a commercial interest in tackling alcohol problems. From a ministerial point of view therefore, it seems sensible to try and work with the industry, rather than against it, at least in the short term. Though in the longer term, if the industry proved intransigent or uncooperative, stronger measures may well be considered necessary.

Generally speaking, most ministers when dealing with the drink industry have sought cooperation rather than confrontation. This, given the industry's stance, has tended to remove control policies from the political agenda. But ministers have not pursued such a strategy against civil service advice, in the main. Control policies have generally been opposed by all except the Health Department. It has therefore been impossible to build a coalition of support for control policies within Whitehall. This situation has been exacerbated by the fact that policy instruments having the potential to regulate alcohol consumption have been largely under the control of departments hostile to alcohol control policies: the Home Office (licensing law), Department of Trade and Industry (alcohol advertising) and the Treasury (alcohol taxation).

Outside central government, control policies have failed to attract the support of a majority in Parliament, and amongst the general public. In Parliament, the opponents of control policies are numerous and would be able to overturn any private member's legislation on the subject, even if introduced with government consent. Moreover the opponents and supporters of control policy are not drawn from any single party - in other words alcohol control is a cross-party issue. This generally prevents government from legislating on such matters in the absence of a clear majority in favour. Normally governments can rely on party discipline in Parliament to ensure that MPs support the measures introduced by ministers. On cross-party issues MPs behave much more independently and consequently the government risks an embarrassing defeat if its proposals do not command the support of a majority of MPs in Parliament. In view of this, governments have tended to avoid legislating on alcohol matters unless (as in the case of licensing reform and the drink driving laws) there is a clear majority of MPs in favour.

The public are also rather lukewarm on the subject of control policies.

Generally, alcohol problems are seen as less pressing than problems associated with illicit drugs, like heroin. In a recent Gallup poll, for example, 50% of the population thought that heavy drinking was a very serious problem. Whilst 84% thought that 'hard drugs' constituted such a problem. (Gallup. 1987) Moreover the level of support for most alcohol control policies is low amongst the general public, as we have seen. As a result, governments have remained unconvinced that the application of comprehensive control measures would have sufficient public support.

Public support is important for two main reasons. First, politicians fear the electoral implications of taking action to restrict alcohol: strong policies may produce a backlash if the policies prove to be unpopular. Secondly, low public support may undermine control policies even if they are implemented. One notes that the ultimate control policy - Prohibition - failed in the United States partly because of a lack of public support and consequent problems of enforcement. In Britain, drinkers comprise a very large proportion of the general public, and policies which have little support amongst the public might be more easily circumvented.

Why has government done anything about alcohol?

If the sources of political inhibition to control policies are so strong, why has the government bothered to do anything at all about the alcohol problem? One reason is of course that the opposition to alcohol policies is not the same as the opposition to control policies. There is a considerable degree of consensus on a range of policy issues within government, and between the drinks industry and the alcohol misuse lobby. Moreover, public support for particular proposals has on occasion been significant. Intervention to prevent drinking and driving, for example, is strongly supported by the general public and by most motorists. But one also notes that the opposition of a majority of the public to licensing law reform did not prevent the government from relaxing the law in England and Wales. (see chapter seven)

Secondly, more effective campaigning by the alcohol misuse lobby has promoted a response from government. As time has passed, the more powerful professions - such as the medical professions, and the law and order professions - have become increasingly concerned about alcohol problems, and have called on government to adopt specific strategies. In response to this pressure, government has legislated against drinking and driving, has introduced safeguards into licensing legislation, and has restricted alcohol advertising, amongst other things. Also, more recently, the government established a ministerial committee (the Wakeham Committee) partly in response to the pressure from the alcohol misuse lobby.

Third, evidence about the causes of alcohol problems can be seen as a significant factor promoting action. The quality of the evidence linking drinking and driving to road accidents has helped persuade policy makers of the need to respond. But evidence alone is not enough. There is plenty of evidence linking the price of alcohol, alcohol consumption, and alcohol misuse, yet this has not been officially accepted by government. Whilst the government's relatively positive support for alcohol education is based on scanty evidence about the effectiveness of education in shaping drinking habits.

Fourth, action on alcohol has been taken because of the willingness and initiative of a number of individual ministers over the years. Lord Joseph, Patrick Jenkin, Sir George Young, David Owen, Barbara Castle, to name a few, have all backed alcohol policy initiatives whilst in office. In some cases their position reflected civil servants' advice, or pressures from Parliament, or the campaigning of the alcohol misuse lobby. But on other occasions it appears that a personal concern about the scale of the alcohol problem was a major reason behind certain policy initiatives - as in the case of Lord Joseph, for example. Such support has on occasion been crucial to the development of alcohol policy responses.

Towards an explanation of alcohol policy

Taken together the above help to explain why British government has been willing to take action on alcohol, but unwilling to adopt control policies. There is however a more general explanation which should be noted. Throughout this study, it has been apparent that the alcohol misuse issue has lacked a certain identity. In other words developments in alcohol policy have in the past often reflected other concerns and broader issues. In chapters two and three for example, we saw how alcohol policy was shaped by more general policy developments, such as community care and preventive medicine. Similarly, the regulation of alcohol advertising has been conducted within the existing framework of advertsing regulation generally. More recently the ideology of deregulation, though not powerful enough to alter Sunday shopping hours, managed to sweep aside those who argued that the licensing laws should not be relaxed. Currently we note that the government is reviewing alcohol policy largely in view of its concern for law and order.

The main reason why the alcohol issue has lacked a specific identity is because alcohol use and abuse has so many ramifications. As we have seen, alcohol has implications for leisure, trade, industry, employment, the wider economy, ill-health, mortality, public order, children and young people, absenteeism at work, safety at work, road safety... one could go on. As a result, concern about alcohol abuse has tended to be rather diffuse. Many organisations have been worried about alcohol abuse, but until recently only a few (the temperance bodies and the voluntary organisations in the alcohol field) have seen alcohol as their central concern.

There are signs, however, that more and more organisations are recognising the role of alcohol in relation to their particular concerns. As a result they are taking more of an interest in the alcohol issue generally, strengthening the alcohol misuse lobby. Ultimately of course this could lead to much stronger pressure on government to introduce alcohol control policies. Much depends on how well the lobby can organise itself, and persuade the public and Parliament and government of the need for such policies.

The Politics of Public Health

As we noted in chapter one, public health issues, such as alcohol misuse, have attracted increasing attention in recent years. This has been reflected in the growing number of studies of public health policy - including smoking and health; the health consequences of environmental pollution; and food and dietary policy. The common theme running through all these policy studies (and indeed this study) is that comprehensive and effective policies to prevent ill-health have been inhibited by a combination of five main factors. These are: the limitations of epidemiological evidence, the weight of libertarian arguments, the existence of powerful industrial lobbies, and departmental conflict within government, the lack of political will. We shall now examine these factors more closely.

Epidemiological evidence

It seems reasonable that those who urge government intervention on public health grounds should have to provide some evidence backing up their case. But on most issues, the burden of proof lies with the public health lobby and not with those whose activities are allegedly responsible for damaging public health. This would not be so much of a problem if conclusive empirical evidence on the effect of certain activities upon public health was available. But epidemiology, the science of establishing such relationships, can only make a limited contribution on issues of this kind. As Erik Millstone, in his study of government policy on food additives, has noted:

"The methods of epidemiology can be very useful when we want to identify the causes of an outbreak of acute illness but they are far less effective when we need to identify the specific causes of chronic problems."

In other words it is difficult to prove what exactly is causing ill health when the symptoms develop over a long period. This problem was clearly illustrated in the issue of alcohol misuse. Of all the alcohol policy issues, the most conclusive evidence linking consumption with harm is found in the area of drinking and driving. This is because here the harm in question is acute (ie: road accidents) In contrast other forms of alcohol-related harm are chronic, occurring after years of excessive consumption - such as liver cirrhosis for example. Evidence linking consumption with these chronic aspects of alcohol misuse is therefore much less conclusive.

But not all epidemiological evidence relating to the causes of chronic ill-health can be so easily discounted. For example, there is an impressive body of evidence linking smoking with lung cancer and other diseases. This has produced a broad medical consensus that smoking is bad for health. Even so, there are a number of scientists who have challenged the empirical evidence on smoking and health, though they have been in a very small minority. (see Collingridge and Reeve, 1986)

Conclusive proof about the effect of certain activities on public health is unlikely to emerge because the activities in question invariably give rise to 'risks' which cannot be accurately measured. The exposure of individuals to food additives, to certain dietary and drinking habits, to tobacco smoke, to lead in exhaust fumes, and so on, does not in every case lead to an identifiable symptom of ill health. Instead, the individuals concerned will face higher risks of ill-health, if these activities are not properly regulated.

In the present political climate, the state generally insists on conclusive proof as a precondition for intervention on public health grounds. On the face of it, this appears quite reasonable. But one soon begins to realise that the difficulties of measurement, not to mention the lack of research resources, are particularly damaging to the cause of the public health lobby. Consequently its adversaries derive much advantaged from the present situation.

Liberty

The idea that government should act with restraint, allowing individuals to enjoy a high degree of personal liberty, is the fundamental principle of a liberal democratic state. It could be argued that the modern public health movement, by urging that the state should intervene to correct individual lifestyles, is operating against this principle. But this depends largely on the degree to which public health issues are perceived as libertarian issues.

It is worth noting that British Governments have often employed libertarian arguments when refusing to adopt stricter policies on drinking, smoking, and dietary habits. The industries involved have also championed the cause of individual liberty by arguing against intervention on the behalf of the consumer. For example, the tobacco industry recently established a pressure group called FOREST (Freedom of the Right to Enjoy Smoking Tobacco) which has fought against tougher anti-smoking measures on libertarian grounds.

Yet consumers are rarely allowed to register their own views independently of the industry. Consumers are generally excluded from consultation processes. As a result, the 'defence of liberty' is left mainly to the industrial lobbies. They are happy to do this, partly because it is good for their image to appear to be on the side of the consumer. But their main aim is to safeguard commercial liberty. This priority is revealed when, as sometimes happens, commercial and individual (or consumer) liberty conflict. In these situations, as one might expect, the former carries more weight. For example, consumers are often denied the kind of information which might help them understand the relationship between the use of certain products and ill-health. The food companies, in particular, have fought strenuously against attempts to inform the public about food additives. (Millstone, 1986) Whilst the tobacco industry, which has never accepted the medical evidence on smoking and health, has sought to misinform consumers by projecting positive images about smoking through promotion (particularly sports sponsorship) and advertising. (Taylor, 1984)

Public health issues have been depicted as libertarian issues - even though the general public themselves have in many cases been denied the information required to make a rational decision on the case against government intervention. Where public knowledge is particularly low - such as in the food additive issue - public interest is also low, and the industry is in a better position to 'hijack' the defence of individual liberty for its own ends.

A further point is that government's reluctance to intervene appears to be inversely related to the proportion of society indulging in the causal activity in question-that is, smoking, eating, drinking, using leaded petrol, and so on. Smoking provides the best example here: it is now a minority habit (compared with twenty years ago when well over half the population smoked) This has been reflected by the more stringent measures- such as prohibitive tax increases- taken by government in recent years. (Calnan, 1984)

Industrial lobbies

A common theme of public health issues is the power and influence of industrial lobbies. In the case of alcohol policy we noted the power of the industry and its allies. On the issue of smoking and health, it appears that the tobacco industry has enjoyed what amounts to a veto power over policy. According to Popham:

"The trump card in the industry's hand... is the recognition it receives from the government as a legitimate interest with a right to negotiate before policy is finally decided." (Popham, 1981)

In the case of food policy, one finds a similar situation. As Millstone notes, the industry's representatives are an important source of policy advice. This, he goes on to say, has serious consequences for other interests:

"Since the dominant interest group influencing the deliberations of the committees is industrial, they will readily assume that what is in the interests of the industry is in the public interest. In practice therefore insufficient consideration is given to consumer interests, and industrial interests massively predominate." (Millstone, 1986)

Industry and commerce can use both economic and political leverage in order to defend their interests. The food industry, according to Millstone accounts for about 10% of manufacturing industry. The tobacco industry, although smaller, is highly profitable and is operated by a few wealthy multinationals. (Baggott, 1987) Similarly the 'anti-knock' industry (those firms which produce lead additives) is partly owned by petrol companies, who are amongst the largest multinationals in the world. (Wilson, 1983)

Earlier we noted that the alcohol producers, rather than retailers or consumers, took the lead role in opposing policies aimed at regulating the industry as a whole. A similar story is found in these other policy areas. In the case of tobacco, the manufacturers' trade organisation, the Tobacco Advisory Council, organises the industry's opposition to health policies. (Baggott, 1987) Whereas in the food industry, according to Cannon and Walker, (1984) 'the industry representative bodies with whom government negotiates in private, like the Food and Drink Federation or the Food Manufacturers Federation, are dominated by the major

158

food manufacturers. Retailers, curiously, do not have much to say when national food policy decisions are made.'

In general the public health lobbies are much weaker than their industrial adversaries. This is largely because, as we saw in the case of alcohol misuse, the industrial lobby has the lion's share of the political resources - particularly economic and social leverage, and political contacts. But this is not to say that these health lobbies are powerless. Their main resources are the social status of the professions they organise (such as the medical profesion) and their ability to mobilise public opinion. Perhaps one of the most successful in this respect has been the Campaign for Lead Free Air, which harnessed public and professional concerns very effectively, putting the industry very much on the defensive. (Wilson, 1983)

Conflict in Whitehall

The ability of government to respond coherently is tested when the issue in question cuts across departmental responsibilities. In general, the greater the number of departments having a significant interest in a particular policy area, the greater the task of coordinating the government's response. This is illustrated by the difficulties which government has faced in formulating public health policies. Each of the issues referred to in this chapter involves at least five government departments. Moreover, these issues have also given rise to serious conflicts between departments, further exacerbating the situation.

The confusion arising out of the clash of departmental interests on the issue of smoking and health, for example, has been noted by Calnan:

"It appears that the government has no overall policy for smoking control and each government department pursues its own objectives in the light of its own policy interests. This... leads to a conflict of interests ـ ie one department pursuing a policy encouraging smoking control and the other discouraging it." (Calnan, 1984)

Here, the Health department's arguments for strong action on smoking are countered mainly by the Department of Trade and Industry (DTI), the tobacco industry's sponsoring department. In similar fashion the DTI's responsibility for the chemical and motor car industries has led it to oppose a ban on lead in petrol. Its adversaries on this issue have been the Department of Environment, in view of its responsibility for pollution, and again the Health Department.

We earlier pointed out that the DTI does not have a monopoly of industrial sponsorship. It is not always therefore the main opponent of public health policies which threaten industrial interests. For example, the alcoholic drink industry's sponsoring department is the Ministry of Agriculture Fisheries and Food (MAFF). This department as a result has been a major opponent of alcohol control policies. It has also strongly resisted pressure from the health departments on dietary policy and food additives, in its capacity as sponsor of farming and the food processing industry.

The DTI also has an interest in domestic and overseas trade in food and drink.

Similarly, other departments have decided to oppose public health policies in view of their general responsibilities. The Department of Employment is concerned about the implications of such policies for the level of unemployment. Whilst the Treasury is mainly concerned about the broader economic consequences of these policies.

In general the departmental conflict on public health issues is based on the division between economic policy and non-economic policy departments, although there are some notable exceptions to this rule. For example the Home Office (a non-economic policy department) has opposed alcohol control policies in the past. Whilst on the issues of smoking and health and alcohol misuse, the Treasury (an economic policy department) has supported the Department of Health's call for an increase in taxes on cigarettes and drink on economic grounds in recent years.

Political will

Ultimately, however, the central government machine can be more effectively co-ordinated if ministers can be persuaded to take an interest in the issue in question. But in general, public health issues have a relatively low political status. Ministers, and politicians generally, tend to see them as vote losers rather than vote winners. This is partly because public health policies take effect over a long period of time; visible benefits do not materialise immediately. Moreover, in the early years they are likely to have high political costs, in the form of industrial and consumer opposition. The distribution of political costs and benefits over time is important because politicians spend a relatively short period of time in office. Accordingly, they tend to attach greater weight to costs and benefits in the short term, whilst discounting long term developments. Put another way, the credit due in the long run for pursuing public health policies is little compensation for the unpopularity politicians' anticipate whilst in office. Indeed if the benefits of the policy take years to emerge, the government of the day - and not the minister who initiated the policy - will get the credit.

Occasionally, though, ministers have taken an interest in public health issues. Indeed an increasing number of health ministers in recent years - Edwina Currie, David Owen, Sir George Young - to name a few, have worked within government to promote public health policies. But in so doing they have met resistance from colleagues both within government and in Parliament. In some cases their activities have led to them being dropped from the government (as in the case of Edwina Currie) or moved to another department (Sir George Young). It is also worth noting that the ministers who have taken an interest in public health have generally held junior posts, and have lacked influence at Cabinet level.

The relatively low political status of public health issues is also reflected by their insignificance in terms of party politics. Public health issues are not party issues, but instead cut across party lines. The major political parties have scarcely mentioned public health issues in the past. Though increasingly the parties have supported particular proposals. For example, both the Labour Party and the Social and Liberal Democrats now support a ban on all forms of cigarette advertising. But these policies do not constitute a priority for either party.

Of all the factors shaping public health policy, political will is perhaps the most crucial. There are signs that public health issues are in future going to generate more interest amongst politicians. At the time of writing food poisoning has become a major political issue (see for example *The Independent* 17 December 1988 p3, *The Economist* 24 December 1988, p33-4). In particular there are worries that food production and processing methods are directly threatening health through the contamination of food. This concern follows on the heels of an official report by the Chief Medical Officer at the Department of Health, which argued that public health should be given priority, particularly at a local level. (Cmnd 289, 1988) International organisations, such as the European Community (European Commission, 1984) and the World Health Organisation (1981, 1985) have added to this climate of concern by calling on member governments to formulate coherent public health policies.

Finally, in 1986 many organisations in the field of public health collaborated in the formation of a public health alliance. The idea being to disseminate information and to coordinate action on these issues. When this alliance becomes fully operative, it should prove a useful platform for the representation and mobilisation of public health interests.

All these recent developments point to a rosier future for public health generally. They also suggest that policy in specific areas of public health - smoking, alcohol abuse, food, and so on - may develop further than hitherto seemed politically possible. Even so any future campaigns in this policy area cannot ignore the political system and in particular the factors operating against effective public health strategies. Preventive action - to protect public health - may be better than cure: but it requires a lot more political will.

Bibliography

Action on Alcohol Abuse *Agenda for Action on Alcohol*, London, Triple A, 1986.

Action on Drinking and Driving *Press Release* 1987.

Advertising Association *Annual Report 1983* London, AA, 1983.

Advertising Standards Authority *The British Code of Advertising Practice* London, ASA, 1980. (Revised 1988)

T. Ambler *Grand Metropolitan: Social Aspects of Alcohol, a Strategy Proposal* Unpublished, 1984.

Anon. 'Alcohol has a lot to do with Alcoholism' *The Lancet* 1, 1981, p425-6.

Anon. Editorial *British Medical Journal* 4, 1972, p625-6.

Association of Chief Police Officers *Public Disorder Outside Metropolitan Areas* London, ACPO, 1988.

R. Baggott and L. Harrison 'The Politics of Self Regulation: The Case of Advertising Control' *Policy and Politics* 14:2, 1986, p143-160

R. Baggott 'The Politics of Alcohol: Two Periods Compared' *Institute of Alcohol Studies Occasional Paper No.8* London, IAS, 1986.

R. Baggott 'Government-Industry Relations in Britain: The Case of the Tobacco Industry' *Policy and Politics* 15:3, 1987, p137-46.

R. Baggott 'Health v Wealth: The Politics of Smoking in Norway and the UK' *Strathclyde Papers in Government and Politics No.57* Glasgow, University of Strathclyde, 1988.

Joel Barnett *Inside the Treasury* London, Andre Deutch, 1982.

R. Barton and S. Godfrey 'Un-health Promotion: Results of a Survey of Alcohol Promotion on Television' *British Medical Journal* 296, 1988, p1593-4.

R. Birch 'Deterring the Drinking Driver' *Deterring the Drinking Driver: Time to Think Again* Proceedings of a Conference organised by Action on Alcohol Abuse, May 1985.

M. Booth, G. Hardman, K. Hartley 'Data Note 6: The UK Alcohol and Tobacco Industries' *British Journal of Addiction* 81, 1986, p825-30.

R.F. Borkenstein *The Role of the Drinking Driver in Road Tarffic Accidents* Indiana University, 1964.

J.A. Brand 'The Politics of Flouridation: A Community Conflict' *Political Studies* 19:4, 1971, p430-9.

Brewers' Society *A Strategy for the Prevention of Problem Drinking* London, Brewers' Society, 1983.

Brewers' Society *Statistical Handbook 1983* London, Brewers' Publications, 1984.

British Medical Association *The Relationship of Alcohol to Road Accidents* London, BMA, 1960.

British Medical Association and Magistrates Association 'Memorandum on Alcoholism' *British Medical Journal* 243, 1961, p190-5.

British Medical Association *The Drinking Driver* London, BMA, 1965.

British Medical Association, Report of the Board of Science and Education *Young People and Alcohol* London, BMA, 1986.

C.F. Brockington *Public Health in the Nineteenth Century* Edinburgh, Livingstone, 1965.

K. Bruun et. al. *Alcohol Control in Public Health Perspective* Helsinki, Finnish Foundation for Alcohol Studies, 1975.

Cabinet Office and HM Treasury *Non-Departmental Public Bodies: A Guide for Departments* London, HMSO, 1986.

M. Calnan 'The Politics of Health: The Case of Smoking Control' *Journal of Social Policy* 13:3, 1984, p279-96.

Campaign for the Homeless and Rootless *Drunken Neglect* London, CHAR, 1974.

G. Cannon and C. Walker *The Food Scandal* London, Century, 1984.

B. Castle *The Castle Diaries 1974-6* London, Weidenfield & Nicholson, 1980.

Central Council of Physical Recreation *Committee of Enquiry into Sports Sponsorship* London, CCPR, 1983.

Central Policy Review Staff *Alcohol Policies in the UK* Stockholm, Sociologiska Institutionen, 1982.

Central Statistical Office *Annual Abstract of Statistics* London, HMSO, 1985.

Central Statistical Office *UK National Accounts: National Income and Expenditure* London, HMSO, 1986.

Central Statistical Office *Social Trends* London, HMSO, 1988.

J.M. Coffey *The Long Thirst* New York, Norton, 1975.

D. Collingridge and C. Reeve *Science Speaks to Power* London, Pinter, 1986.

Cmnd. 2859 *Road Safety Legislation 1965-6* London, HMSO, 1965.

Cmnd. 7047 *White Paper on Prevention and Health* London, HMSO, 1977.

Cmnd. 9571 *Lifting the Burden* London, HMSO, 1985.

Cmd. 289 *Public Health in England* London, HMSO, 1988.

Confederation of British Industry *Price Controls and the Price Commission: The Business View* London, CBI, 1979.

Conservative Party *The Next Moves Forward* (1987 Election Manifesto) London, Conservative Party, 1987.

J. Cook and C. Kaufman *Portrait of a Poison* London, Pluto Press, 1982.

R. Cyster and A. McNeill 'Alcohol Education and Training at Work' *Institute of Alcohol Studies Occasional Paper Number 4* London, IAS, 1985.

M. Daube 'Disorderly House' *Times Health Supplement* 25 December 1981, p14-15.

P. Davies 'The Relationship between Taxation, Price and Alcohol Consumption in the Countries of Europe' in M. Grant, M. Plant, A. Williams *Economics and Alcohol* London, Croom Helm, 1983, p140-58.

P. Davies and D.Walsh *Alcohol Problems and Alcohol Control in Europe* London, Croom Helm, 1983.

J. de Lindt and W. Schmidt 'Consumption Averages and Alcoholism Prevalence: A Brief Review of the Epidemiological Investigations' *British Journal of Addiction* 66, 1971, p97-107.

Department of Employment *Employment Gazette* London, HMSO, 1986.

Department of Environment *Report of the Committee on Drinking and Driving* (The Blennerhasset Report) London, HMSO, 1976.

Department of Health and Social Security *Community Services for Alcoholics* Circular 21/73 London, HMSO, 1973.

Department of Health and Social Security *Better Services for the Mentally Handicapped* London, HMSO, 1971.

Department of Health and Social Security *Better Services for the Mentally Ill* London, HMSO, 1975.

Department of Health and Social Security *Prevention and Health: Everybody's Business* London, HMSO, 1976.

Department of Health and Social Security, Advisory Committee on Alcoholism *Report on the Pattern and Range of Services for Problem Drinkers* London, DHSS, 1977a.

Department of Health and Social Security *Priorities in the Health and Social Services: The Way Forward* London, HMSO, 1977b.

Department of Health of Social Security *Circular LASS L(78)33* 1978a.

Department of Health and Social Security, Advisory Committee on Alcoholism *Report on Prevention* London, DHSS, 1978b.

Department of Health and Social Security, Advisory Committee on Alcoholism *Report on Education and Training* London, DHSS, 1979

Department of Health and Social Security *Care in Action* London, HMSO, 1981a.

Department of Health and Social Security *Drinking Sensibly* London, HMSO, 1981b.

Department of Health and Social Security / National Council for Voluntary Organisations Joint Committee of Enquiry *National Voluntary Organisations and Alcohol Misuse* London, DHSS, 1982.

Department of Health and Social Security *Health and Personal Social Service Statistics for England 1987* London, HMSO, 1987.

Department of Trade and Industry *Overseas Trade Statistics* London, HMSO, 1986.

Department of Transport *Road Traffic Law Review* (The North Report) London, HMSO, 1988.

J.C. Duffy and G.R. Cohen 'Total Alcohol Consumption and Excessive Drinking' *British Journal of Addiction* 73, 1978, p259-64.

J. Dunbar, A Pentilla, J. Pikkarainen 'The Success of Random Testing in Finland' *British Medical Association* 295, 1987, p101-3.

K. Dunjohn 'Advertising, Broadcasting and Alcohol' *Report of a Symposium held at the House of Commons* 28 January 1981.

J.M. Eagles and J.A.O. Besson 'Changes in the Incidence of Alcohol-Related problems in North East Scotland 1974-82' *British Journal of Psychiatry* 147, 1985, p39-43.

M. Emery 'Alcohol and Safety in Industry' *Journal of Social and Occupational Medicine* 36, 1986, p18-23.

European Commission *Recommendation 76/2* 5 December 1975

European Commission *Commission Communication to Council on Cooperation on Health-Related Problems* COM(84)502, 1984.

M. W. Flinn *Public Health Reform in Britain* London, Macmillan, 1968.

G.R. Foster, J.A. Dunbar, D. Whittet, G. Fernando 'Contribution of Alcohol to Deaths in Road Traffic Accidents in Tayside 1982-6' *British Medical Journal*, 1988, 1430-2.

W.M. Frazer *A Study of English Public Health 1834-193* London, Balliere Tindall Cox, 1950.

P. Friend *Nursing 1974-6* London, DHSS, 1977.

G.H. Gallup *The Gallup International Public Opinion Polls: Great Britain 1937-75* New York, Random House, 1976.

G.H. Gallup *Gallup Political Index* London, Social Surveys Ltd, February 1986.

G.H. Gallup *Gallup Political Index* London, Social Surveys Ltd. November 1987.

M.M. Glatt *Alcoholism* London, Teach Yourself Books, 1982.

C. Godfrey, G. Hardman, A. Maynard 'Data Note 2: Measuring UK Alcohol and Tobacco Consumption' *British Journal of Addiction* 81, 1986, p287-93.

C. Godfrey, G. Hardman, M. Powell 'Data Note 1: Alcohol and Tobacco Taxation' *British Journal of Addiction* 81, 1986, p143-9.

W. Grant 'Insider and Outsider Pressure Groups' *Social Studies Review* 1985, p31-3.

C. Grattan and P. Taylor 'The Economics of Sports Sponsorship' *Nat West Bank Quarterly Review* August 1985, p51-6.

B.S. Greenberg, S. Fazal, B. Wober *Children's Views on Advertising* London, Independent Broadcasting Authority, 1986.

C. Ham *Health Policy in Britain* London, Macmillan, 1982.

A. Hansen 'Alcohol and Drinking on Television' *The Presentation of Alcohol in the Mass Media* Proceedings of a Conference held at IBA House, January 1985, London IAS, 1985.

A. Hansen 'Alcohol, Television, and Young People' *Brewing Review* Summer 1988, p16-19.

L. Harrison 'Data Note 7: Drinking and Driving in Great Britain' *British Journal of Addiction* 82, 1987, p203-8.

L. Harrison and P. Tether 'Alcohol and Fire Accidents' *British Journal of Addiction* 81:3, 1986.

A. Hawker *Adolescents and Alcohol* London, Edsall, 1978.

S. Haywood and A. Alaszewski *Crisis in the Health Service* London, Croom Helm, 1980.

Health Education Council *Beliefs About Alcohol* London, HEC, 1986.

Health and Safety Executive *The Problem Drinker at Work* Occasional Paper Series No.1, London, HMSO, 1981.

H.W. Henry 'Advertising Alcohol: An ITV View' *The British Journal of Addiction* 15:3, 1980.

R. Hodgkinson *Public Health in the Victorian Age* Farnborough, Gregg, 1973 (2 vols.)

Home Office *Circular 129/67* London, HMSO, 1967.

Home Office *Report of the Working Party on Habitual Drunken Offenders* London, HMSO, 1971.

Home Office *Report of the Departmental Committee on Liquor Licensing in England and Wales* (The Erroll Report) Cmnd. 5154, London, HMSO, 1972.

Home Office (Research Unit), M. Tuck *Alcoholism and Social Policy: Are We on the Right Lines?* Home Office Research Study No.65, London, HMSO, 1980.

Home Office *Liquor Licensing Statistics for England and Wales* London, HMSO, 1984.

Home Office *Statistical Bulletin, Issue 40/87* London, HMSO, 1987a.

Home Office, Standing Conference on Crime Prevention *Report of the Working Party on Young People and Alcohol* (The Masham Report) London, Home Office, 1987b.

Home Office *The Licensing Act 1964: Government Proposals for Reform* London, Home Office, 1987c.

House of Commons *First Report of the Select Committee on Violence in Marriage Session 1974/5* London, HMSO, 1975.

House of Commons *First Report of the Select Committee on Expenditure, Sub-committee on Employment and Social Services on Preventive Medicine Session 1976/7* London, HMSO, 1977a.

House of Commons *First Report of the Select Committee on Expenditure, Sub-committee on Employment and Social Services on Preventive Medicine Session 1976/7: Minutes of Evidence* London, HMSO, 1977b.

House of Commons *Report of the Select Committee on Expenditure, Sub-committee on Employment and Social Services on Perinatal and Neonatal Mortality Session 1978/9: Minutes of Evidence* London, HMSO, 1979.

House of Commons *Sixth Report by the Treasury and Civil Service Committee on Budgetary Reform Session 1981/2* London, HMSO, 1982a.

House of Commons *Observations by HM Treasury on the Sixth Report of the Treasury and Civil Service Committee Session 1981/2* London, HMSO, 1982b.

House of Commons Session 1983/4 *Early Day Motion No. 542* 1984a

House of Commons Session 1983/4 *Early Day Motion No. 524* 1984b

House of Commons Session 1985/6 *Early Day Motion No.372* 1986

House of Lords *Thirteenth Report of the Select Committee on European Communities: Cooperation at Community Level on Health-related Problems Session 1984/5, with Minutes of Evidence* London, HMSO, 1985.

Howard League for Penal Reform *Control By Consent: Towards a Penal Philosophy* London, HLPR, 1974.

Independent Broadcasting Authority *The IBA Code of Advertising Practice* London, IBA, 1979. (Revised 1989)

Institute for Alcohol Studies *Proceedings of a Conference on Alcoholism, November 1984* London, IAS, 1984.

Institute for Alcohol Studies *The Presentation of Alcohol in the Mass Media: Report of a Seminar held at IBA House, January 1985* London, Institute for Alcohol Studies, 1985.

Justices' Clerks' Society *Licensing Law in the Eighties* Bristol, JCS, 1983.

R.E. Kendell 'Alcoholism a Medical or a Political Problem ?' *British Medical Journal* 278, 1979, p367-71.

R.E. Kendell, M. de Roumanie and E.B. Ritson 'The Effect of Economic Changes on Scottish Drinking Habits 1978-82' *British Journal of Addiction* 78, 1983, p365-79.

Labour Party Research Department *Company Donations to the Conservative Party* Information Paper No.24, London, Labour Party, 1981.

J. Laurance 'Drinking Scottish Style' *New Society* 16 August 1984.

S. Ledermann *Alcool, Alcoolism, Alcoolisation* Paris, Presses Universitaires de France, 1956.

C. Lee, M. Pearson, S.Smith ' Fiscal Harmonisation: An Analysis of the European Commision's Proposals' London, Institute of Fiscal Studies, 1988.

J.M. Lee 'The Political Significance of Licensing Legislation' *Parliamentary Affairs* 14:2, 1961, p211-28.

W. Leedham 'Data Note 10: Alcohol, Tobacco and Public Opinion' *British Journal of Addiction* 82, 1987, p935-40.

E.G. Lucas 'Alcohol in Industry' *British Medical Journal* 294, 1987, p460-1.

R. McDonnell and A. Maynard 'The Costs of Alcohol Misuse' *British Journal of Addiction* 80, 1985, p27-35.

A. McNeill 'Alcohol Problems and Employment' *Institute of Alcohol Studies Occasional Paper No.1* London, IAS, 1984.

Market Opinion Research Institute (MORI) *Opinion Poll* 18/19 December 1980.

P. Marsh 'Alcohol Advertising: the ABM View' Speech given to the Media Committee of the Backbench Conservative Party, April 1981.

J.N. Martin *Paterson's Licensing Acts* London, Butterworths, 1988.

A. Maynard, G. Hardman, A. Whelan 'Data Note 9: Measuring the Social Costs of Addictive Substances' *British Journal of Addiction* 82, 1987, 701-6.

Medical Council on Alcoholism *Annual Report 1970* London, MCA, 1970.

Medical Research Council *The Effect of Small Doses of Alcohol on a Skill Resembling Driving* (The Drew Report) London, HMSO, 1958.

E.H. Miller and N. Agnew 'The Ledermann Model of Alcohol Consumption' *Quarterly Journal of Studies on Alcohol* 35, 1974, p877-98.

E. Millstone *Food Additives* Harmondsworth, Penguin, 1986.

Ministry of Health *The Hospital Treatment of Alcoholism* Memorandum HM(62)43, London, HMSO, 1962.

Ministry of Health *The Treatment of Alcoholism* Memorandum HM(68)37, London, HMSO, 1968.

Ministry of Transport *Road Accidents; Great Britain* London, HMSO, 1960.

Monopolies Commission *Beer: Report on the Supply of Beer* London, HMSO, 1969.

G. Morgan 'All Party Committees in the House of Commons' *Parliamentary Affairs* 32:1, 1979, p56-65.

D. Murphy 'Alcohol and Crime' *Home Office Research Bulletin* 15, 1983, p8-11.

National Audit Office *Department of Transport, Scottish Development Agency, Welsh Office: Road Safety* London, HMSO, 1988.

National Consumer Council *MORI Opinion Poll* July 1981.

National Council on Alcoholism *The Alcohol Explosion* London, NCA, 1970.

National Council on Alcoholism *Annual Report 1982* London, NCA, 1982.

National Economic Development Office, Brewing Sector Working Group *Report on Brewing* London, NEDO, 1977.

National Economic Development Office, Distilling Sector Working Group *Scotch Whisky* London, NEDO, 1978.

National Economic Development Office Distilling Sector, Working Group *Distilling - Gin and Vodka* London, NEDO, 1982.

National Economic Development Office, Brewing Sector WorkingGroup *The Outlook for the Brewing Industry* London, NEDO, 1983.

National Economic Development Office, Distilling Sector Working Group *Scotch Whisky in the 1980's* London, NEDO, 1985.

National Economic Development Office, Agriculture, Food and Drink Economic Development Committees *Foodlink* 4 March 1988.

Office of Fair Trading *Review of the Self-Regulatory System of Advertising Control* London, OFT, 1978.

Office of Health Economics *Alcohol Abuse* London, OHE, 1970.

Office of Health Economics *Alcohol: Reducing the Harm* London, OHE, 1981.

Office of Population Censuses and Surveys (OPCS) *General Household Survey* London, HMSO, 1986a.

OPCS *Mortality Statistics: England and Wales 1986* London, HMSO, 1986b.

OPCS, A. Marsh, J. Dobbs, A White *Adolescent Drinking* London, HMSO, 1986c.

OPCS, E. Goddard *Drinking and Attitudes to Licensing in Scotland* London, HMSO, 1986d.

J. O'Beattie, D. Hull, F. Cockburn 'Children Intoxicated by Alcohol in Nottingham and Glasgow 1973-84' *British Medical Journal* 292, 1986, p519-21

A.C. Ogborne and R.G Smart 'Will Restrictions on Alcohol Advertsing Reduce Alcohol Consumption?' *British Journal of Addiction* 75, 1980, p293-6.

P. O'Neill *Health Crisis 2000* London, Heinemann, 1983.

B.G. Peters *The Politics of Bureaucracy: A Comparative Perspective* Longman, New York, 1984.

M. Plant and B. Ritson *Alcohol: The Prevention Debate* London, Croom Helm, 1983.

M. Plant and J.C. Duffy 'Scotland's Liquor Licensing Changes: An Assessment' *British Medical Journal* 292, 1986, p36-9.

A. Pollitt 'Promise and Product: Can Health Education Deliver?' *Paper Presented at the 6th International Conference on Alcohol-Related Problems* Liverpool, April 1984.

G.T. Popham 'Government and Smoking: Policy Making and Pressure Groups' *Policy and Politics* 9, 1981, p331-47.

R.E. Popham, W. Schmidt and J. de Lindt 'The Prevention of Alcoholism: Epidemiological Studies of the Effects of Government Control Measures' - *British Journal of Addiction* 70, 1975, p125-44.

Price Commission *Beer Prices and Margins* London, HMSO, 1977.

Price Commission *Allied Breweries UK Ltd: Brewing and Wholesaling of Beer in Managed Houses* London, HMSO, 1978.

Price Commission *Whitbread Ltd. Wholesale prices and prices in managed houses of beer, wines, and spirits, soft drinks and ciders* London, HMSO, 1979a.

Price Commission *Bass Ltd. Wholesale prices of beer and prces in managed houses* London, HMSO, 1979b.

Registrar General Scotland *Annual Report* London, HMSO, 1986.

J.J. Richardson and R. Kimber 'The Role of All Party Committees in the House of Commons' *Parliamentary Affairs* 25:4, 1972, p339-49.

D. Robinson *Talking Out Of Alcoholism* London, Croom Helm, 1979.

D. Robinson and B. Ettore 'Special Units for Common Problems: Alcoholism Treatment Units in England and Wales' in G. Edwards and M. Grant (eds) - *Alcoholism Treatment in Transition* London, Croom Helm, 1980.

A. Roth *Business Background of MPs: 1972 Edition* London, Unwin, 1972.

A. Roth *Business Background of MPs: 1975-6 Edition* London, Unwin. 1975.

Royal College of General Practitioners *Alcohol: A Balanced View* London, RCGP, 1986.

Royal College of Physicians, Faculty of Community Medicine *Recommendation for the Prevention of Alcohol Related Disorders* London, RCP, 1980.

Royal College of Physicians *The Medical Consequences of Alcohol Abuse: A Great and Growing Evil* London, Tavistock, 1987.

Royal College of Psychiatrists *Alcohol and Alcoholism* London, Tavistock, 1979.

Royal College of Psychiatrists *Alcohol: Our Favourite Drug* London, Tavistock, 1986.

C. Sandford and A. Robinson *Tax Policy-Making in the United Kingdom* London, Heinemann, 1983.

W. Saunders 'Licensing Law; The Scottish Experiment: A Reply to Clayson' *Triple A Review* July-August 1985.

W. Schmidt 'Cirrhosis and Alcohol Consumption: An Epidemiological Perspective' in G. Edwards and M. Grant (eds) *Alcoholism: New Knowledge and New Responses* London, Croom Helm, 1977, p15-47.

Scottish Home and Health Department *Report of the Departmental Committee on Scottish Licensing Law* (The Clayson Report) Cmnd. 5354, London, HMSO, 1973.

Scottish Home and Health Department, OPCS, S.E. Dight *Scottish Drinking Habits* London, HMSO, 1976.

Scottish Home and Health Department *Statistical Bulletin* May 1988.

J. Shepherd, M. Irish, C. Scully, I. Leslie 'Alcohol Intoxication and Severity of Injury in Victims of Assault' *British Medical Journal* 296, 1988, p1299.

A. Sippert in Medical Council on Alcoholism *Notes on Alcohol and Alcoholism* London, Edsall, 1975.

R.G. Smart 'The Effect of Licensing Restrictions during 1914-18 on Drunkenness and Liver Cirrhosis Deaths in Britain' *British Journal of Addiction* 69, 1974, p109-121.

R. G. Smart and R. B. Cutler 'The Alcohol Advertising Ban in British Columbia: Problems and Effects on Beverage Consumption' *British Journal of Addiction* 71, 1976, p13-21.

R. Smith 'An Overview of Alcohol and the Media' *Paper given to a Seminar on the Presentation of Alcohol in the Mass Media, IBA House, January 1985* London, IAS, 1985.

R. Smith *The National Politics of Alcohol Education: A Review* School of Applied Urban Studies Working Paper No.66, Univerity of Bristol, 1987.

D. Steele *Politics or Policy ? The National Organisations and Alcohol Misuse* Unpublished Pamphlet, 1984.

W.S.R Stewart *Drink, Drugs and the Family* London, NSPCC, 1971.

L. Taylor 'The British Drinker Exposed' *New Statesman* 97, 22 June 1979, p906-8.

170

P. Taylor *Smoke Ring* London, Bodley Head, 1984.

The Times *Top 1000 Companies* London, Times Publications, 1986.

Transport and Road Research Laboratory (TRRL) *Road Accidents:Christmas 1959* Road Research Technical Paper No.49 London, HMSO, 1960.

TRRL *Fatal Accidents at Christmas 1963* Road Research Technical Paper No.70 London, HMSO, 1964.

H.M. Treasury *Economic Progress Report* Volume 161, October 1983.

V. G. Treml 'Production and Consumption of Alcoholic Beverages in the USSR' *Journal of Studies on Alcohol* 36, 1975, p285-320

T. Ward 'PESC in Crisis' *Policy and Politics* 11:2, 1983, p167-76.

M. Waterson, Advertising Association *Advertising and Alcohol Misuse* London, AA, 1981.

A. Weir 'Obsessed with Moderation: The Drinks Trades and the Drink Question (1870-1930)' *British Journal of Addiction* 79, 1984, p93-107.

G.P. Williams and G.T. Brake *Drink in Great Britain 1900-79* London, Edsall, 1980.

D. Wilson *The Lead Scandal* London, Heinemann, 1983.

G.B. Wilson *Alcohol and the Nation* London, Nicholson and Watson, 1940.

Wines and Spirits Association *A Statement by the Wines and Spirits Association on the Social Aspects of the Sale of Alcohol* London, WSA, 1984.

Wines and Spirits Association *Alcohol Policy Guidelines for Companies* London, WSA, 1987.

World Health Organisation *Report of an Expert Committee on Alcoholism* Geneva, WHO, 1951.

World Health Organisation *Report of an Expert Committee on Alcoholism* Geneva, WHO, 1966.

World Health Organisation *Problems Related to Alcohol Consumption: Report of the WHO Expert Committee on Alcoholism* Geneva, WHO, 1980.

World Health Organisation *Global Strategy for Health for All by the Year 2000* Geneva, WHO, 1981.

World Health Organisation *Targets for Health for All* Copenhagen, WHO Regional Office for Europe, 1985.

Index

health education 77-81
Health Education Authority/Council
26, 77, 79-81, 85
Health and Safety Executive 76
Hicks, Robert 67
high risk offender procedure 144,
146-7
Hogg, Douglas 128-9
Home Office 12, 19, 42, 49, 65, 79, 85,
89, 92, 117-18, 122-4, 127-131,
136-139, 141-4
Home Office Working Party on
Habitual Drunkenness 12, 15, 22
Home Office Working Party on Young
People and Alcohol 49, 90, 107, 128
Hooley, Frank 36, 98, 141
'The Hospital Treatment of
Alcoholism' 10, 16
Houghton, Lord 87
House of Commons Expenditure
Committee 24, 36-7, 80, 82, 91, 97,
121
House of Commons Select Committee
on Violence in Marriage 82
hostels 14, 21-22, 23
Howard League for Penal Reform 17
Hurd, Douglas 49

Incorporated Society of British
Advertisers 85, 88
Independent Broadcasting Authority
83-5, 90, 92
Independent Television Companies
Association 83, 86-88
Ingrow, Lord 68
Institute of Alcohol Studies 26, 127,
148
Institute of Practititioners in
Advertising 88

Jenkin, Patrick 41, 46, 68, 70
Joseph 15, 20, 70
Justices' Clerks' Society 34, 78, 128,
145

Kendell, Professor 33
Kessel, Professor, 20
Kinnoull, Lord 109

Lawrence, Ivan 68
Law Society 137, 143
lead in petrol 2
Ledermann hypothesis 30
Lewis, Ron 18, 36, 121
licensing laws 114-132
Licensing Act 1988 127-30

Mackay, Andrew 131
Magistrates' Association 10, 13, 34,
45, 143
Marples, Ernest 136
Marsh, Peter 88
Masham, Baroness, 49
Mawhinney, Brian 36
Medical Council on Alcoholism 11,
17, 20, 24, 26, 34, 61
medical profession 10-11, 33-4, 48-9,
119, 127
Members of Parliament and the drinks
industry 66
Monopolies Commission 117
Montgomery, Lord 126
Moonie, Lewis 127
Moyle, Roland 40

National Association for the Care and
Resettlement of Offenders 12, 23
National Association of Licensed
House Managers 71, 119, 121, 125,
127-8
National Association of Probation
Officers 12, 34,
National Audit Office 148
National Consumer Council 72, 100
National Council for Voluntary
Organisations 25-6
National Council on Alcoholism 9, 10,
14, 17, 18, 19, 20, 24, 26, 34, 36, 37,
76, 82, 98, 108, 143, 145